Views Of An

EARLY BIRD

Views Of An
EARLY BIRD

Life in the Army's Air Corps

By Edmund C. Lynch
USAF, Major General, Ret.

EAKIN PRESS ★ Austin, Texas

FIRST EDITION

Published in the United States of America
By Eakin Press
An Imprint of Eakin Publications, Inc.
P.O. Drawer 90159 ★ Austin, TX 78709-0159

ISBN 0-89015-730-8

The photographs in this book were selected by the author from his personal collection as relevant to his stories.

Library of Congress Cataloging-in-Publication Data

Lynch, Edmund C.
Views of an early bird : from Jennys to jets, pioneering in the Army Air Corps and the USAF / Edmund C. Lynch.
p. cm
Includes index.
ISBN 0-89015-800-2 $19.95
1. Lynch, Edmund C. 2. United States. Air Force — Biography. 3. Generals — United States — Biography. I. Title.
UG626.2.L96A3 1990
358.4'0092--dc20
[B] 90-3356
CIP

Souvenir Edition — 1990
Ninetieth Anniversary
of the Author

Credit

My Mother, for my basic values,
My Memory, for I kept no diary.
My son Edmund, for checking details.
Margrette, my Wife, who reduced distractions,
Virginia, my Sister-in-Law, who represented the Reader.
Colonel Glenn L. Davasher, a very old friend,
one of the few who could check my veracity.
Kimo Dunn '36, my advisor on Style.
West Point for a solid foundation.
My effort which speaks for itself.

Contents

Forewords

Edmund Clayton Lynch asked me to read a manuscript copy of *An Early Bird's View* in late 1987. Frankly, I tend to be a little wary of autobiographical works, but this one struck me at once as something different, perhaps even unique. Its approach is unconventional, episodic, and completely human. Its author is a natural story teller. He has selected the most memorable episodes and the most interesting people encountered during his first two careers (as military aviator, 1922–1953, and as civilian educator, 1954–1971) and he shows how they helped shape his own life.

The author was in his *third* career by the time I first met him in 1983. As co-editor with his wife, the poet Peggy Zuleika Lynch, he was helping produce books. That year they had published *Behold Texas: As Seen by Texas Poets,* and they were already working on *From Hide and Horn: A Sesquicentennial Anthology of Texas Poets,* timed to celebrate 150 years of Texas history throughout 1986.

The three of us became acquainted at a writers' conference in the summer of 1983. After the conference General Lynch spotted me in a parking lot, struggling to dismantle my bicycle to fit it into the car for the trip back home; he immediately offered help. He reached into a neat mechanic's tool box in the trunk of his own car and selected a wrench of the exact size needed to solve my problem. Returning my pliers to a back pocket, I knew at once that this aviator was a pilot of the pioneer school, who had always known more about maintaining his aircraft than mechanics and crew chiefs charged with such tasks.

Several episodes early in his book bear out my first impression of the author; but one of them that sticks most forcibly in my mind is "The Tennessee River," which recounts how young Lynch and a fellow second lieutenant, U.S. Army Air Service, with mission-type orders and a camera mounted in a DeHaviland-4 biplane, executed a four-month aerial photo-mapping mission, the first of its kind in that area. All details of the job were left to their judgment. They maintained their airplane and all other equipment themselves; they finished the job ahead of schedule; and to the great satisfaction of the District Engineer in Chattanooga, they photographed an extra section of the Duck River area. The mission was a complete success — quite remarkable when we think of how rare is such true delegation to youngsters in today's world.

The Early Bird's tale begins as the story of a teen-aged Pennsylvanian, son of a National Guard officer who was killed in action while serving with the U.S. 28th Infantry Division in France during World War I. The loss of his father undoubtedly influenced Edmund Lynch to scrap his plans to study mechanical engineering at the University of Pennsylvania, and instead, accept an appointment to the U.S. Military Academy at West Point. Thus, he became a cadet in 1918 with the unique "Orioles" of the Class of 1922.

Like two pioneer American aviators of his age group, Amelia Earhart and Charles A. Lindbergh, Edmund possessed an inquiring mind. He quite naturally chose the Army's fledgling new Air Service, which had been barely baptized in World War I. He found the 1920s a fascinating period of experimentation.

As a freshly minted West Point graduate with gold bars on his shoulders, he found that he had to resist his tendency to be a perfectionist and make adjustments to the world around him: his willing, but green airmen, his skilled, but set-in-their-ways NCOs. He grew in tolerance, never losing his sense of humor, of wonder, of optimism about his country and human nature throughout his thirty years as an officer in the service that grew into the U.S. Army Air Corps, and later, the U.S. Air Force.

Early on, he learned to be skeptical of people who thought they had "the right answers." The accidental death of an instructor pilot — a victim of his own "right way to fly" — impressed this lesson on him indelibly.

Many of his associates described in the book became famous figures in U.S. national defense, e.g., certain of his classmates who became four-star generals, like Orval Cook and Maxwell D. Taylor; contemporaries like Hoyt Vandenberg, destined to become head of the U.S. Air Force when it became a separate service; superiors like General Hap Arnold who created the World War II Army Air Forces; General George C. Marshall, Chief of Staff of the

Army and architect of the World War II victory, who was his top boss during the author's wartime Pentagon service; and Anna Rosenberg, Assistant Secretary of Defense for Personnel, who was his immediate superior during the postwar years. Lynch has written short sketches about these and many other famous people he knew. But of all his character sketches, one that will perhaps stay in my own mind longest, is entitled "Daddy Baker." It's about one of this country's pioneer flight surgeons, a plain-spoken Arkansas doctor, who got his early practical training in medicine as a low-paid county doctor, healing patients at the prison and poor farm run by his home county.

Both of the first two careers of Edmund Lynch — military aviator, civilian educator — were voyages of discovery, full of surprises for himself, and happily for his readers also. This is a book that is hard to put down, and it is one that may be picked up at any starting point the reader may choose from the long list of episodes — each a self-contained little story to be savored many times.

General Lynch is a man who will never stop learning and growing, and as of 1989, I find his buoyant sense of humor still intact. In this book the author, in my opinion, accomplishes what his introduction tells us he sets out to do. Some day in the future his *third* career should make an interesting sequel.

EDWARD CLARE DUNN
Major General, U.S. Army, Retired

I had the pleasure of reading and of commenting upon the stories about our cadet life and our experience at Brooks Field while they were in the formative stages. They stirred memories for me.

Marge and I had married upon graduation and we lived near Brooks Field in the Hot Wells section of San Antonio. Upon the move to Kelly Field we were assigned quarters in one of the four tiny apartments in a one-story structure built during World War One. There were two other student couples with us in that building, both lighter-than-air pilots. I soloed on the DH airplane and shortly thereafter was told by the *Benzine Board* that I "lacked natural flying ability." That was when we flew by the seat of our pants. I continued to fly as an observer while awaiting the orders for my transfer to the Coast Artillery Corps. We departed for Fort Adams, Rhode Island in mid-October. Our son William Junior was born at Fort Sam Houston Hospital on September 14th, 1923, a reminder of those days.

P. D. has done a magnificent job of reliving for us some of the efforts and exploits of the daring young men who flew Jennies and DHs in the formative period of the Army Air Service. My flying helmet is off to him.

I was stirred to do research of my own on the *Orioles* who reported to Brooks Field in September 1922. Of the original ten, six survived to participate in World War Two. These six provided the Army and Air Force with two full generals, three major generals, and one brigadier general. This group earned seven Distinguished Service Medals, seven Legion of Merit Awards, one Distinguished Flying Cross, a Silver Star and numerous other awards.

WILLIAM S. LAWTON

Lieutenant General, U.S. Army, Retired

Preface

"Observations from a Lifetime of Learning" was my first title for this project because I disliked the conventional biographic form which includes the routine or humdrum detail of living along with its more important aspects. My project began as a collection of stories about my personal learning experiences through what I did or what I saw. As the collection grew I discovered that I was actually writing a biography in a unique form. I then changed the title, but the underlying theme remains.

Life is a learning process with ideas gleaned from a variety of sources, should one be curious about what makes things tick. The intent herein is to share with others the knowledge that I gained. The following stories are short and to the point, each seeking to paint a picture to arouse interest, with the hope that it will make the reader think. These are vignettes rather than the total story.

Episodes were selected to illustrate events from which I had learned something during my thirty years in the Army and Air Force, followed by eighteen years as an educator. Some of the major ideas to be found in these stories include:

When you help others, you help yourself.
Cooperation benefits all who work together.
Seek a better way to do your work.
One should concentrate on *ends* rather than means.
Develop confidence and self reliance.
Be certain that you know your purpose.
Be suspicious of those who have the right answers.
It is important to know what you do *not* know.
A sense of humor is always a help.

Introduction

I was an Early Bird in the Army Air Service joining it seven years after the first tactical air unit had been organized in 1915, the First Aero Squadron. That unit scouted for General Pershing during the Punitive Expedition into Mexico during 1916. While pursuit pilots harvested glory during World War One, their reason for being was to protect the observation aircraft from the enemy fighters seeking to prevent the air observer's extended view of the battlefield.

My selection of the Air Service upon graduation from West Point was based on the thought that it would be nice to get in on the ground floor and grow with a new military service. My active duty career spanned the entire growing period of the Army Air Corps and I retired from the United States Air Force in 1953.

My early days of flying were an adventure for we were all in the same state of ignorance, the war period having been too brief to tell us much. The Twenties were a period of active experimentation in the use of the airplane in aerial photographic mapping and for dusting crops. I was fortunate to have several independent assignments and spent much time in training rather than in flying with a tactical unit. The events which I have selected relate to people and experiences that shaped my career and personal growth, interwoven with Air Corps history as I experienced it.

I was not alone on this journey. Though my wife, Edith does not appear frequently in these stories, she contributed her full share of support and assistance as a military spouse. She enjoyed Army life at our various posts, and meeting new people. She did her share of volunteer activities, singing in the choir at Randolph Field. As the wife of a commanding officer, she held the view that the ladies should conduct their own affairs and that her role was an advisor, that her status derived from her personal experience and not from my rank.

Career One

Flying With my Britches Firmly in the Seat

Assignments

United States Military Academy, West Point, New York	1918–1922
Brooks and Kelly Fields, San Antonio, Texas	1922–1924
Pope Field, Fort Bragg, North Carolina	1924–1925
Scott Field, Belleville, Illinois	1925–1926
Brooks and Kelly Fields	1926–1929
France Field, Panama Canal Department	1929–1931
Brooks and Randolph Fields	1931–1936
Maxwell Field, Montgomery, Alabama	1936–1937
Fort Leavenworth, Kansas	1937–1938
General Headquarters Air Force Langley Field, Virginia and Bolling Field, District of Columbia	1938–1942
The War Department, The Pentagon, District of Columbia	1942–1944
Key Field, Meridian, Mississippi	1944–1945
Headquarters Third Air Force, Tampa, Florida	1945–
The Alaskan Department	1945–1947
Headquarters United States Air Force, The Pentagon, District of Columbia	1947–1950
Department of Defense — The Pentagon	1950–1953

West Point

Little did I know when I graduated from Darby High School in June 1918 that I would be a West Point cadet by November of that year. I had established my intention of entering the University of Pennsylvania to study mechanical engineering and had signed up for a summer job as a student-apprentice electrician with the Philadelphia Electric Company which was building a coal-fired electric plant near Chester.

That summer job was an on-the-job training program for engineering students. It was special in the sense that the student moved through a sequence of operations under an experienced electrician. My team did all the work to wire up an electric motor which drove an indirect draft blower for the boiler. We installed the conduit, pulled the wires through that conduit, built a switching panel for the remote control of the motor and ended up pushing the button to see the motor respond. The instructor demonstrated a task, then we showed him that we understood and we went to work. The instructor returned periodically to inspect our work, should it not suit him, we would tear it out and do it over. I learned a lot that summer. My pay was $3.50 for a ten-hour day plus train fare. One beneficial aspect was that I had a firm model for on-the-job training.

My father, Captain of "B" Company in the 111th Infantry, 28th Division, was killed in action at Fismet, France, on August 18, 1918. I knew that he had been working to obtain an appointment for me to attend West Point. Having heard nothing I entered the University of Pennsylvania that fall as planned. On September 15th I received a telephone call to go to West Chester and see Congressman Thomas S. Butler who represented the 7th Pennsylvania District. I was met at his home by his son, Major General Smedley Butler of the Marine Corps who told me that his father was at a nearby barbershop. I learned about my appointment while Congressman Butler was being shaved and that I would hear more about it from The Adjutant General of the Army.

A few days later I had instructions to go to Princeton University and report for the mental and physical examinations and that procedure took several days. I then withdrew from the University of Pennsylvania and waited for the next move and that was a letter stating that the class would begin on November first. On that date I took an early train to Weehawken and changed to the West Shore Railroad to arrive at West Point before noon. There I learned that my name was not on their list and that I should have received a telegram from The Adjutant General ordering me to report. Knowing that the local Adjutant's Office was the administrative center I went there to explain my predicament and learned that I was not alone. A kindly clerk in that office helped us word a telegram to The Adjutant General and we each sent our own telegrams. From there we walked to the Thayer Hotel to wait for our instructions. That was the old hotel near Trophy Point which had been built many years before. My orders came in and I was sworn in as a cadet on November 6th, 1918.

MY PLEBE YEAR

We were assigned rooms in North Barracks and my first task was to draw bedding from a store room in the West wing. My bundle included a mattress, pillow, linens and two blankets. There were upper classmen dressed in cadet gray in the area who urged us to move on the double. An unfortunate cadet ahead of me tripped and fell with his load as a cushion. An upper classman cried out, "Mr. Dumbjohn, what do you mean taking a nap in the area at this time of day?" My room was on the fourth floor of the Third Division and four of us shared that room designed for two as the iron beds had been double decked.

At the Cadet Store we were fitted with the standard olive drab uniform including the campaign hat. Our distinguishing insigne was an orange yellow felt hat band, our special mark and we were dubbed *The Orioles*. Our civilian clothes were packed in our suitcases and stored in the basement, not to be used until Christmas 1919.

Our instruction began with close order Infantry drill provided by the upper classmen who had entered in June 1918. We had massed calisthenics conducted by Colonel Koehler, Master of the Sword, who stood on an elevated platform with the new cadets on three sides, about four hundred of us. When the Armistice was declared on November 11th, we were told that any one who wished to do so could go home immediately, or we could wait until the situation cleared. Two left from the four in our room while Arthur Klein and I decided to stick it out. We continued with drill and calisthenics, the normal program for new cadets known as Beast Barracks. Shortly we were informed that our program would be for three years and there was another opportunity to go home. Those who departed during November and December 1918 were not included in the class records.

During the war period the various classes were graduated early. The Register of Graduates noted that the cadets who entered in June 1916 were under the War Emergency Course, a three-year program. The cadets who entered in June 1917 were graduated on November 1, 1918 and then recalled as second lieutenants on December 3, 1918 for further training to graduate again in June 1919. This class was known as the Student Officer Class, but we saw very little of them.

With our program established and our performance at drill satisfactory we were merged with the cadets who had entered in June 1918 and clad in cadet gray. We were sized for our parades with the tall men or flankers at each end of the line, grading smoothly to the shorter men at the center. Since I was a flanker at six foot two, I was assigned to "A" Company to live on the fourth floor of the First Division. My roommates were Howard (Bull) Davidson, Alfred (Aaron) Kessler and Paschal (Pat) Strong. My former roommate, Art Klein was now in "D" Company.

Alfred A. Kessler, better known as Aaron, was my roommate for the three years I was in "A" Company. He was already a second lieutenant when he reported for he had attended an Officer's Training Camp. Aaron had graduated from the Passaic High School, New Jersey, where he had played basketball with a team noted for having won more than one hundred games without a loss. As a cadet he played varsity basketball. I was fortunate for we were like-minded about making good grades, avoiding demerits and graduating.

Each cadet company had a tactical officer and ours was Major E. J. Dawley of the Field Artillery. When we left our room for our morning classes, everything had to be in apple-pie order. Bedding stacked just so, our locker doors open to view as Major Dawley made his morning inspection. The floor had to be clean and no dust on the mantel. Infractions brought demerits to be avoided. Major Dawley also made an evening inspection during study hours or as a bed check.

The reveille gun went off at ten minutes to six in the morning and we were serenaded by the Hell Cats. All our duty calls were on the drum, an entirely new language for me. A sympathetic drummer could space out his final taps to permit a laggard to get into line before his final tap. Several of our upper classmen had salvaged castoff trousers from an earlier class and had sewed the bottom section from the knee down over their pajama legs so they could make reveille by wearing their overcoat over their pajamas. The uniform of the day was given us by flag signals flown at the Guardhouse on the South side of the area of North Barracks.

ODE TO THE HELL CATS

[Hell Cat — a member of the Fife and Drum Corps]

Oh, it was nice to be a plebe dressed in Cadet Gray, assigned to Company "A," living on the fourth floor of North Barracks in the First Division. We were surrounded with tradition, our room had changed little during the past fifty years. We now had steam heat instead of the fireplace and our modern facilities were in the basement, replacing the pitcher, wash basin and slop jar.

Oh, it was nice to lie abed in the winter mornings after being awakened by martial music, the traditional fife and drum, and to know that it was music made by real people for the sounds petered out as the cold got to the fifer's fingers and his breath froze. The snare drums persisted in their urging to get going for the new day. Such drums had sounded the traditional military calls for centuries. This was my first experience with specific messages and I learned a new language, all our duty calls were on the drum with Taps the three final beats of the day.

Our eyes and ears were completely surrounded with tradition every hour of the day, reminding us that we were following the path of those who had marched before us to the same martial music, The Long Gray Line. Our life may have been Spartan, but it was rich in values for a growing young man to emulate for a lifetime benefit. We were initiates in a new culture and the Hell Cats reminded us of that fact, the call to duty for each and every day.

The Fourth Classman or plebe was subjected to a culturalization process called *Beast Barracks* provided by a selected group of upper classmen. Despite our hazy status and olive drab uniform we had the traditional treatment intended to convert a raw civilian youth into a model cadet. The key exercise was *bracing* to develop an erect posture with shoulders back, chin in and belly sucked up. To this end an upper classman is always critical of your posture and seeking to improve it by urging you to pull your chin back, suck up your gut or to pull your shoulders back, to encourage a habit. This activity goes on until graduation parade when you become recognized. Plebes always move at the double but come to a walk when saluting officers. For this reason the Student Officer Class was a pain in the neck for our class because they were very punctilious about being rendered a proper salute. Obviously, our goal was to be inconspicuous and to avoid such meetings.

There were numerous funerals at West Point during the early months of 1919 due to the influenza epidemic and the Cadet Corps was turned out to escort the cortege and fire the customary salute. The cadet companies rotated that firing and on one occasion "B" Company had the duty. An upper classman of that company asked me to exchange rifles so that I would have the task of cleaning my rifle, but I refused on the basis that an Infantryman should never be separated from his piece. Ford Trimble who was in charge of my platoon backed me up and I thought the matter closed. As luck would have it, I was on interior guard that evening and drew that upper classman's division to walk my tour, back and forth on the first floor for about two hours. He gave me a hard time during numerous visits to the basement facilities while urging me to pull my shoulders back and suck up my belly. His behavior was proper because he kept moving, but slowly.

Our academic classes, including gymnasium, were in the morning. For such classes we were organized in groups of twelve with a designated section marcher and were marched to the classroom in a military manner. The section marcher reported those present and absent to the instructor.

I still remember my first class in English for we entered the class room to see this title on the blackboard, "Is Vicarious Atonement Justifiable?" and we were to write a theme of 300 words, or so. We sat stupified for a few minutes until one brave student asked permission to ask a question. That was granted and the instructor explained vicarious atonement. I was able to do a passable job as I had written pieces for my high school paper.

With the small sections we were expected to recite every day. My instructor in mathematics would place twelve cards on the front edge of his desk and we would each draw one. Six of the cards were for problems to be worked out at the blackboard and then explained to the class. Four cards were for problems to be worked out at one's seat in class and handed in. Two called for an oral quiz and those students stayed in front of the instructor's desk. When we had written reviews in mathematics we were not permitted to erase anything. False starts were to be "X-d" out and you started over. The instructor could examine everything on the paper and judge your thinking. We were taught to budget our time and make an effort on every problem.

Afternoons were devoted to the riding hall, intermural athletics, practical military engineering (drawing & surveying) and various activities under the Tactical Department.

A plebe spent much of his spare time in shining his shoes and brass. Shoes were to be shined for every formation whether needed or not and the plebe would be quizzed on that point to develop a habit. We used a liquid water based polish which appeared to do little good at first and built up slowly.

Our traditional brass belt buckles and the breastplate came from the Cadet Store with a coat of lacquer which had to be removed before getting down to the brass itself. After the lacquer was off the surface would have minor imperfections visible to a keen eye. The ultimate goal was to wear down the brass until a mirror-like finish had been achieved, perhaps after a year's hard work. For the breastplate I had rigged a holder from a piece of wood to hold the plate while polishing it. The cadet store provided us with scraps of uniform cloth which were suitable for working down the finish. I also made pouches for my belt buckle and breastplate to preserve the shine, hand sewn of course.

The insigne on our full dress hat and the side buttons were stamped out of sheet brass. We used Electro-silicon to polish those items because it was a powder and left no deposit when used with a nail brush. The cadet had no easy way out, just persistance and elbow grease.

We were marched to all meals and sat ten to a table in the Mess Hall. My table commandant was Ford Trimble the cadet lieutenant in charge of my platoon. At the other end of the table, one plebe served the milk and another the water and were referred to as "Corporals." We sat on the edge of our chairs and brought the food to our mouth by a vertical lift until opposite our mouth and then straight in, for slumping was discouraged. Should a plebe leave the spoon in his cup, he would be directed to "Ship your oar!"

An element in the culturalization of the plebe was *The Plebe Bible,* a compilation of "What every plebe should know." It ranged from the trivial to commendatory remarks about West Point, all to be memorized. A plebe would be called upon to recite at any time by an upper classman. The most obscure request was, "Mr. Dumbjohn, what should be done whenever possible?" The answer was, "Sir, the troops should be supplied with fresh beef!" This was a direct quotation from an Army training manual. A plebe, having no identity, was always addressed as Mr. Dumbjohn.

Another piece always memorized was a statement of General Winfield Scott in his letter to the U.S. Military Academy Commission, 1860:

> . . . I give it as my fixed opinion, that but for our graduated cadets, the war between the United States and Mexico might, and probably would have lasted some four or five years, with, in its first half, more defeats than victories falling to our share; whereas, in less than two campaigns, we conquered a great country and a peace without the loss of a single battle or skirmish . . .

During the summer of 1984, I was sitting at the bar of the Hilton Hotel in Dallas, nursing a brew. To my right was a young man talking to a civilian on his right. I paid only casual attention until I heard West Point mentioned and then I really did eavesdrop. The young man was telling his neighbor about the plebe recitations. When he began the Definition of Leather, I chimed in about the middle and we finished in duet. He gave me a startled look and I gave him a bland smile, introducing myself. I had often recited that piece at appropriate times during the past sixty-odd years. That young man had graduated in June 1984 and was on his way from Fort Polk, Louisiana, to Fort Sill in Oklahoma, by automobile.

The definition was a quote from the Chemistry Textbook written by Samuel E. Tillman, Professor of Chemistry after he became professor in 1880. In 1918, Brigadier General Tillman was Superintendent.

> If the fresh skin of an animal, cleaned and divested of all hair, fat and other extraneous matter, be immersed in a dilute solution of tannic acid, a chemical combination ensues, the gelatinous tissue of the skin is converted into a nonputresable substance, imper-

vious to and insoluble in water. This, Sir, is what we are having for dinner (steak.)

We had a well equipped gymnasium. I was six foot two and weighed about 125 pounds with legs half my height. My classmates called me *High Pockets*. I was not built for doing gymnastics such as the parallel bars. We had to qualify in swimming, so I learned the breast stroke hooked to a lanyard until the instructor judged me safe enough to solo.

Our introduction to the gym came through bayonet drill with ancient rifles fitted with spring bayonets and the barrels filled with lead. Two lines of cadets would advance executing in cadence the long thrust, short thrust, butt stroke and jab. At the command, "Drop and Pass Over!" we would drop our piece, run to the other side and pick up the dropped rifle for the next advance. It was hard work and when we would begin to slack off our instructor would cry, "Come on men, rest has not been given!" and that became one of our class slogans. That instructor was Francis (Blinky) Dohs who had been a professional gymnast before coming to West Point as an instructor.

During the evening hours we were confined to our rooms for that was the study hour, seven until bedtime. I programmed my study time, concentrated at the task and sought to finish about nine-thirty to read interesting books from the Library, the dessert so to speak.

All cadets attended chapel on Sunday. Otherwise they were confined to their rooms during the chapel period. Chaplain Clayton Wheat, the Protestant Chaplain, conducted the services in the main Cadet Chapel. The Choir Master and Organist, Frederick Mayer screened us as potential Cadet Choir members with a short voice test which I flunked, the only test at West Point that I flunked. Aaron and I generally spent our Sunday afternoons hiking around the reservation both for exercise and to avoid the upper classmen and student officers. On one hike toward Storm King we met Colonel Wirt Robinson our Chemistry Professor. He was out birding for he was a well known amateur ornithologist and had identified more birds in Eastern New York than anyone else. He greeted us briefly and went on his way.

We were in a meritocracy and our relative standing within our class was determined by academic grades and by our grade in Military Efficiency and Conduct. That was where the demerits would lower your grade and were to be avoided. Some cadets with an excessive number would spend their free time walking off such demerits in the area of barracks under the supervision of the Officer of the Guard.

The Student Officer Class graduated on June 11, 1919. At the end of that graduation parade we were duly recognized by our upper classmen. A new class of cadets was due to arrive and we moved to Summer Camp to free the barracks for the Beast Barracks to welcome them.

SUMMER CAMP

The Summer Camp area was at the Northeast corner of the Plain at the edge of the bluff, an established area with wooden floors to keep us out of the mud and fence-like structures to anchor the tent guys instead of stakes. It got off to a dreary start with a week of cold rainy weather and we had much sack time.

The summer was devoted to learning the basic skills of an Infantryman. We had practice marches with a full pack and would practice making camp with our pup tents. After the tents were pitched we would display our packs for field inspection. At the end of one of the practice marches with full pack the Tactical Department pulled a surprise inspection. Several cadets were indeed surprised for they had a piece of stove pipe in their packs to lighten the load. That trick was not approved.

Aaron and I lived in a standard wall tent with a fly to keep it cooler in the summer. During the rainy period we had practice in adjusting the tension of the canvas during the intermittent rains.

Interior guard was a twenty-four hour stretch from the guard mount one afternoon until the next. Such guard mounts were usually formal with music. There were old fashioned sentry boxes around the perimeter of the camp area. We marched post from one box to another doing a snappy about face at each end of the post. I enjoyed the early morning tour when the camp was sleeping, particularly when I could watch the break of day and the sun rise over the Hudson River from my vantage point on the bluff.

We learned to shoot the Springfield rifle and the Colt automatic pistol to fire for record at the end of the course. I qualified as a sharpshooter with the rifle and as an expert with the pistol, to have two nice silver badges to wear with my full dress uniform. Our instructor in musketry was Major Paul W. (Pablo) Newgarden, informally referred to as *Pistol Paul,* who was the top gun in the Army. Some cadets could not get the hang of the rifle and would completely miss the target which was quite sizeable. Major Newgarden formed them into the *Bolo Squad,* had them fix bayonets and marched them down the range to attack the targets hand-to-hand.

Cadets manned the Butts and marked the targets. There were two targets for one firing station, arranged on a metal frame and chains so that when one was in firing position the other one could be marked. We had colored round disks on a long pole to indicate the value of the hit on the target and laid the disc over the center of the hit. A field telephone line led to the firing point for communications. At that time our target range was on the flats by the West Shore Railroad and a short distance from our camp.

Toward the end of the summer we marched with our full packs to a campsite near Monroe, following Central Valley. We lived there for several days in our pup tents before marching home. We would march for fifty minutes and rest for ten out of each hour, the standard routine. On our return we were met by the Academy Band for the last mile or so. What a difference the music made! While tired after several hours of marching, we stepped out at our smart parade cadence to complete the march.

Our Commandant of Cadets Colonel Jens Bugge, who had graduated in 1895, died during July 1919. During his funeral we stood at ease outside the Main Chapel while it rained. My full dress hat came apart for the glue was not waterproof.

Cadets celebrate special occasions and Summer Camp ended with *Camp Illumination,* a play written by cadets and acted by cadets for the interest of the faculty and other cadets, a spoof on the highlights of that summer. We returned to barracks about the first of September to begin my Third Class or Yearling year.

THE YEARLING YEAR

Our Third Class year was known as the yearling year. Based on my grade in Military Efficiency and Conduct during the Fourth Class year I was made a Cadet Corporal, and lost no time in having my stripes sewn on at the Cadet Store with one narrow row of braid to show that I was a Third Classman and a squad leader in "A" Company for all formations. Aaron was also a cadet corporal, but a

Color Corporal and marched with the colors.

Our academic program was the basic civil engineering program with a military bias. For most of the nineteenth century, West Point was the sole source for engineers who provided the know-how for the opening of the West, first by canals and later by the railroads, not to overlook the protection of those people who were moving westward. That program was strong on mathematics, so we went through The Calculus. I had had a solid foundation from Darby High School, found descriptive and analytic geometries no problem and wound up in the first section of mathematics.

Before Summer Camp was over, Aaron and I learned that we would be housed three to a room in barracks, so we selected Gordon S. Armes from the uncommitted list and he was happy to join us to make a comfortable roommate. While an average student during his Fourth Class year, he could have done better, but he marched to a different drummer than Aaron and I. He liked to read subjects that interested him, not necessarily class assignments. For instance, he read Schopenhauer and marked pages he thought would appeal to me. So, I became acquainted with that philosopher. Gordon stood number two in the class in Spanish and had a copy of the *Four Horsemen of the Apocalypse* by Ibañez in Spanish which he read for his pleasure. Aaron and I would help him in mathematics as needed.

Our Class Committee decided that members of the first section in mathematics should help the *Goats* in our class to get ready for the written reviews. They obtained permission from the Commandant for us to visit during study hours for that purpose. I did not like that idea, having my own plans to prepare for the written reviews, but could think of no excuse to evade the task. So I became a reluctant tutor.

I do not recall who I tutored, but when I would make a self-evident statement, he would challenge me with "Why?" He controlled the review and I spent my time reviewing basics. I made a good grade on those written reviews and came to the conclusion that he had helped me as much as I may have helped him. From then on I would volunteer to tutor when needed.

Cadets received information from sources other than the classroom or from military instruction. Our wrestling instructor, Tom Jenkins was a prolific source of worldly wisdom acquired in the school of hard knocks. He had worked his way up to be World

Champion Heavyweight Wrestler before World War One. He had honed his skill against numerous opponents when winning was a necessity.

His homilies were based on his experiences and one that I recall was with an opponent known as The Terrible Turk. This opponent wore a charm in a chamois sack around his neck. Tom's manager assured him that his opponent's strength depended upon this amulet, and suggested that Tom go for that sack. Jenkins was an excellent story teller and described in detail the moves he made to seize the sack in his teeth and jerk it free.

After a dramatic pause, Tom said, "He tru me outada ring!" (Tom had his own brand of English.) After a second pause Tom added, "When ur wrassling, stick to wrassling!" All his stories had a piece of sound advice.

Jenkins had his own way of holding our attention. One time he thought that I was slacking off and chose me as a partner to demonstrate a "Holt." He flipped me over his hip and let me have a free, horizontal fall to the mat.

Physically, Tom Jenkins was designed by nature for his calling, no neck to speak of, a barrel of a trunk with long arms and short legs. Despite his weight of 250 pounds and all muscle, he was light on his feet and as agile as a cat. He had one of his eyes gouged out by an opponent. On that point Tom remarked, "A feller what'll stick his finger in another feller's eye aint no gent. I bruke his leg!"

There were many ways of stating Tom's message. Perhaps the circumstances were special, but whenever I hear someone talking about the "Principle of the Objective" my mind always goes back to Tom's way of stating that principle. Truly, he was one of a kind.

As a cadet corporal I was on the roster for duty as Corporal of the Guard that year. The main task of that position was to make certain that the sentry on duty knew the rules, his general and special orders, other than to march back and forth in a military manner. I would post the sentries and relieve them at the proper time. In between I kept busy visiting those I thought needed help, that is, make them repeat the rules to me.

The Cadet Store dressed us from the skin out. Our long drawers (Scrivens I believe) protected our knees from the chafing of our starched white duck trousers. There were no pockets in our uniforms so we carried our handkerchief tucked in our sleeve. The flat clerical style white collar was clipped in the standing collar of our dress and full dress uniforms. Our cuffs were pinned to our sleeve with cuff links bearing the West Point Seal. Our white duck trousers came back from the laundry stiff as a board, so we had to open up the crease and form the break at the ankle before wearing them. It took some time to get ready for a parade.

General Douglas MacArthur became our Superintendent in June 1919. He initiated the intermural athletic program with the following purpose:

Upon the fields of friendly strife
Are sown the seeds
That upon other fields, on other days,
Will bear the fruits of victory.

It was based on the concept that the peace-time Army officer was a teacher and that he should know enough about several sports that he could teach his men to play a sport and to referee a game with a rule book in his hand. Naturally, it would benefit the cadet as well. I chose lacrosse, soccer and tennis as my sports. Aaron was an excellent player at lacrosse and a member of the Army Varsity Team.

As Third Classmen we had training in the social graces for we were eligible for the dances (Hops) in Cullum Hall each Saturday evening. Mr. Vizet, our dancing master, assisted by his daughter who played the piano, taught us the waltz, foxtrot and one step. Two cadets would dance together taking turns as lady or gentleman. Sometimes, Miss Vizet would demonstrate a position. We had been issued patent leather dancing pumps with sedate flat bows and could break them in.

An invitation to a West Point Hop was prized by the young ladies on the East coast and their mothers who would chaperone them. It was customary that a cadet who had a date would start his date's dance card well beforehand to assure that she would have a busy evening. I did not date my Third Class year, but would sign up for dances with those who did so. In between such dances I would line up with the Stags, so I enlarged my acquaintances.

My first leave of absence and opportunity to return home came at Christmas 1919, about ten days. Aaron's father drove up from Passaic to take Aaron home and they dropped me off at Newark, New Jersey to catch my train for Philadelphia. It turned out that I was not the only West Pointer visiting Sharon Hill, for Christian Hildebrand who had graduated in June with the Student Officers Class was home on leave. He and his sister Rose invited me to one of their parties. Mainly I stayed close to home to relate all my experiences.

On my return trip my train was late getting into Grand Central Terminal in New York City and I caught the last train for West Point on a dead run just as it began to move. What a relief! Ordinarily the trains at that time seldom ever were more than a minute or so off from their published schedule. You could set your clock by them. But, from then on I always allowed myself ample time for making a connection. I rode the New York Central to Garrison and crossed the Hudson to West Point on the ferry.

During the Spring of 1920 we learned that Congress had authorized the normal four-year program and we were given the option of graduating in 1921 as planned before, or extending our graduation to 1922. I elected to go the full four years as I was enjoying my studies and thought the extra year would be beneficial.

Horseback riding was a new experience for me though I had ridden bareback on a farm horse on the way to the blacksmith for a new shoe. By the end of our plebe year I began to feel comfortable and was reasonably proficient by the end of our yearling year. The riding hall was immense with the ground covered by six inches or so of a mixture called tanbark to provide traction for the horse and a cushion when we fell off. We rode in a large circle, first at a walk. The instructor worked on our posture and the handling of the reins until we had that pat and then increased to the trot to learn how to post with the horse's gait. My long legs were an advantage here. Eventually we would increase the gait to a canter or easy gallop; all exercises designed to learn how to control the change of gaits. We rode the flat or English style saddle for our training and used the McClellan or field saddle on field exercises.

We wore a wide web belt with our riding breeches and our last names were printed on the belt in letters about an inch and one half high. Major Crittenberger the instructor for our group always called me Mr. Strong, for Pat Strong and I were built alike. One day Major Crittenberger said, "Mr. Strong, are you chewing gum?" looking square at me. I replied, "Yes, Sir!" Chewing gum was forbidden but it helped keep the saliva flowing with the dust. I was curious about that skin, but it was posted to Lynch, E. C., so Crittenberger had done his homework. Gordon would cut up a plug of chewing tobacco into small cubes and keep a cube in his mouth during riding. He was from Kentucky and used to riding a horse. Gordon never got skinned for his chews.

The cadets who entered during June 1918 graduated as the Class of 1920 on June 15th. We began our Yearling Furlough, a full summer at home to relax and have fun. Our class celebrated this event by publishing a *Furlo Book*.

YEARLING FURLO

That long summer at home was busy and enjoyable. I made myself useful about the house and all my friends were interested in my life at West Point. There was plenty of entertainment in Philadelphia such as Vaudeville, then in its heyday and the silent movies. In some instances the news reels were better than the feature picture. Also, I spent several days with my two aunts who lived in Collingswood and Island Heights, New Jersey. I usually wore civilian clothes for there were no pockets in my uniform.

One set of cousins on my grandmother's side lived on a real farm at Gwynedd Valley near Norristown. They had a small dairy and kept a number of riding horses. I had visited them with my family at an early age, their six children being comparable to my brothers and sister. As a teenager I had ridden my bicycle and visited solo. This family also had an advertising agency in Philadelphia, so I rode home with them for a week's visit.

My cousin Violet Haines operated a riding school for the children in their vicinity so I wore my uniform and took along my riding breeches to demonstrate my riding skill. My visit coincided with a local horse show where Violet's students were to display their talents before their parents. I tagged along properly mounted and was greeted cordially to feel quite at home.

Another special event of that summer was a canoe trip up the Schuylkill River from Fairmont Park in Philadelphia to Valley Forge. I went with a high school classmate and the two of us camped out along the way as we took it easy. I learned how to handle a canoe and got a good sunburn. I knew that we had some canoes at West Point, so on my return I felt confident in checking out a canoe for a paddle on the Hudson.

Toward the end of the summer I began to miss the cadet routine and busy life and looked forward to the summer's end with no regret.

A SECOND CLASSMAN

With the four year program now in effect we were officially second classmen and wore our two rows of braid on our sleeve. Although seventeen of our class had opted to graduate in June of 1921, there was no distinction for them in our class during that year. There being no class ahead of us, we held all the cadet appointments from sergeant to first captain.

My appointment was that of Regimental Supply Sergeant and I roomed that year with Walter R. Hensey the Regimental Staff Sergeant, for all the regimental staff were housed in the tower rooms at the West end of North Barracks, known as the Eighth and one-half Division. Others in that division were: First Captain and Adjutant, William Kyle; Captain and Supply Officer, David Crawford; and three lieutenants — Battalion Adjutants, Frederick Lee, Henry McGrath and Lemuel Mathewson. Alfred Kessler became a Cadet Lieutenant in "A" Company and Gordon Armes a Sergeant.

I now carried the Cadet Sword instead of the rifle and wore a red sash at my waist. Since we were sergeants we wore the standard pompom on our full dress hats. We marched directly behind the colors at formations with Hensey on the right.

As far as the hops were concerned I was now in the midst of social activity as several were on the Hop Committee. I became a *Hopoid* or regular attendee and had a number of dates. Walter Hensey's sister was a regular visitor and sometimes brought one of her friends with her. When Walter had a date I would step in and escort his sister. When the young lady was unknown to me before the hop, I had a *blind date.*

Social activity did not interfere with my study habits. With the small size of our class sections we were likely to recite every day, but it did not always work out that way. The department heads made a practice of visiting each section from time to time. Colonel Echols, Professor of Mathematics would treat us to mathematical tricks or oddities. Colonel Willcox, Professor of Modern Languages quoted amusing incidents caused by literary translators working on the manual for the French 75mm field piece to emphasize the difference between technical and literary French. Several instructors had pet topics and could be induced to switch from the topic at hand. Major Arthur, our instructor in Military History, had an intense dislike for Sherman's March to the sea during the Civil War, Arthur being from South Carolina. When he got off on that tangent, he was good for using up twenty minutes.

My four years of Latin at Darby High School were of great help in the Romance Languages, more so in Spanish than in French. Our Spanish instructor, Jose M. Ascensio had a beautiful speaking voice; quite musical. When he lectured the class on Spanish art, I became so enchanted listening to him that I almost forgot my note taking for our required paper.

French was my poor subject of the two for I did not have the ear to distinguish subtle differences in tone. Louis Vauthier, one of our instructors in French, had been on the Academy Staff before World War One and spoke Cadet French because he stressed the accent to help the student. I could understand him rather well. Jean Gauthier, the other instructor, spoke with a Parisian accent, quite difficult for me to comprehend.

My regular instructor was Major Adam E. Potts of the Coast Artillery Corps. Daily work in class consisted of a series of short exercises, vocabulary, dictation and translations both ways, French to English and the reverse. Each exercise was graded as completed and we posted our grade in colored chalk under our names. At the end of that class, Major Potts would tell us to write down .5 and then add up the rest of the several grades. Then, he would post his record book during the final minutes. Finally, one member's curiosity got the upper hand and he asked about that .5. Potts replied, "That is a gift from the Department!" That gift kept me proficient in French.

My riding had improved and I was confident enough to sign up for recreational riding on a Sunday afternoon. We would ordinarily ride in groups of two or more, walking to the stables near the South Gate where the horses would be tied to a rail about saddle height. We generally rode up the hill to Fort Putnam and over the reservation on established trails. They were typical Cavalry horses that worked better in groups, liked each others company, and were familiar with cadet riders. One had to be careful to maintain control, for they were hard to hold back when they thought they were headed for their stable. The idea was to return to the stables on the back of the horse you started out with.

One of our interesting Practical Military Engineering exercises was to build a section of a pontoon bridge at one of the lakes on the reservation. We had four wooden pontoons, each on its separate wagon which was horse or mule drawn. These were the same type as had been used during the Civil War. The *balk* or timbers which bridged the pontoons were on their separate wagon as were the *chess* or flooring planks. We built the starter section of a pontoon bridge. We also made the pontoons into a large raft for use in ferrying heavy equipment.

Our class was one of the last to have instruction in the care of the feet, both of horse and of man. Such courses were taught by the Tactical Department. Our course in *Hippology* or the anatomy of the horse, emphasized the proper fitting of a new horseshoe. The key was in the "Frog," that triangular elastic horny pad in the middle of the sole of the hoof. The pumping action of the frog assists the circulation of blood in the leg, and the frog should make contact with the ground when the shoe is properly fitted. A horse should be warmed up before moving at a pace faster than a walk to get the blood circulating properly. Conversely, a horse should be walked after exercise to cool it down. Such knowledge was important to the well-being of the horse.

The Infantry officer should know how to fit a new boot or shoe, neither too loose or too tight, and how to break them in properly. Foot inspections were the rule after the hikes we took in summer camp. A junior officer may not depend on his men to take care of their feet, especially recruits.

Recognizing the role of the Army motor truck in World War One, we had a course on motor transportation. This included the internal combustion engine and various considerations in the maintenance of such vehicles.

In my time the Army-Navy Football games were held in the Polo Grounds. We rode the train to New York and then marched to the Polo Grounds with our band in the lead. I do not recall a long march, but we always had an enthusiastic audience along the way. After the game was over I usually headed for the Astor Hotel, the conventional Army hangout when in New York. My problem was to find the way there. The return trip to West Point left from Grand Central Station about ten the same night. I usually carried an extra white collar for my dress coat, pinned to my shirt in case I needed a change for dinner.

The Corps of Cadets went to Washington during the spring of 1921 to head the parade which was part of the dedication of the Memorial to General Grant at the end of the mall adjacent to the capitol, a tribute to one of the Long Gray Line. The midshipmen from the United States Naval Academy were also in that parade. Vice-President Calvin Coolidge gave the principal address. The ceremonies over, we gathered at the Willard Hotel to spruce up and for some entertainment before leaving for West Point later that evening. That was a long day!

Seventeen members of our class graduated on June 13, 1921 and the rest of us were off on a series of visitations and summer training at Fort Dix, New Jersey, to begin our First Class Year.

SUMMER 1921

We boarded the Army Mine Planter Brigadier General Absalom Baird at the West Point dock while the other two classes moved directly to Camp Dix near Trenton, New Jersey. General Baird, a member of the Class of 1849 had earned a Medal of Honor during the Civil War. We were bound for Fort Wright on Fisher's Island to learn about the Coast Artillery. We had a sightseeing cruise down the Hudson and through the East River into Long Island Sound as Fisher's Island is at the extreme end of Long Island.

Fort Wright was equipped with 12-inch mortars and disappearing rifles and we learned how to load and fire both types under supervision as well as to track moving targets in the control center. Our target was towed about five miles distant, away from shipping.

It was not all hard work for we had plenty of time for recreation. The swimming was good and there were boats available. I rowed out to watch a fisherman work his lobster pots and we enjoyed lobster salad at one of our meals.

The mine planter returned us to New York where we boarded the train for Aberdeen Proving Ground to learn about the Ordnance Department. That was where new weapons were developed and tested and we had some demonstration firings. Edgewood Arsenal, the Chemical Warfare Testing Station was next door to the proving ground. There we were introduced to poison gases, just a sniff, and the gas mask. The main weapon of chemical warfare was the four-inch mortar which used smoke projectiles to cover the Infantry advance as well as explosive and phosphorous rounds. These demonstrations over, we boarded the train again for Camp Dix for the remainder of the summer.

Camp Dix had an excellent artillery range and we were introduced to Corps Artillery, the gun and howitzer of the 155mm bore, about six inches. Again, we learned to fire them doing the work of a typical gun crew. The howitzer was towed by a ten-ton Holt tractor which was new for me. I learned to drive it around in a large open field until I could handle it with accuracy. One steered it by slowing down (braking) one of the treads.

The Air Service gave us a demonstration of their activities. An Army Non-rigid Airship (blimp) of the C-3 Type was flown up from Langley Field, Virginia, to give us demonstration rides. I enjoyed that ride for it was the first time that I had been airborne and could look down at things on the ground. Then, another day, there were several Curtis JN-4 type airplanes flown down from Mitchell Field on Long Island. I found that ride noisier, but much faster than the airship.

That summer ended with the Cadet Corps marching back to West Point in easy stages. There were about 350 cadets plus tactical officers and enlisted men, mainly horse handlers. The column was mixed: Infantry, Cavalry and Artillery, one battery of 75s and one howitzer. I had made a nuisance of myself until given permission to drive the tractor back to West Point. While the cadets who rode horses fed and watered them after a day's march, I filled my tractor with fuel, oil and water, plus greasing the tracks. I rode at a stately pace of five miles per hour.

We marched by back roads and camped at Princeton, Somerville, Morristown and Pompton Lakes to head up Central Valley. At Pompton Lakes I developed a stomach ache and the doctor thought that it might be appendicitis, so I rode into West Point in an ambulance to the Station Hospital where they decided that all I needed was a dose of castor oil. It was an interesting summer.

MY FIRST CLASS YEAR

I felt quite the thing wearing a feathered pompom on my full dress hat and proud to be a cadet lieutenant leading the second platoon of "A" Company. That was far and beyond my expectations as a plebe. Pat Strong was leading the first platoon and Bull Davidson the third. Aaron Kessler was now Cadet Captain of "C" Company. The four of us had roomed together as plebes on the fourth floor of the First Division. Aaron and I now lived on the second floor of the Second Division.

While it was tedious to prepare for our full dress parades, particularly when wearing white trousers, once we were in formation our anticipation was high. The rhythm and cadence of the martial music stimulated our spirits. Marching shoulder to shoulder gave us a sense of unity. These combined for high esprit and an enjoyable experience. Also, there was the stimulation of our audience and reviewing party. It was amazing how much support the bass drum gave to the ceremony, for on one occasion the drum became silent for a while and we could note the difference.

My daily routine remained unchanged and I studied to improve my class standing, or to maintain it. I attended just about every hop that year and did my duty dances with the wives of the senior staff. Aaron and I no longer hiked on foot but rode horseback on the reservation when the weather was nice. Again, we were able to go home for Christmas and I rode to Newark with Aaron and his father in the family car. We also had six-hour leaves on weekends that year, so one Sunday I rode the West Shore Railroad to Newburgh to have Sunday dinner with a young lady and her family. She was one of the locals who regularly attended the hops and I had danced with her many times.

That fall, Lieutenant Mosely of the Air Service had landed an SE-5 (Sopwith) Pursuit airplane on the plain for an overnight stay and visit with the cadets. He talked to those interested in flying, but I did not hear that talk.

A First Classman at West Point led a cloistered life with an exalted status within his environment. The radio was yet to come and I seldom saw a newspaper or popular magazine. We had a speaker program to broaden our view and prepare us for the real world we were about to enter.

Colonel Lucius Holt, our Professor of English, brought home

the point that we really knew little within the total field of knowledge. We entered the classroom to see the blackboards listing all the known fields of knowledge springing from the roots of polytheism and monotheism. He had examined our records before our entrance and during our work at West Point. He then proceeded to underscore, in colored chalk, every field in which one of us had taken a course. The underscoring was very sparse and his message was clear. There was much that we did not know, and that led to the point that it was important to know what you don't know.

We had a civilian chemical engineer lecture on the topic, "I believe because I know!" He was forty years in age before he had taken a close look at the Bible. By that time he thought in chemical terms and decided to check out any chemistry in the Bible. Chapter 32 of Exodus tells that, when Moses was up on the Mount, Aaron and the Israelites had made a Golden Calf to worship and the Lord did not like it. Moses' action in Verse 20 had all the earmarks of a chemical reaction:

> And he (Moses) took the calf which they had made, and burned it in the fire, and ground it to powder, and strawed it upon the water, and made the children of Israel drink of it. (King James version)

The engineer was able to replicate that process after doing some research through a Rabbi friend on the etymology of the original Hebrew text, since gold could not be burnt. Another meaning was *bubble* and that could be done. The local stone at the site of the Biblical incident was magnetite from which he made a mortar and a pestle. He passed around a bottle of a red-brown powder which he had made, assuring us that it would turn water blood-red. From his point of view the Bible was to be believed.

Speakers on the military side were senior members of the staff who spoke from their experiences on suitable behavior, both social and financial, to avoid trouble in adjusting to garrison life as a second lieutenant. They dealt with practical issues such as advice not to sign a friend's note unless you were willing and able to pay it yourself.

The countdown for our graduation began with the *One Hundredth Night Celebration*, written and staged by the cadets. Plebes were called upon to recite the number of days remaining, each day. We wore our class rings with the seal reversed and ordered our uniforms from the Cadet Store. I ordered Peal boots and their representative had an interesting method for measuring me. He used a paper tape about three foot long and made his measurements in a sequence such that each one was greater than the one before, ending up with the height of the boot. For each measure he would make a neat tear in the edge of the tape, about one-fourth inch deep. My name was the only writing on that tape.

The First Class preceding us in 1920 had a one-day field trip to the Army's arsenal at Watervliet near Troy, New York, some ninety miles north of West Point on the Hudson River. We were fortunate in having a week-long field trip to visit three arsenals in the New England area, traveling by railroad. Our first arsenal was Watervliet. It had been in existence since Revolutionary War days; then manufacturing heavy artillery. However artillery was not the highlight of the stop for we were entertained with a dance at the Emma Willard School for Girls at Troy. We had been forewarned and had our full dress coats with us.

The Watertown Arsenal was our next stop, located in a suburb of Boston, Massachusetts. Seacoast Artillery was manufactured there, such as we had learned to operate at Fort Wright on Fisher's Island. At Watertown we were also instructed on the organization and management of such facilities. My interest was captivated by their method of casting the steel billet from which the rifle barrel would be manufactured. The mold was in a vertical position and on a turntable which slowly rotated. The idea was that the centrifugal force from the rotation would concentrate any impurities at the center to be removed when the billet was bored. In the course of manufacture, several sleeves would be shrunk on the breech section of the barrel to pre-stress that barrel to the extent that it would always operate within the elastic limit of the steel when the gun was fired. Incidentally, I saw my first dial telephone at Watertown. It was used for the telephone interconnecting their buildings.

From Watertown we headed for Springfield, Massachusetts, to visit the factory where the Model 1906 rifles were made. This was the standard weapon for World War One and we used them at West Point. The Commanding Officer, Colonel Thales L. Ames and his wife arranged a reception and dance for us on the large veranda of their quarters and the adjoining lawn; the local ladies being augmented by students from Smith and Vassar Colleges. My classmate William S. Lawton kindly provided me with a clipping from the *Springfield Union* dated June 3, 1922, reporting on our visit to that city. We left for West Point that afternoon in time for the hop that evening.

General and Mrs. Douglas MacArthur held the traditional reception for the graduating cadets and distinguished visitors in the garden of the Superintendent's Quarters. When I entered through the front door to where Mrs. MacArthur was receiving, I was taken by surprise when she greeted me by name. While I had danced my duty dances with her at the hops, I did not expect her to remember me that well. There was a large gathering, the Secretary of War, the Honorable John M. Weeks who would make the address, senior members of the staff and faculty and others in uniform.

I expected that General William Weigel, Commander of the First Corps Area, would be present for we were located in his area. General Weigel was commanding my father's brigade at the time he was killed in August 1918. He knew that I was a cadet at West Point and had inquired about me from other cadets he would meet through happenstance, on the train or in New York City.

He was at the reception so I had a short but interesting conversation with General Weigel during which he remarked that it was customary for "Old Grads" to pass on words of wisdom to new graduates, and that such pearls were largely ignored. However, he felt impelled to pass on a warning from his experience: "Do not permit yourself to become dependent upon another person, but get rid of him before dependency develops. Should money matters be involved, get rid of him sooner!"

General Weigel's theme was to develop self-reliance and that matched my own views. I was strongly inclined to do things by myself and in my own way; to find my own solutions. That bent had been encouraged at home by my mother.

The old Thayer Hotel at Trophy Point had limited facilities for the families that gathered for graduation. I was able to secure accommodations in a private home in Highland Falls for my mother, three brothers and sister to attend my graduation and they were present for the big day.

Aaron and I had had numerous discussions regarding the merits of the various arms and services during our first class year. By the spring of 1922 I was down to the Corps of Engineers because of its technical nature and the Air Service, also technical. Aaron was enthusiastic about the Air Service because it was quite new and we could get in on the ground floor and grow with it. We both signed up for the Air Service when the time came and received our choice because Aaron graduated ninth in class standing and I seventh.

To sum matters up, West Point took in a callow youth and made him a man in four years.

THE CLASS OF JUNE 13, 1922

We were graduated on June 13, 1922, the first class to have completed the normal four-year academic program since the cadets who had entered in June 1913 and who were graduated on April 20, 1917. The intervening classes had academic programs of three and two years. After the Armistice in November 1918, we began a three-year program which was extended to four years by an Act of Congress in March 1920. Cadets in the class following ours also had entered under a three-year program and thirty of that group exercised their option to graduate in three years. They became the Class of June 14, 1922.

Our class was also unique in that we had members directly commissioned in the Air Service upon graduation, and the following were assigned to the Air Service and sent to Brooks Field at San Antonio, Texas, for the primary phase of their pilot training:

Benjamin W. Chidlaw	Alfred A. Kessler
Orval R. Cook	William S. Lawton
Howard G. Davidson	Edmund C. Lynch
Mervin E. Gross	James W. Spry
Francis B. Kane	Fred J. Woods

While prospective promotion opportunities in the Twenties were dismal, those who selected the Air Service and who qualified as airplane pilots, all ended up in the general officer grades with Chidlaw and Cook to become four-star generals.

Brooks Field — 1922

Carlstrom Field at Arcadia, Florida, was the sole remaining primary flying training station after World War One. In the spring of 1922, that school was moved in two troop trains to Brooks Field at the south edge of San Antonio. I became a member of the first class of the rejuvenated flying training program which began at Brooks Field in September 1922. Arriving by the "Katy" train on Sunday, I put up at the St. Anthony Hotel and had the opportunity to stroll around downtown before reporting to that station on Monday.

Major Ralph Royce had made the move from Carlstrom to Brooks as Commanding Officer and had participated in the Punitive Expedition under General Pershing. Lieutenant Pardoe Martin was his Adjutant and all the permanent party were first lieutenants. The hierarchy in that group was based on flying skill rather than on date of rank. Johnny Corkill who was checkout pilot had that position because he was acknowledged number one, based on the way he could handle the JN-4E he used in that task. The students were a mixed lot, forty-seven officers ranging from major to second lieutenant and several flying cadets brought from Carlstrom Field.

One student from the California National Guard had driven his Stanley Steamer automobile to Brooks, about fourteen hundred miles. That was no mean feat because that machine used up water for the boiler about as fast as the kerosene for making steam. We had demonstration rides and it was a revelation to me for I had never ridden in a steam car before. After a few minutes to get up steam, you were off by opening the throttle, no gears. Acceleration was smooth and powerful and maximum speed depended upon steam pressure. While the car was on standby, a pilot light kept the burner ready for ignition. One night when the car was parked outside our bachelor quarters, the guard saw the flickering light and doused it with a fire extinguisher.

Our bachelor officer quarters were adjacent to the Officer's Club and mess. My room was small but adequate with the common bath midway down the hall. We had no heat in our rooms, but the bath was warm with plenty of hot water. The large social room at one end had a fireplace, our sole source of heat in the building. The

Officers Mess was excellent, three meals each day for one dollar. The "Mess Officer" was elected and anyone who complained vociferously was an automatic candidate for election, the assumption being that he should be able to correct his complaints. All the staff were Chinese, brought back to San Antonio with General Pershing when he returned from Mexico. The soldiers on the Punitive Expedition were all combat troops and Pershing had hired the Chinese to work in the kitchens and to do the laundry. They were from among those trapped in Mexico by the Chinese Exclusion Act of 1912.

Ruth and Chink Rust lived in a set of married officer quarters next to bachelor quarters, so we soon became acquainted.* One day that fall, Chink invited three of us to ride with him on a visit to his bootlegger and to see the country. Leaving San Antonio on the old Austin Highway in his Model-T touring car, we turned south at the Blackjack country, a wooded area about halfway to New Braunfels. Following a winding lane through the brush, there were sandy places where we had to get out and push because the Model-T did not do well in deep sand. The bootlegger lived in a small shack several miles from the highway and we were invited in to sample his wares. The inside board walls had the cracks papered with magazine covers to stop the drafts. During the initial proceedings I had noted the bootlegger eyeing Chink's boots which were Quartermaster issue for enlisted troopers, made of soft chrome tanned leather.

Chink bought a gallon of clear corn whiskey for six dollars, brought from a cache some distance away. When the bootlegger returned he began dickering with Chink to trade his boots and a deal was struck for another gallon, not bad as the boots cost about seven dollars new. Since the boots fitted, Chink drove home in his socks.

From September until Christmas we attended Ground School classes in subjects such as Theory of Flight, Meteorology, Navigation and Radio Code. At the end we had a celebration dinner at the Officer's Club with all the staff present. The feature event that evening was a skit prepared by the students on the various mannerisms and classroom behavior of the instructors. The center piece was a jerry built airplane powered by an electric fan. This craft was fastened together in a way to collapse when the trigger was pulled.

* Lieutenant Charles (Chink) Rust was Commandant of Flying Cadets.

The gist of the skit was that the student pilot became confused with all the advice he had received and crashed. It was a hit.

Flying training began after the first of the year, the instruction being in the master — apprentice mode. The instructor would describe a maneuver, demonstrate it to the student who would then do it with corrections from the instructor. For instance, the normal takeoff requires application of right rudder to offset the engine torque. When I was too easy on the rudder bar, I could feel the increased pressure applied by the instructor on our dual controls.

The "Jenny" we trained on at Brooks was the JN-4D Model made by Curtiss and had a more powerful engine than the JN-2 used on the Punitive Expedition, this Hispano Suiza was rated at one hundred fifty horsepower. The "E" Model engine developed twenty-five horsepower more than the "D" Model. The fuselage of the Jenny was constructed of wooden longerons and struts braced by steel wires and turnbuckles for tension. The wings were made of wood, both ribs and spars, covered with a closewoven cotton fabric which was shrunk by the application of a nitrocellulose plastic called "Dope." The various control surfaces were made the same way. The upper and lower wings of this biplane were separated by struts and braced by flexible steel cables, tensioned with turnbuckles. The control column or "Joystick" operated the horizontal and vertical controls, and was operated by the right hand. The rudder had a foot bar. The throttle or engine control was operated by the left hand. The only instruments were for engine temperature and revolutions. It was up to the pilot to judge his air speed through the *feel* of the controls, customarily referred to as, "Flying by the seat of one's pants."

The Jennies used by the flying instructors had two sets of airlerons on each side, right and left. They were hinged to the upper and lower wings and interconnected with two wooden struts. There were a number of Jennies on the solo stage with but one set of airlerons on each side, those on the upper wings. One soon learned that there was a difference in the airleron control to be taken into account when turning; the reaction was slower of course.

Lieutenant Frederick Patrick, my flying instructor, had been a pursuit pilot in World War One. His key theme was *smoothness,* to work through the momentum of the airplane with the controls, rather than to use brute force. From time to time, and without warning, he would close the throttle as a signal for a forced landing.

You were supposed to put the nose down to keep up your speed, look around for a suitable field and begin your maneuver to land. It was a test of your control of the situation, or your reaction, rather than to make a landing.

When Patrick thought that I was ready to solo, to take off and land by myself, we landed at an auxiliary field away from Brooks, he climbed out and told me to make several landings. After two or three, he signalled me to taxi to him, he climbed back in the front cockpit and I was then ready for the solo stage. We flew in the front cockpit on that stage for sandbags had been secured in the rear seat to maintain the balance. From then on my instruction periods were intermittent, to teach me new maneuvers and to see that I had acquired no bad habits on the solo stage.

While San Antonio had excellent weather for flying, I recall one March day when the wind was blowing at least twenty miles per hour and I thought that flying might be cancelled, but no, we were scheduled for instruction in cross wind landings. The technique was that the pilot side slipped into the wind at a rate to offset the drift and maintain alignment with the landing direction of roll. At the instant of touchdown, you would pick up the low wing, straighten out and apply hard rudder to avoid a ground loop, not easy to do smoothly. The Jenny had wing skids that would protect the wing tip from dragging during a moderate ground loop.

When I passed my checkout ride with Lieutenant Corkill, the Patrick's took me to the Menger Hotel for a celebration dinner. That was when I say my first live alligator, perhaps three feet long and confined to a cage at the entrance to the dining room.

During that spring our afternoons were spent in the maintenance shop to learn about rigging an airplane and to overhaul an engine. We were in teams to take a Jenny apart and then put it back together again the proper way. The key tool there was a steel tape, for the crew chief had all the dimensions of the various cables in his black book, which I copied. The engine was completely disassembled, cleaned and parts replaced as necessary before reassembly. I learned how to fit piston rings and to scrape bearings. That engine was given the standard run-in on the test stand and was then installed in the airframe we had rigged, to be flown for the final adjustment, or trim. The message was clear, that knowledge of our equipment was part of flying safety. The other part was an understanding of your own capability.

Public transportation from downtown San Antonio to Brooks Field was the trolley car from Alamo Plaza South on Presa Street to the city limits. From there we took a "Jitney" for the ride to the Officers Club, a five-cent fare. It was adequate for normal travel but not for social activity. Frank Kane and Freddie Woods of my class had touring cars on station. They had struck up an acquaintance with three young ladies, close friends from high school days, who preferred multiple dating. Frank was dating Pauline Palmer and Freddie was dating Anita Culp and I was brought in to date Edith Hightower. Our primary interest was dancing, so we would make the rounds on weekends. The St. Anthony and Gunter Hotels then had roof gardens with good bands. There were dances at Brooks Field, Kelly Field and Fort Sam Houston, to visit two or more on a Saturday evening. I saved my pennies that winter and bought a Model-T coupe for six hundred and thirty dollars delivered.

When the class moved to Kelly Field, I continued to date Edith Hightower and we were married in June 1923. Anita later married Jimmy Daniel from another class at Brooks Field. Pauline went to the West coast hoping to break into the movies, but married instead.

The forty-seven officers in the first primary flying training class which began in September 1922 included seventeen recent graduates of West Point:

Ten members of the Class of June 13, 1922:

Benjamin W. Chidlaw	Alfred A. Kessler
Orval R. Cook	William S. Lawton
Howard G. Davidson	Edmund C. Lynch
Marvin E. Gross	James W. Spry
Francis B. Kane	Fred J. Woods

Four members of the Class of June 14, 1922:

Landon C. Catlett, Jr.	Townsend Griffis
William B. Goddard	Hilbert M. Wittkop

Three members of earlier classes:

Frederick von H. Kimble, June 1918
Cornelius E. O'Connor, June 1919
Hugo P. Rush, June 1920

In 1922, an aeronautical rating was required for membership in the Army's Air Service. Fourteen newly minted second lieutenants from West Point had to qualify as an airplane pilot to retain that status. Fourteen who then held lighter-than-air or observer ratings were seeking to up-grade their future status. One of that group was Major Oscar Westover who would become Chief of the Air Corps in 1935. The remaining nineteen were, in effect, applying for admission. Also, there were ten national guard officers seeking to qualify for the Air National Guard and a large number of flying cadets who could receive a reserve appointment in the Air Service with a flying rating.

Howard G. Davidson of my class was held over because of being hospitalized due to an aircraft accident. Francis B. Kane did not qualify and transferred to the Coast Artillery Corps.

Army Officer students in the class of September 1922:

Bender, W., Capt., A.S.	
Boudinot, T. E., Capt.	
Burt, B. T., 1 Lieut., A.S.	Graduated
Bushey, O. J., 1 Lieut., A.S.	
Candee, R. C., Capt.,	Graduated
Catlett, L. C., 2 Lieut., A.S.	Graduated
Chidlaw, B. W., 2 Lieut., A.S.	Graduated
Cook, O. R., 2 Lieut., A.S.	Graduated
Davidson, H. G., 2 Lieut., A.S.	Holdover
Duty, W. A., Major	Graduated
Fenters, C. E., Capt.	
Fisher, A. G., Lieut. Col., A.S.	
Gardner, 2 Lieut., A.S.	Holdover
Giles, B. F., Capt., A.S.	Holdover
Goddard, W. H., 2 Lieut., A.S.	Graduated
Gray, H. C., Capt., A.S.	Graduated
Greenslade, R. H., 1 Lieut., A.S.	
Griffiss, T., 2 Lieut., A.S.	Graduated
Griffith, J. S., 2 Lieut.,	Graduated
Gross, M. E., 2 Lieut., A.S.	Graduated
Hale, W. R., Capt.	Graduated
Healy, M. V., 2 Lieut.	
Hill, R. S., 2 Lieut., A.S.	Graduated
Holden, H. W., 1 Lieut., A.S.	
Hopkins, F. M., 1 Lieut., A.S.	
Kane, F. B., 2 Lieut., A.S.	
Kessler, A. A., 2 Lieut., A.S.	Graduated
Kimble, F. H., 2 Lieut.	
Lawton, W. S., 2 Lieut., A.S.	Graduated
Long, N. F., 1 Lieut.	Graduated

Lynch, E. C., 2 Lieut., A.S.	Graduated
Morrow, J. C., Maj.	
O'Connor, C. E., 1 Lieut.	Graduated
Peak, L. J., 1 Lieut., A.S.	
Peterson, L. J., 2 Lieut.	Graduated
Powers, J. D., Capt.	
Pughe, K. F., 2 Lieut.	
Rush, H. P., 2 Lieut.	Graduated
Simpson, F. W., 1 Lieut.	
Snavely, R. A., 2 Lieut.	Graduated
Spry, J. W., 2 Lieut., A.S.	Graduated
Terry, D. A., 2 Lieut.	
Westover, O., Major, A.S.	Graduated
Turnbull, W. R., 1 Lieut.	
Wittkop, H. M., 2 Lieut., A.S.	Graduated
Woods, F. J., 2 Lieut., A.S.	Graduated
Zelner, W. A., 1 Lieut., A.S.	

Kelly Field

The Air Service emerged from World War One with three well defined specialties: Pursuit (Fighter), Observation and Bombardment Aviation, according to their military function. During that war, bombardment training had been at Kelly Field while pursuit training was located at Ellington Field near Houston, and observation training was located at Fort Sill, Oklahoma. By 1922, all advanced training was concentrated at Kelly Field.

By the end of World War One there was a felt need for an aircraft to attack enemy ground troops using machine gun and cannon fire. This need related to the armored vehicles (tanks) which were an innovation of that war. Experiments had been made at Kelly Field to install additional machine guns on the DH-4 aircraft, but without success because the machine guns outside the propeller arc upset the flying characteristics. When I returned to Kelly in 1927, the specialty of Attack Aviation had been added to the advanced training courses.

I was assigned to the observation training section to learn how to fly to DH-4B airplane. That program was much the same as that at Brooks, but the DH-4 was a heavier airplane with the Liberty engine which developed 400 horsepower in contrast to the 150 used with the JN-4. Bigger and more powerful, the DH-4 handled differently.

During the early stages while we were practicing landings and take-offs, we had a dramatic and unintended demonstration of a stall followed by a spin. I was with a group of students and a flying instructor out in the middle of the field, grouped at the ending of the landing roll. Each student would make circuits to land and take off immediately. After several circuits you would be called in and replaced by another student without stopping the engine. I was waiting my turn and watching the approaching airplane, it was apparent to me that the glide was too flat and the speed too low. Quite suddenly the plane stalled and whipped into a spin from an altitude of a little over one hundred feet. The rule in the Cavalry was that when one was thrown from a horse, you immediately climbed back on and took a ride to establish confidence. My instructor followed that practice and I was sent off to make my landings. As to be expected, I came in with too much speed and was halfway across Kelly before I was able to touch down. It took several landings before I calmed down.

Edith and I had decided to marry during a short break in the class schedule when I could get a few days leave of absence. The wedding was at Edith's home, a quiet ceremony in which I was supported by my classmates and their wives. Lillian Chidlaw was Matron of Honor and Aaron Kessler was my Best Man, with others in support. We took an auto trip to Dallas in my Model-T Coupe to visit one of Edith's aunts and to see the sights along the way. That trip was an adventure as there were few road signs to mark the way in those days.

Edith and I were assigned tiny quarters on Kelly Field and made-do with the minimum government furniture that came with the quarters. We made our duty call on Major and Mrs. Hickam, my Commanding Officer, and were invited for dinner in their quarters. Then, it was our turn to reciprocate, should we take them out to dinner or should we have the dinner in our quarters? We decided that the proper thing was to entertain at home. The dinner was quite successful with Mrs. Hickam relating her early experiences in the Army. Her philosophy was to do the best you could with the means at hand.

In contrast to my smooth progress through the course at Brooks Field, I had troubles at Kelly Field, some of my own making. Our wedding did not please officialdom and I had been having problems with my flying instructor. For one thing, his methods of making the 180° and 360° maneuvers for a forced landing were different from those I had learned at Brooks. When I had a new instructor whose pattern I understood and could do well, I was transferred back to Brooks Field in August of 1923 to wait for the next class to move to Kelly. Edith and I were fortunate in retaining our quarters and I commuted each day.

I then became Commanding Officer of the Photographic Detachment which had about twenty men in it. This unit performed public relations and historical photography. There were several old time noncommissioned officers in that detachment and I learned more than photographic techniques. I was clearly a *Perfectionist* and thought that activities should be governed by logic. My education began with the allocation of flying pay to the noncoms in my detachment. My position was that flying pay was for actual flying duty, while past allocations had been based on seniority. I lost out on any ideas to change the past routine!

When I returned to Brooks I was greeted as an old member of the family. At my move to Kelly I sensed a cooler atmoshpere, principally as between students and staff, attributing it to the larger size of Kelly and the specializations. The fact that the personnel at Brooks had moved in a body from Carlstrom Field could have drawn them together. At any rate, I was given a free hand to fly with the solo group to build up flying time and practice.

I performed normal station duties. As a detachment commander I inspected supplies delivered to the Enlisted Men's Mess, for quantity and condition. My first inspection was an order of whole chickens packed in wooden barrels, supposed to be *hens*. When the burlap cover was removed from the first barrel, I saw a set of spurs on a chicken. I asked the Mess Sergeant whether he had seen a hen with spurs. Since he had not, I told him to reject the entire order and tell the supplier to sort out any other hens with spurs. That was to let the supplier know that someone did inspect their orders in detail.

Social activity for Edith and me was confined to weekends,

usually a dance at Fort Sam Houston or Kelly Field. One weekend there was a gigantic reception and dance at Fort Sam Houston to honor General Pershing's visit. The Commanding Officer at Kelly reminded us of the reception and said that he would like to see a good turnout. Edith and I had planned for dinner in town but did not plan to go to the reception because of the crush. However, dinner over and dressed in party clothes, we decided to take a look. As we expected the receiving line was a block long, and we began to dance. Colonel Sheplar Fitzgerald, the Executive, with his wife, as well as Major and Mrs. Hickam were also on the floor, so we said our "Good Evenings." As the line shortened, we joined and met General Pershing. The next day there was a notice on the Bulletin Board to report whether we had been to the reception. The lesson there was that when the Commanding Officer expressed a "desire" about a social occasion, it was equivalent to an order.

Aaron Kessler was dating his future wife "Polly" who was visiting her sister Blanch Walker at Kelly Field. Captain Ralph Walker who was in the maintenance department, liked to cook nice sirloin steaks outside over a mesquite fire and knew a meat wholesaler in town who supplied the hotels with Kansas City corn fed beef, properly aged. Aaron and I would go with him into the cold room and look for a steak with the proper *marbling* of the meat and test our choice in the eating. By the time Edith and I left for Fort Bragg, they were engaged to be married. However, we were unable to attend their wedding.

The second time around at Kelly I thought that I was making satisfactory progress during the first three months when, to my surprise, I was suspended from flying by the Evaluation Board, but not terminated (washed out), with no explanation made to me. I made no effort to appeal that decision and waited for further word. It did remove me from flying status, a penalty in effect. Thinking things over I could only relate it to my overall judgement, since I had not been involved in an aircraft accident. As to judgement, it could have been due to a lack of maturity or sophistication. On the other hand it could have been due to my independence, as in the case I decided to get married. I never did find out. Whatever the reason, it did not alter Major Hickam's attitude toward me.

Shortly thereafter, Major Hickam called me to his office to ask whether I would be interested in flying as an aerial photographer with Captain Calvin E. Giffin on a mapping project which had been assigned to Kelly Field for execution. That sounded interesting and I agreed. This project kept me busy until September 1924 when I was ordered to Fort Bragg, North Carolina, for duty with the Field Artillery Board.

Horace M. Hickam

Major Horace Meek Hickam, West Point 1908 had taken a look at the future and transferred from the Cavalry to the Air Service during World War One. After a tour as Public Information Officer for the Chief of Air Service, he had moved to Kelly Field as School Group Commander and was my Commanding Officer in 1923.

When Edith and I married, Major and Mrs. Hickam were kind to us and instrumental in our keeping our quarters on Kelly Field while I was assigned to Brooks Field for five months. In one of our conversations he told me about escorting Thomas Edison on a tour of Bolling Field to show him the various aircraft. Edison was not interested in looking closely at detail. He told Hickam that his laboratory was concerned with evaluating ideas for their economic potential and that only about one in a thousand proposals were given serious consideration.

Shortly after I was suspended from the flying training program in 1924, he called me to his office to ask whether I would be interested in flying as an aerial photographer on a special project authorized by the War department. I agreed and was returned to flying status. He knew that I was familiar with surveying and mapping from my courses at West Point, and would be a suitable counterpart to Captain Calvin E. Giffin who had been a topographic engineer before he took his pilot training.

While this project was under way, he asked me to substitute for him as speaker for a Lion's Club Luncheon at the St. Anthony Hotel, remarking that skill in public speaking was important for all Army officers. Since he had no topic, I suggested that I describe the mapping project and went to work. My theme was about what the Army could do for the civilian community during peacetime. I took the Bagley Camera and samples for display at the luncheon. Just before the luncheon began, Major Hickam came in to sit beside me. I was certain that he had maneuvered me into this opportunity for my benefit and was on hand to support me. He was that kind of a person, helpful to junior officers.

Major Hickam took me fishing with him on the Gulf of Mexico. He landed our DH on a meadow at the north end of Matagorda Island across the inlet from Port O'Connor where a commercial fisherman picked us up to head out through Cavallo Pass. We trolled offshore for Spanish Mackerel using spoons and towing four lines. The fish were plentiful near a submerged wreck and we caught about two hundred in a few hours, the locker was full and our fish paid for the trip. The fisherman unhooked our fish for us as the mackerel had sharp teeth. He had the knack of grasping the flapping fish between his knees and wore cotton gloves. We both took home fish for our suppers that evening. My contribution was to start the Liberty engine when we were ready to go home to Kelly Field.

At that time, Matagorda Island was vacant other than for cattle grazing on its grass. It was later developed as a range during World War Two for aerial gunnery practice over the Gulf of Mexico.

By the time I returned to Randolph Field from Panama, Hickam had been promoted to Lieutenant Colonel and was in command of the Third Attack Group at Fort Crockett, Galveston, Texas, a former seacoast artillery post. My classmate Harold Conway was the Aviation Ordnance Officer for that group, so I made frequent visits to Galveston. When I arrived on station, I always paid my respects and some conversations with Colonel Hickam ran long. For one thing he was interested in what I had been doing in Panama and topics related to the future development of the Air Corps. Colonel Hickam had graduated from the Army War College and suggested several books which he thought would be helpful to me, including Admiral Mahan's work, *The Influence of Sea Power Upon History,* and General Douhet's book, *The Command of The Air.*

In one discussion, Colonel Hickam made the remark that the Air Corps needed officers who could bridge the gap between research and application. Scientists tend to seek perfection and delay the application of their knowledge. Hickam's idea was that there was a need for someone to tell the scientists when to put their *Know-how* to work for the benefit of the tactical units. Years later I heard the same thought expressed by the Englishman who ram-rodded the radar screen which enabled the Royal Air Force to counter the moves of the German Air Force in the Battle for Britain. The speaker said, "We had to do the best we could with the means at hand, for the next best would come too late and the best would never come!"

Major Hickam's intercession on the mapping project proved beneficial to me. As a mentor he listened to my ideas and suggested professional readings. The Air Corps lost a Potential Chief and a superior officer when he was killed in an aircraft accident at Fort Crockett in 1934, a sad day for me. Hickam Field was named in his honor.

The Right Way

The pioneer Army pilots were largely self taught, expanding from a base of two qualified by the Wright Brothers in 1909. Lieutenant Benjamin Foulois, with a Wright "C" airplane (operating off skids), was sent to Fort Sam Houston in 1911 to teach himself to fly. After April 1917, the great expansion of the Army's air arm created urgency, coupled with hustle and bustle. Student pilots were turned loose as soon as they could make safe take-offs and landings, to build proficiency. With limited supervision, they developed their own techniques for various maneuvers. There had been no standardized method developed.

This situation was brought home to me by my first instructor on the DH-4 airplane at Kelly Field. He had been a pursuit pilot during the war, short in stature and of a cocky attitude. He had no doubts about his ability to handle an airplane telling me, "There is my way of flying an airplane, and there is the wrong way."

I had no problems with his ways until we came to the 180° maneuver for a forced landing which differed from that learned under Lieutenant Patrick at Brooks. On the 180° approach, the airplane was headed downwind over the intended landing spot at one thousand feet above it. His first turn was 90° to fly away from the final glide path, followed by a second 90° turn, counting seconds for the estimated time to obtain clearance. The last two turns were also 90° but the target was in sight. The pattern which I had learned called for a turn of about 60° to start so that you could see the landing spot, followed by a long sweeping turn into the final landing approach, the target always in sight and adjustments could be made continuously in the glide path.

Before matters came to a head, that instructor had the misfortune to collide with an oil derrick near Laredo, and was killed. He was replaced by Lieutenant Westside T. Larson who used the pattern I was familiar with. The concentration of flying training at Brooks and Kelly began a period of standardization in teaching methods.

That experience left an indelible impression on me. Ever since I have distrusted anyone who stated or implied that they have *The Right Way* and my mind switches back to that flying instructor.

The De Haviland Airplane

The De Haviland Airplane (DH-4) was designed by Sir Geoffrey De Haviland and powered by the Liberty engine. It came too late for our use in World War One, but was the Army's mainstay until the late Twenties. While the *Jenny* had all the glamour, the DH did all the work. There were three versions based on the rear cockpit arrangements: the training version with dual controls, the observation type with a ring mount for a flexible machine gun support, and a photographic version to accommodate an aerial camera shooting pictures through the floor. In Panama, we used the photographic version converted with a winch for tow target work through 1931. The front cockpit of the DH-4 had a full complement of instruments. The bank and turn indicator was adequate for rudimentary instrument flying, and to avoid vertigo. I spent many enjoyable hours riding in that aircraft as pilot, observer or photographer.

The JN-4 (Jenny) was designed by Glenn H. Curtis and produced in quantity for training purposes. After the war they were used for barnstorming by civilians and in a number of experiments by the government. American manufacturers were supposed to build the DH-4 for use in the war and plans were available in August 1917, but manufacturing delays resulted in not one being shipped before the Armistice. The "A" model had the front cockpit immediately behind the engine and the fuel tank between the two cockpits, no doubt to improve the pilot's visibility forward. Being unsatisfactory to the pilots, the front cockpit and fuel tank were interchanged for the "B" model which became standard. The fuselage of the DH was similar to that of the Jenny in construction in the early versions, but some were produced using steel tubing in place of the wooden longerons and struts. The DH-4 which we used for tow target work in Panama had steel tubing construction. It had decidedly different landing characteristics due to being heavier. The wooden version which we used at Kelly would float just before the touchdown in landing. The steel version would settle down like a brick with no float.

The Liberty engine was designed by a committee, fortunately that committee was a team of automotive engineers. Guided by the basic policy that there would be no innovations, just tried and true elements from internal combustion engines then existing, it represented the state of the art in 1917. Until then the magneto had been standard for the ignition system on aircraft engines. The Liberty was to have dual ignition systems (dual spark plugs) for reliability, so the Delco system developed by Mr. Kettering was used. This was a low voltage system with a battery and generator. The low voltage pulses were stepped up by a transformer and distributed to the proper spark plugs. This system has been universal in automobiles for the past seventy years.

After I moved to Austin in 1953, I met Mr. Williams who had been a member of that committee representing Packard Motor Company. He had served in the Navy during World War One and was a crew chief for one of the NC-4s flown by the Navy to the Azores in the early Twenties. After that he served as a civilian employee in the Navy, retiring from the Naval Air Station at Corpus Christi. He confirmed my information about the policy used in developing the Liberty engine and was very proud of the record it had for reliability.

There was only one minor modification that I know of and this was replacing the *Standard Tooth* gears driving the camshafts with *Stubnosed* gears to avoid possible binding which caused camshafts to shear. I can testify to its reliability because I had only one malfunction in ten years behind that engine, a broken rocker arm which caused one cylinder to *miss* and the other eleven took me back to base.

The Liberty engine was used in the Loening Amphibian in an inverted position. That involved no basic change in the engine. In the upright position the engine oil is retained in the crankcase (wet sump type).When inverted it was converted to a *dry sump* type where the oil is pumped out of the crank case into a separate oil reservoir or cooler.

I saw only one Liberty engine which had been equipped with an exhaust driven supercharger; that was when I was on temporary duty at Wright Field, Dayton, Ohio, during 1929. That engine was installed in a LaPere biplane used by Lieutenant John Mcready in setting an altitude record of 40,000 feet in 1921. The LaPere had a high-lift wing section with wings much longer than those for a conventional biplane such as the DH-4 (high aspect ratio.) In 1929, that airplane was being used for experimental purposes and could only be flown when the ground wind was less than ten miles per hour. When that airplane was being taxied, there was one man on each wing in case of gusts.

A Bird's Eye View of Texas

The utility of the airplane for military purposes had been clearly demonstrated during World War One, but little work had been done to apply the talents of the airplane to civil use, other than through barnstorming. The Twenties were an active period for experimentation in various uses for the airplane, further, the War Department encouraged such experiment. For instance, when I was in charge of the photo detachment at Brooks Field in 1923, the War Department authorized us to loan film to an Army reserve officer who was starting out in the field of aerial photography, there being no local source for such film. When his order came in from Eastman Kodak at Rochester, he would return the fresh film. We benefited as that type of film was soon out-dated.

The Texas State Board of Water Engineers faced the problem of flooding along the Rio Grande River and other large Texas rivers as well. They were handicapped in locating and designing suitable dams by a lack of up to date maps. Most of the topograhic maps had been made by the Army during the 1880s at the time they were fighting the Indians. At that time the topographers rode along the roads in a horse draw buggy and worked from the highway, so the maps (other than railroad surveys) were not trustworthy.

Aerial photography was the answer and the Army had a unique mapping camera designed by Major Bagley of the Corps of engineers, quite new in 1924. Essentially, it was three cameras in one case and arranged to take simultaneous pictures; one a vertical picture and two chambers shooting to the right and left of the flight path. The three exposures were all on one roll of film. The ground covered was about two by seven miles from an altitude of 12,000 feet above the ground. The two oblique pictures had to be *transformed* to the horizontal plane of the center vertical by using a special printer, the composite photograph looking like a bow tie in outline. The Bagley camera was really a mapping *instrument* since the transforming printer and various templates were specially made for one particular camera. This machine was outside the experience of the typical aerial photographer.

The War Department approved a joint project; the Air Service would provide the aerial photographs and process the film, the U.S. Geological Survey would make the maps from the aerial photographs, and the Texas Board of Water Engineers would put up some money for the maps they needed. The Bagley camera was shipped to Kelly Field for that station would provide the photographic work.

Captain Calvin E. Giffin was selected to fly the mission, an experienced topographic engineer having mapped in Alaska and on the Arizona border before he took pilot training during World War One. He was in charge of the project and I became his assistant. We began by making a trip to Austin to consult with the State Board of Water Engineers landing our photographic DH on the Camp Mabry parade ground and going to the State Capitol Building by staff car. They provided maps with the desired areas marked out and I noted that one of the maps had a date of 1874, the best one that they had. The main parts were along the Pecos and Devils Rivers which fed water into the Rio Grande. In Central Texas there were the Colorado and Nueces Rivers. We photographed 11,500 square miles in 23 flying days, but the time-consuming part was the work on the ground.

Captain Giffin did all the planning of the flights to conserve time, fuel and film to get the most out of each roll of film and tank of fuel. The camera had to be reloaded in complete darkness because of the special film. He gave me a quick course in the operation of the Bagley camera and we were off. My task in the air was to keep the camera level, using the bubble on the top, and snap a picture every 30 seconds along the flight line to obtain an overlap of about sixty percent. I also recorded the exposure numbers from the counter on the camera for each strip.

It got cold over Texas at 12,000 feet, so we wore furlined flying suits and gloves. We also wore parachutes, my first experience. The West Texas country provided few emergency fields in the area we were covering and we were prepared to bail out if necessary. The Liberty engine ran smoothly and we had no problem. Before each mission Captain Giffin would run through his checklist to see that everything was ready before we started the engine. We covered the entire area without gaps for I knew enough to snap an extra picture if there was any yaw in the flight line when Giffin made a correction. He had a streamer on the trailing edge of the wing to indicate proper overlaps of the flight lines.

On the ground work, Captain Giffin set up the plan and I did the work and wrote up the report. The laboratory work was done by the Kelly Field Photographic Detachment and I had my space in their building. When the film had been developed, I numbered each exposure with India ink, and made a visual inspection of the film checking the numbers against my record from the counter on the camera. The film then was turned over to the laboratory to make the necessary prints, each carrying its number from the film. While waiting, I made index maps to show the location of each composite against the flight line, using a template shaped like a bow tie.

When the prints were ready, I assembled the composites by trimming each print with its special template and cementing them to a light cardboard backing with rubber cement. Two sets were made, one for the U.S. Geological Survey and one for the Texas Board of Water Engineers. The set for Washington was sent by mail while Captain Giffin and I flew to Camp Mabry in Austin to deliver the Texas set.

Lieutenant Dache M. (Dash Madly) Reeves was the Commanding Officer of the Kelly Field Photographic Laboratory. He had been an air observer during World War One and was interested in photographic mapping, so he viewed what I was doing with interest. All the people I worked with were competent. In working up his report, Captain Giffin thought that we should have a picture of our photographic airplane, so I took care of that item. An old-time master sergeant was designated to take the picture and showed up at the airplane with an apprentice carrying a view camera. The sergeant set up the camera, took one exposure and packed up. His nonchalance stirred my curiosity so I trailed along back to the laboratory and looked over his shoulder while he developed the film. It was a beautiful shot, showing that it pays to know what one is doing.

The talk which I had made to the Lion's Club resulted in a request from the San Antonio *Express* that I write a story for their Feature Section of the Sunday Edition. That article ran over two thousand words and was printed verbatim. It described just what we were doing, the technique of aerial mapping with the Bagley Camera and expanded on the theme of the potential contributions by the Air Service through an organized reserve and the promotion of civilian aviation as in the flying of mail. The sub-heading of that article stated, "Air Service men of Kelly Field get a real 'Bird's eye' view of magnificent distances in Texas . . ." the source of my title.

I learned a lot from working with Captain Giffin for he was a meticulous worker, strong on planning and in checking ever detail before we took off on a mission. He was the first to use a check list with whom I had worked. He also taught me to read the drainage as a means of orientation in addition to man-made features. In West Texas that was about all we had to go by. I taught the reading of drainage to my classes in air pilotage later on.

Kelly Field Polo

One hundred years after Stephen F. Austin brought his first settlers to Texas in 1821, the horse was still a primary element in ground transportation, particularly in the area west of San Antonio, where the Cavalry were dominant. The Field Artillery at Fort Sam Houston was horse drawn and the Texas National Guard at Camp Mabry in Austin had stables full of horses. The rodeo was the mounted sport for the civilian community, while the military preferred polo.

Kelly Field had an allotment of horses for recreation, and since many of the early aviators in the Air Service had been Cavalrymen before taking up flying, their interest in polo was obvious. However, the aviators had an "edge" in that they could fly to the Army's Remount Depot at El Reno, Oklahoma, and look over the two-year-old horses bought by the Army for potential polo ponies to fill their allotment at Kelly Field. Any Army officer could buy a government horse and keep it on station by paying a modest fee for its room and board. Some of the polo players at Kelly Field owned their horses.

My interest in polo was due to my next door neighbor, E. D. Jones being a member of the Kelly Field Polo Team. He had been raised in East Texas and was saddle-wise. Another member of that team about 1923 was "Sunny Jim" Reinhardt who had the distinction of silver plate in his head to cover a polo wound received several years before. The Kelly Team were hard riders and dominated polo in the San Antonio area during the Twenties. Their champion team of 1925 included Lieutenants George H. Beverly, Harold K. Coutler, Demas T. Craw and Thomas W. Hasty, all aviators. Craw had played polo at West Point.

Polo games were held on Sunday afternoons and well attended. The field would be surrounded with the parked automobiles of the spectators, not carriages. Games were played at Kelly, Fort Sam Houston and at Camp Mabry in Austin, that I attended. There were at least five teams in the area. There was also a team of Mexican Army Officers led by their Commanding General* which came up from the Border from time to time. The games rotated in

* General Quinones as I recall.

the area with Fort Sam Houston as the site for the important games.

When I returned to Randolph Field in 1931, Tom Hasty and several others still owned horses. Since there were no stables provided at Randolph, they organized a Riding Club in the town of Schertz nearby. There was no longer any polo in the military for it was a victim of the depression.

Pope Field

Edith and I arrived in Fayetteville, North Carolina, after a tedious train trip. There had been heavy rains in South Georgia with damage to bridges and we were routed over back roads. Since we missed connection with the dining car, we had to make do with sandwiches bought at stops along the way. That was offset by being met by Ray and Harlan Holden who took us to Pope Field and got us settled in our quarters. They were old friends from Brooks Field when Harlan had attempted to qualify as an airplane pilot without success. During World War One he had been an airplane observer and then the Commanding Officer of Pope Field.

Pope Field was in the northeastern corner of the huge Fort Bragg reservation so the Air Service was distant from the main post. It was the home for a flight of the 22nd Observation Squadron to provide support for the Field Artillery. There were four DH-4s with five officers on duty when we arrived in September 1924. Our quarters were in a four-unit building which had been rehabilitated by Air Service personnel. Marie and Walter Meyer were our neighbors, living above us. Since the field was about a half-mile distant, I rode to work in a motorcycle sidecar until the Model T arrived by freight.

Shortly after our arrival, Marie and Walter took us to the "Harvest Ball" at the country club outside of Fayetteville. They already had an invitation and their hosts kindly included us. That Ball was an eye-opener on how North Carolinians can play. It opened at seven and most everyone was there to participate in dancing until a break at midnight when everyone went home for supper. Then, back to the dance which ran until dawn, followed by breakfast. Two bands were used, one before midnight and the other after midnight. The four of us from Pope Field were not used to such activity and we ran out of steam about three in the morning.

Lieutenant John B. Patrick and his bride were the next arrivals. He had been working on an experimental project with the Department of Agriculture at Tallulah, Louisiana, where he met his wife and they married. Our social group included the Holdens, the Meyers and the Patricks, plus two bachelors, Glenn Lampton and Don Mayhew.

Patrick had been a member of the South Carolina National Guard before the war and transferred to the Air Service. He described the work at Tallulah which was to determine the best way to dispense insecticides from the air. At that time the boll weevil was the source of interest. The Air Service provided the JN-4s and the pilots, while personnel from the Department of Agriculture installed various types of dispensing systems for test. It was this group which learned that the slipstream of a low-flying airplane would swirl the dust to reach the underside of the leaves on the cotton plant. The information gleaned from these tests was passed on to civilian pilots and agricultural aviation was born. When discussions of derring-do were a topic, Pat always said, "I do not want to be the best pilot in the Air Service, I just want to be the oldest pilot!"

While I was working on the project for the Field Artillery Board there was a representative of the Department of Agriculture who was interested in learning whether aerial photographs could be used in crop reporting. I took some photographs for him and Glenn Lampton flew him over several selected areas which I had photographed. I never learned what his study determined. But years later, the Agriculture Stabilization Program used mosaics in their work since they showed clearly the vegetation. That was a boon to civilian aerial photography.

There were numerous forest areas on the Fort Bragg reservation and forest fires were always a concern. While range guards were on the alert, lightning caused forest fires from time to time. Holden worked up a project to use an air observer to direct such fire-fighting operations. He was an avid hunter and had walked over most of the area to know that swampy areas would block a fire. His idea was to place the effort where it would do the most good; Troops being called out, as many as needed. Jess Balmer, the Range Officer had a headquarters for directing the fight. We had a field telephone line run from that headquarters to our base communications trailer. Holden would send instructions to me by code and I would then relay them over the telephone line. Holden as the director speeded up the action through concentrating the ground effort, but a large factor was his knowledge of the terrain.

Hunting was strictly controlled under the Federal Game Laws. Fees were charged for hunting permits and such funds were used for purchasing game chicks to stock the range. The range guards would watch over the chicks until they were old enough to fend for themselves. I never heard of any wild animal or bird being killed by artillery or small arms fire. For one thing, the target areas were on high ground while game congregated in the low swampy areas. Years later, when the Air Force was planning a bombing range in Alaska, there was lot of whoop-de-du about killing game. I suggested that they obtain data from Fort Bragg on their experience.

The highlight of our tour at Pope Field was our Christmas visit to my family in Sharon Hill to introduce Edith to my various relatives in the Philadelphia area who extended a warm welcome to a Texan addition to the family. My Uncle John had a small crystal set and we listened to John McCormack and Lucrezia Bori sing on the radio on New Year's Day, 1925, our first experience with a radio broadcast.

My brother Walter, an engineering student at Drexel Institute, had built a radio receiver with parts arranged on a wooden base, and it worked. He took me to a Philadelphia store which sold radio parts and I returned to Pope Field with a kit of parts to make my own receiver. That winter we enjoyed listening to the Kansas City Nighthawks over that battery operated receiver.

Walter and I had built a spark transmitter in 1915 using the battery and spark coil from the gasoline engine in our basement used to pump water from the well to the tank in the attic. The circuit was based on an article in a popular magazine. We were able to generate dots and dashes in the basement and read them in the attic for we had learned the Morse code in the Boy Scouts. The fact that it did work was enough at that time because pumping water was more important, as we found out.

Our social activities centered on Pope Field. Other than the weekly dances at the Officers Club at the main post, some distance away, we did not socialize with the Field Artillery group.

Brigadier General Albert J. Bowley, the Post Commander, believed that a soldier in the stockade should not live an easier life than a soldier in a training unit. Army Regulations in 1925 permitted a soldier sentenced to hard labor to be worked from sunrise to sunset, and General Bowley saw to it that they did so at Fort Bragg. They worked on clearing brush from the fire trails, repairing gravel roads around the reservation and similar projects calling for manual labor. The guard detail for such prisoners worked in two shifts, one from sunup to noon. The other detail took over after dinner until sundown. Breakfast was served before sunrise and supper after sunset.

The Chief of Field Artillery, Major General William J. Snow, paid Fort Bragg a visit during the spring of 1925. All the officers on station gathered for a formal dinner at the Officer's Mess in his honor and he responded with a short talk. General Snow had graduated from West Point in 1890 and was the First Chief of Field Artillery, serving from 1918 to 1927.

Edith being pregnant, we spent a number of Sundays that spring roaming the countryside to visit Pinehurst, Wrightsville Beach on the Atlantic Ocean and other points of interest. We were in a tobacco growing area, a new and interesting crop for us with its glossy, luxuriant leaves. The plants grew about three feet high and came right up to the farmhouse. We watched as the pickaninnies picked the tobacco worms off the leaves and dropped them in their tin cans with kerosene. The children were just the right size to see the worms.

As the project with the Field Artillery Board was winding down and I had been told by Captain McDonnell to expect another assignment for the summer, Edith decided to return to San Antonio to stay with her parents until the baby was born. Edmund Clayton Junior was born at the Fort Sam Houston Hospital on June 3, 1925.

After Edith left I ate my main meal at noon with Glenn Lampton and Don Mayhew. During the summer training period that mess expanded to about two hundred seated at tables of eight and the food was served home style from serving dishes. The orderlies were enlisted men. The trainees were reserve officers on their two week active duty period. That was when I met Maxwell T. Smith from Morristown, Tennessee, who extolled the country fried chicken served in that town. He invited us to visit should we be in that area.

Muscadine grapes were native to North Carolina and the reservation had numerous patches of their vines. When ripe the grapes could be readily stripped from their clusters into a bucket. One of the bachelor officers had made a batch of wine from their grapes and had it stored in two wooden kegs, about five gallons in size. He had buried the kegs under his quarters for an aging period of six months, due to end that spring. I was invited to the wine tasting party and watched as the kegs were unearthed. We were greatly disappointed to find that the termites had gotten to the kegs first and the wine had leaked out through the honeycomb of holes.

I left Pope Field early in July when Jim Fitzmaurice came to pick me up for the mapping project in Tennessee. Our few household goods were packed and placed in storage.

The Field Artillery Board

My switch from the flying program at Kelly Field turned out to have interesting and beneficial aspects. I had gained knowledge and practical experience under Captain Giffin's guidance. That project finished, I was soon on my way to Fort Bragg, North Carolina, for duty with the Field Artillery Board.

Each of the combat arms had a central board made up of senior officers to keep that service up to date and look toward the future. It was the source for doctrine and technique. Generals George Marshall and Omar Bradley had served on the Infantry Board.

The Field Artillery Board was interested in knowing whether aerial photographs could be of help in field artillery firing, either with maps or as a substitute for maps. My task was to provide any photographs desired and information to go with them. Dache Reeves had a small library of books related to aerial photographic mapping, so I consulted him as to which books might be helpful. I sent that list to the Chief's Office and asked that they be sent to me on loan for the project, but I do not recall their being needed.

As soon as I had settled down at Pope Field, Lieutenant Glenn Lampton flew me to Washington to visit with Captain John C. McDonnell in the Munitions Building, and learn what we could from him. In my assignment, I was responsible to Captain McDonnell and under Lieutenant Holden at Pope Field for administrative control and assistance. Captain McDonnell had sent a K-3 Fairchild Camera to Pope Field and ordered Langley Field to send me a Field Photographic Laboratory with a detachment of three men. Lampton flew practically all my missions and enjoyed flying to Washington when we made progress reports.

While I was riding to work in the motorcycle sidecar, the driver said one morning, "The detachment from Langley Field came in and Sergeant Scott said that he thought that he knew you." Scott had been a member of Company "B," Sixth Pennsylvania Infantry, and I had met him as a teenager before World War One. He came out of that war as a Second Lieutenant and went into business as a professional photographer in Chester, but failed during the postwar depression. He had then enlisted in the Air Service as a photographer. I was fortunate for he knew all the laboratory tricks, especially fast work as with news photos.

We set up the laboratory in an old building with a scullery sink and water supply. Our main problem was to create a light tight room as we needed full darkness for working with the aerial film. The field laboratory normally handled full rolls of film, so we had to devise our own method of developing short strips. Since we had extra magazines for the camera, we could keep one for use when only a few exposures were to be made, cutting off the exposed portion without disturbing the unexposed portion left in the magazine.

Major Falkner Heard, West Point 1913, was the Board member in charge of this study which would involve single photographs, some arranged in strip form and a mosaic where the photographs were assembled into a small map. Major Heard would tell me what the Board wanted to know and I would work up the air part of a test problem, Major Heard would flesh it out and submit it for Board approval. Then we would get to work. The test became a series of problems, about a dozen.

Since few Army officers were familiar with aerial photographs, I suggested that we start with a direct comparison under controlled conditions. We selected a section of the target range (Fort Bragg had excellent maps) with lots of detail and I took a photograph at about ten in the morning when the shadows were well marked. I then marked True North and Magnetic North as well as a linear distance scale, having laid out a base line on a level stretch of road with end markers. On every mission we began and ended with a picture of the base line for scale. The idea was that the test battery could fire a problem from the data on the photograph, first registering fire on the map location of a point (also on the photo) and then shift fire using the photo to some selected target. Other tests, shifted fire when the registration point and the target were not on the same photo. One problem often suggested another. In each test we kept considerable data regarding the length of time involved. For instance, one test called for an aerial photo requested by a commander in the field with the airplane on the alert. We flew out, took the picture, quick-developed a print and then dropped it at the commander's location, with each stage timed.

Major Heard wrote the report to the War Department for the Board and I added an appendix to cover the Air Service contribution, the record of the flying time and other aspects I thought to be of interest.

Lieutenant Lampton became as interested in the project as I and suggested a parallel project. He had heard about a coming night march and camouflage exercise planned for a 155mm howitzer regiment through conversations at the Bachelor Officer's Mess. He thought that it would be interesting to see whether the camera could penetrate the camouflage, but the area for the test was a secret. I enlisted Major Heard's assistance and we were able to photograph the area at ten in the morning, several days beforehand. We repeated the photos the morning after the bivouac while the guns were still concealed.

We had no difficulty locating several of the guns because of the tractor tracks in the white sandy soil, so I showed them to Major Heard. We then became a part of the critique of the exercise. For that I made a series of lantern slides with the before and after sections side by side. The theater projector enlarged them nicely for everyone to see. Our part was actually a lecture on photo interpretation and created a lot of interest as it was new to many present.

We flew to Washington about once each month to make reports to Captain McDonnell. The Photographic Section had a civilian employee, Mr. Albright who had been a professional photographer, and his portrait camera must have been twenty years old in

1924, if not older. He still used that same camera in 1953 when he made my portrait upon my retirement, in color that time. He used the silent shutter that opened with a press on the bulb in his hand. The lens for that camera was huge, perhaps four inches in diameter. His main problem was to have the various stations send in their pictures for historical use, for he maintained the photographic library in the Chief's Office. I always supported his efforts when I was in the GHQ Air Force, and whenever possible.

The Willard Hotel was our favorite place to stay in Washington for it was only a few blocks from the Munitions Building where Air Service Headquarters were located. We could travel light because we could buy our shave at the hotel barber shop. On one occasion during the winter, I did not wear my face mask so my face was chapped due to the cold wind. The barber suggested a *Lemon Steam* which was most effective in relieving the soreness.

On one such visit I learned that Captain McDonnell had another mapping project in mind for the Summer of 1925, this time of the Tennessee River and that I could expect orders.

Air-Ground Communications

I saw my first and only radio frequency, wind driven spark transmitter on a DH-4 at Pope Field in the Fall of 1924, still operational. The entire transmitter was in one unit mounted on the landing gear strut. It included a low voltage alternator (400 cycles) driven by a constant-speed impeller. This voltage was stepped up by a transformer to generate a spark to jump the rotary gap and create a broad tone modulated signal. The operator made dots and dashes by breaking the low voltage circuit. The radio frequency section was in the bullet shaped rear section where the antenna connected to the tip of the cone. The antenna was a long wire with a weighted end and the output could be maximized by adjusting the antenna length. The receiver was a small battery operated unit based on the Armstrong superhetrodyne circuit, suspended on shock cords behind the observer.

This unit could only communicate with an Air Service ground station housed in a communication trailer. In order to work with a Field Artillery unit on a firing problem, field telephone wire was strung from the trailer to the field artillery unit. The message from the air observer in Morse code was translated by the ground operator who relayed the data by voice over the telephone line. Lieutenant Holden used this transmitter on several occasions and I operated the base station for I knew the Morse code.

In the observation training program at Kelly Field the standard method for communicating with the Infantry and Cavalry used cloth panels laid out on the ground in prescribed patterns (standard messages). The air observer called for, and acknowledged such panel messages with a *Very pistol* which fired colored flares; red, white and green. The Very pistol looked like a sawed-off shotgun and the flares were used singly or in combination, so the amount of information that could be sent was limited. There was also the *drop message* in a weighted pouch with a streamer. The reverse of this was to pick up a message on the fly. The message bag was attached to a large loop of light rope, and that loop was elevated about ten feet with two poles about twenty feet apart. The air observer had a pronged graphnel on a line which he could lower and the pilot would maneuver the plane to hook the loop, no easy task. I saw the technique demonstrated but never used it.

By the time I joined the 7th Observation Squadron in 1929, we had tube type transmitters capable of either the code or voice mode, but we always used code transmissions. Frequencies were designated for each mission and the ground crew would set such frequencies before takeoff. All the observer had to do was turn the set "on" and operate his key.

In working with strange operators on the ground, one of our problems was that some of the operators like to show off and *dazzle* the air observer with their skill to the detriment of the message information. We coped with this problem in Panama by inviting the ground operators to communicate with their buddies on the ground by taking a sightseeing ride with us. Our goal was to teach them to follow the speed set by the observer, when he speeded up they could speed up, or when he slowed, they should slow. An open cockpit was not the best place since it was cramped and one had his seat belt on. Should one drop a pencil, it was difficult to pick it up. That solved the problem and we made friends. On some missions they would get chatty and ask who was on the key.

We still did not have radio contact with the Infantry in 1929. Panels were of little use because of the thick foliage over the trails on the Atlantic side. We tried to work some experiments to spot the head of a column on the trail but the Infantry were not interested.

The Tennessee River

The Army's Corps of Engineers had an interest in the Tennessee River well before World War One when they built a canal to bypass Muscle Shoals. Then came a defense plant to use the *Haber* process to make nitrogen from the air by electricity, for nitrates were used in explosives and fertilizers. Mapping of the river began after World War One using aerial photographs taken with a Fairchild single lens camera, the K-3. By 1925 all the river had been photographed other than the Northeastern tributaries: the Holston, Hiwassee and Nolichucky Rivers. Such maps were to serve as the basis for developing the water power and navigation of the river under the Tennessee Valley River Authority. Our project was to photograph the Northeastern tributaries.

James M. Fitzmaurice, West Point 1923, and a recent graduate of the Air Service Photographic School, was designated as pilot and I was to be the photographer. We had letter orders to report to Major Harold C. Fiske, the District Engineer, and to do what was needed on the Northeastern tributaries.

Major Fiske had been a classmate of General Douglas MacArthur at West Point (1903) and had commanded an engineer regiment in Europe. He was very knowledgeable about maps and topography. Jim flew him between Nashville and Chattanooga, following the Tennessee River so that Fiske could take a close look. When they returned to the office, Fiske followed the trip on his wall map in detail. As this was his first air trip over the route, it was clear that he could change his orientation from ground to an air view. His Chief Engineer, a civilian named Mr. Hooper was in charge of the entire mapping project, and provided the flight maps along the Holston, Hiwassee and Nolichucky Rivers.

That Spring at Fort Bragg I had met an Army reserve officer from Morristown, Maxwell T. Smith, when he was attending a training program. Since Morristown was central to our mapping area, we decided to look there for a base, and landed in a field north of town and close to the highway. Maxwell Smith was happy to welcome us and Mr. King who owned the farm kindly gave us permission to use his pasture. He also stored our film for us in his cool root cellar. Maxwell Smith had been a dirt track racing driver before World War One. After the war he had set up an automobile supply business, so we appointed him our supply officer to handle all our needs for fuel and oil. Through Smith and his wife Edith, we were soon well acquainted in the town.

Jim and I put up at the local hotel, The Hodges House with a long veranda. That was a pleasant place to sit in the afternoons while Viola Hodges, the daughter would clue us in on all the local news. She knew everyone as she worked as a cashier of the local movie house several doors away. When the Ku Klux Klan would march by in their regalia (hoods), she identified the men by their shoes. There were no secrets in a small town.

We were in complete agreement that the taking of pictures came first and we were ready to go whenever we had a clear sky required for the mapping photographs. When the weather was in doubt, we would get airborne in case the few clouds would burn off. Sometimes, on such days, we would go on to Chattanooga and visit with Mr. Hooper to review the prints that had recently arrived. As soon as we had exposed a roll of film, we mailed it to the Photographic Laboratory at Wright Field where it was processed and the prints sent directly to Chattanooga. The laboratory also mailed us a fresh roll of film as a replacement.

One day when unable to fly we visited a field party working near Morristown to see what happened to our photographs. The first work was in the office where a draftsman with a stereoscope sketched in contours to highlight the relief and marked control points and ground features to show on the final map. A stereoscope brings the terrain into relief when two overlapping pictures are examined at the same time, similar to binocular vision. The men in the field then complete the data. After such data were marked with India ink, the photographic image was bleached out to leave a line drawing in black and white. This drawing, in turn, was copied on the master sheet in the office at Chattanooga.

Jim and I were also the ground crew for the project. Jim took care of the DH-4B photographic airplane (AS 24-55), while I looked after the Liberty engine. After every flight I cleaned the two distributors of the carbon residue from the soft brushes, checked the clearance of the breaker points, and looked things over such as oil and water. My tools were an ordinary pencil eraser, a feeler gauge and a small wrench. After twenty-five hours of flying time, we changed the sparkplugs as we had an extra set. We made one trip to Chanute Field and another to Pope Field to get new sparkplugs and to have the rocker arms adjusted. The Liberty ticked along smoothly and I was the official starter, by hand.

On our trip to Chanute we ran into heavy rain showers and landed in an old corn field close to the Cumberland River not far from Burnside. The farmer, a taciturn type, invited us to share his porch, took a store made cigarette, but provided no conversation. Soon a group of young men who had been bird hunting further up the mountain came by. We struck up a conversation and they surmised that our Army plane was suspect; that we might be looking for whiskey stills. They told us that our host lived alone and had a self-sufficient life, asking them to bring salt or other needed items on their next trip. Our host was about as close to nature as anyone could get.

When the weather cleared we took off to continue our flight and made about fifty miles more before the heavy rain forced us to land again at Junction City. This was a small town where two railroads crossed; just south of Danville, Kentucky. We spent the night there in a small hotel by the railroad tracks. The weather cleared during the night and we had an uneventful trip to Chanute Field, near Urbana, Illinois, the next morning.

In those days, every pilot had an allowance of shotgun ammunition for skeet shooting, to learn how to lead a bird when shooting. On our trip to Pope Field for extra sparkplugs and for engine maintenance, Jim and I picked up our annual allowance so that we could do some dove hunting at Morristown, for there were plenty in the upper pastures along the ridges. We could easily borrow a shotgun from our friends in town and cooked up one batch in the Smith's kitchen following their instructions.

Toward the end of July, Edith brought baby Clayton to Morristown to stay for about three weeks. Jim and I were then living in a private home with no housekeeping and we ate at Mamie's Restaurant which was nearby. From then on we spent a lot of time in the kitchen of the Smith's home; a large old-fashioned type. Edith Smith made delicious angel food cakes, all beaten separately by hand and then baked while we watched. Watermelons grown along the Holston River were famous for their size and flavor and Max Smith always had several in the ice house keeping cool. Today, that land is under a lake.

As the work around Morristown had been completed ahead of schedule, Major Fiske asked us to do some work on the Duck River near Columbia, Tennessee. The nearest flying field was at Nashville near the Hermitage. Edith and the baby took the train for Sharon Hill to stay with my family and show off the new grandchild. Jim and I bid farewell to our friends in Morristown and moved to Nashville for the short period to complete the work on the Duck River.

This project was *heady* experience for two second lieutenants with five years of experience between us. We had an airplane, photographic gear and a free hand, responsible for our own performance. We completed the project well ahead of Mr. Hooper's schedule and he was happy. Early in the project we had tried to have Hooper pay for a rented car for our transport to and from town and our field, with no success. Before we left for Nashville, Hooper raised the rented car question himself and asked for our total expense. We then got a check to cover it, a windfall. Hooper was well ahead of schedule and his expense had been less.

Jim and I worked well together for we were like-minded. We became life-long friends serving together in the 7th Observation Squadron at France Field and at Langley Field. Jim later became a Brigadier General in command of Hunter Field, a staging base at Savannah, while I was in the Third Air Force.

WAR DEPARTMENT

AG 580.8 Tenn. River
(6-20-25) (Misc.) June 27, 1925.

Aerial photographs of Tennessee River and Northwestern Tributaries.

The Commanding General,
Sixth Corps Area,
1819 W. Pershing Road
Chicago, Illinois

1. Send . . . 2nd Lieut. J. M. Fitzmaurice, Air Service, now on duty at Chanute Field training center, with photographic airplane obtained from the Photographic School, Chanute Field, by air, as photographic pilot to Pope Field, Fort Bragg, North Carolina.

2. At Pope Field this officer will obtain a K-3 camera and other necessary photographic equipment and will be joined by 2nd Lieut. Edmund C. Lynch, Air Service, now at that station, who will act as photographer.

3. These officers will then proceed by air from Pope Field to Chattanooga, Tennessee, reporting upon arrival to Major H. C. Fiske, District Engineer, 40 Municipal Building, and obtain maps and detailed instructions for carrying out certain mapping work desired by the Chief of Engineers.

* * *

5. Before proceeding with the photographic operations, such aerial reconnaissances as may be necessary will be made, in order to locate a suitable landing field to be used as a base for refueling.

* * *

8. Upon completion of this duty the personnel concerned will return by air to their proper stations.

By order of the Secretary of War:

H. H. TEBBETTS,
Adjutant General

(The paragraphs omitted were instructions for the supply and processing of the film and the proper appropriations for the expenses.)

HEADQUARTERS
CHANUTE FIELD RANTOUL ILLINOIS.

NOTICE TO DEALER

You are hereby requested to sell gasoline and lubricating oils and render services other than personal to the Aviator presenting this notice. After proper notations as to quantities are made, this notice is to be signed in triplicate by the officer to whom supplies have been issued and the following certificate signed in triplicate by the dealer. This invoice in triplicate, together with three copies of the Operations Order, will be presented to the Finance Officer, Chanute Field, Rantoul, Illinois, for payment.

INVOICE

Place Morristown, Tenn.

Name of Dealer Auto Tire & Supply Co.

Date Oct. 30, 1925.

Date of Delivery	Quantity	Unit	Description	Unit Price	Amount
10/28	43	gal.	Gasoline	$0.18	$ 7.74
				Total	$ 7.74

CERTIFICATE TO BE SIGNED BY DEALER

I certify that the above account is correct and that payment therefor has not been received.

Auto Tire & Supply Co.
Maxwell T. Smith
Signature of Dealer
per: Maxwell T. Smith, Prop.

STATEMENT FOR OFFICER TO SIGN

Expendable property listed hereon is for immediate consumption in current service in U.S. Airplane # 24-55, and will not be taken up on stock record cards. The non-expendable property checked thus (x) is accounted for on stock records of Property Officer at Chanute Field, Illinois. Payment to be made by Finance Officer, at Chanute Field, Rantoul, Illinois.

Edmund C. Lynch
Edmund C. Lynch.
Signature of Aviator.
2nd Lieut., A.S.

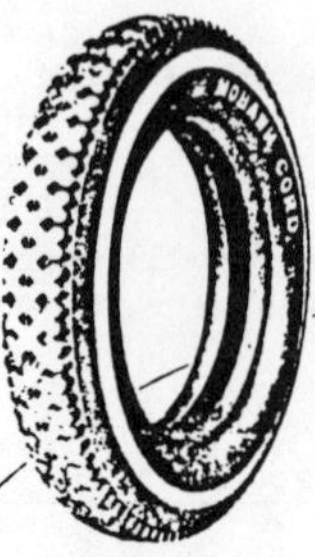

MOHAWKS
Go Farther!

AUTO TIRE & SUPPLY COMPANY

MAXWELL T. SMITH, Proprietor

Tires
Accessories
Replacement Springs
Vulcanizing

OLD PHONE 45
308 North Cumberland St.
MORRISTOWN, TENNESSEE

Gas
Oil
Car Greasing
Car Washing

Aug. 27, 1925

for airplane
A.S. 24-55

	unit price	Amount
151 gal. gasoline	$0.23	$34.73
20 qt. mobil B oil	$0.30	$6.00
1 lb. Alemite grease	0.25	.25
		$40.98

Cast Tenn Woodworking Co.
Roswell E. Smith

Aug. 28, 1925

Rental of 3 jacks for 7 days at $.50 per day. $10.50
" " 1 truck load of housemoving blocks 7.00
for 7 days at $1.00
$17.50

Clinch Mountain Culture

Morristown was then (1925) a small friendly town. The young men who we met either worked in the family business or for themselves. We toured several of the businesses, one a chicken processing plant, another a coffee roaster. Our friends could get away in the late summer afternoons when business was slack for a little sport such as seining fish in the river, or for dove shooting later on. Such gatherings usually ended with a libation and a singsong. One of the popular ballads at that time dealt with a train wreck in western Virginia where the engine driver was scalded to death by the steam from the wreck. The opening line we used was "It wasn't 38 but old 97." One of our friends hired a local sign painter to decorate both sides of our DH from the rear cockpit aft with the logo, "It's OLD 97," our theme song and quite unauthorized.

Another friend had several kegs of well-aged bourbon whiskey in his cellar, unlike the ordinary white lightning in a fruit jar. When asked about his source he said, "I had to work for that whiskey," and then told us this story.

He had grown up with a family in the Clinch Mountains some thirty miles from Morristown. Such folk were noted for their clannish notions, but he had hunted and fished with them and was considered a member of the clan. Whiskey making was a family affair and for their use, not for sale.

The patriarch kept the family recipe in his head and passed it on to his successor. Whiskey making was combined with hunting, so the patriarch started several barrels of mash fermenting to be ready to cook at the beginning of the season, usually birds. The location would be passed around and the clan would gather.

Each member brought his camping and hunting equipment, plus his food and a keg for his share of the whiskey. The patriarch scheduled the work so that everyone had time for hunting, contributed to tending the still and cutting firewood. It was a cooperative effort and they all shared in the output, not to overlook the companionship and the pleasure of hunting.

There were several Civilian Conservation Corps camps in the Clinch Mountains and the Army provided support, including a Chaplain who visited the camps frequently. I met one later when he was on duty at Barksdale Field and he told me about his difficulty in breaking through their clannishness to make friends with the locals. He was a jovial, outgoing Irishman but it took him several months of persistent effort.

The Airship School

When the work was completed on the Duck River, Jim dropped me off at Pope Field with a hasty "goodbye" on his way to Chanute Field. I lost no time in flying to Washington to see Captain McDonnell to learn about my next assignment. Our few household goods had been packed for months and I had been living out of a suitcase. Captain McDonnell told me that orders were being issued for me to attend the Airship School at Scott Field, Illinois, but that I should see Colonel Sheplar Fitzgerald, the Executive, before I left to return to Pope Field. Fitzgerald, who knew me from Kelly Field days, said that the class was already in progress and that I could expect some "Static" when I reported, but not to worry, and he advised me on how to meet any objections.

The Commandant of the Airship School was Lieutenant Colonel James Mars. When I reported he promptly said, "It can't be done!" It was as Fitzgerald had predicted and I almost broke out in laughter. After Colonel Mars had cooled down I pointed out that I already had had a ground school at Brooks Field and flying had not yet begun. I suggested that he let me give it a try and reserve judgement.

My orders provided leave for a few days en route to Scott Field, so I visited my family at Sharon Hill for an early Christmas, since my visit was in early December 1925. I knew that I would be busy catching up with the class in progress, so we decided that Edith and the baby should stay with my folks until after the first of the year and I could get a place to live in Belleville.

There was only one significant new course in the airship program and that dealt with the specifics of operating an airship. The course was *Aerostatics,* involving the action of helium gas in the airship envelope under varying conditions of temperature and atmospheric pressure. This course was taught with a special manual prepared for that course with daily problems to illustrate the assignment. It dealt with "Why?" certain changes occurred and what to expect (The heat of the sun will increase the lift of the gas.)

In my conference with the instructor, Lieutenant Harvey Holland, I suggested a plan for his approval, since I was generally familiar with the physics of gases. That plan was to work the next daily assignment and hand it in with the class, and then continue to submit the problems should I be able to cope. On the prior problems the class had submitted, I would work them and hand them in before the course was over and take an oral if need be. Needless to say, the first problem took hours because I had to scan the manual for the proper formula. I managed to keep up and was soon working several back problems each evening, so I passed that course. Two years later, Harvey Holland and I would be working together in the Ground School at Brooks Field.

I attended all the remaining ground school courses for a good review. The course on Meteorology was taught by Captain James C. Van Ingen of the Signal Corps. He used the system of forecasting developed by the Weather Bureau which was empirical based on the study of thousands of weather maps and their associated weather. Seven different types of isobaric or pressure patterns had been identified, each with characteristic weather. The two major patterns were the cyclone, or low pressure system, and the anticyclone, or high pressure system. Such patterns were the starting point for a particular forecast because local conditions could influence the actual weather; for instance, the presence of a large body of water such as Chesapeake Bay or the mountains with their uplift effect. Forecasting at that time was hampered by too few reporting stations and the forecast was for an eight hour period. As flying activity increased, we had six hour forecasts of the weather for flying.

Military interest in having an observer spy on the enemy from an elevated platform went back a long way. The Chinese built large kites capable of lifting an observer. The French had the Montgolfier balloon in 1790, and there was a sporadic use of the balloon in our Civil War. I made several flights in the kite balloon used in World War One, a more stable type due to its peculiar shape. This sausage shaped envelop was attached to a ground winch through a steel cable which had a telephone line as its inner core. Should the cable break, as it sometimes did, the observer landed his balloon as a free balloon. He would be hampered by the tail riding up against the basket, so any kind of landing was his goal.

We learned to fly the Army's C-3 type of nonrigid airship which had an open gondola or car with two Hispano Suiza engines mounted on an outrigger, the same type used on the Jenny. Usually four students rode with one instructor, so we could learn by observing and doing. For landing we needed a ground crew of fifty men or so depending upon the wind. We had long ropes to drop on the landing approach to be caught by the crew and they would walk us into the hangar.

The shape of the envelope was maintained by air pressure, one and one-half inches of water on the manometer, or gauge, not large by the usual idea of pressure. When the pressure became too low to maintain the shape, the patches cemented to the envelop from which the car was supported, would pull off. While the airship was in the hangar there was a gas guard to inspect the pressure at intervals and make any adjustments.

The envelope had internal compartments at the front and rear called ballonets. These could be inflated with air to provide the pressure and were also used to control the trim or flying attitude. Air had weight and a nose down attitude was achieved by having more air in the forward compartment. A nose down trim with forward movement would offset the lifting power of the helium when the airship was in a light condition and was useful in the landing maneuver. Similarly, a nose up trim with forward movement would increase the lifting power of the gas. Learning the proper use of trim was an important element in flying an airship.

The main control in the gondola was the elevator between the two seats at the front. The rudder was operated with foot pedals and the throttles were at the front handy to both pilots. Since the lift of the gas varied due to heat primarily, the pilot juggled the factors of speed and trim in his maneuvers.

On one flight with Lieutenant Karl Axtater as instructor we went over a farm house several miles from Scott Field where that farmer was a friend of Axtater's. While we circled the farmer came out with two bottles of beer fastened at the necks with wire. The crew chief lowered a sandbag on a long line and we maneuvered the craft for a pickup. Anyone should know what happened when we were successful. However, it was no easy task to make the pickup on a hot afternoon with no wind. We had to trim the nose down and maintain forward speed to offset the lift due to the heat. So, we would be going to fast, or too high for the pickup. Only one was made while I was aboard. However, it was good practice for a very light condition.

One Saturday during the spring of 1926, Karl invited me to accompany him on a trip to St. Louis, Missouri, purpose not stated. We arrived at a lithographic plant in the industrial area to be met by the proprietor as the plant was closed on Saturdays. He gave us a tour of the plant explaining the various steps in the sequence of operations. The copy which I saw related to advertising layouts for newspapers or magazines. He told us that when he had learned the trade through apprentice training some years before 1900, he had learned to do every step in the process. However, in 1926, there were six unions involved in the work, each deemed a specialty. He showed us the six union cards which he held as a consequence of his training and explained that he was able to step in and keep the work flowing should anyone be absent.

That story was interesting to me because my father had completed apprentice training as a machinist about the same time and was superintendent of a machine shop when called to active duty in 1916. As I was growing up there had been some discussion as to whether I should be enrolled in apprentice training, rather than to attend high school as that training began after the eighth grade. When our tour was over we returned to the proprietor's office where he opened a large safe, took out a bottle and handed it to Karl. The only thing in that safe was a partially empty case of Gordon's gin.

Edith and I were fortunate in renting a furnished home in Belleville while the owners were on an extended visit to Europe that Spring, for we had practically no furniture. We had a closed garage for the Model T and I could warm the engine during the winter with a kettle of hot water and an old towel while eating breakfast. Two of my classmates lived close by and we rode to Scott Field together from Belleville, leaving their cars for the ladies. One was Lieutenant William O. (Bill) Eareckson who completed the course and then went on to qualify as an airplane pilot. He made a name for himself in the Battle for the Aleutians as described by Brian Garfield in *The Thousand Mile War,* published by Ballentine in 1975.

Lieutenant Leslie A. (Les)Skinner was the third of our trio. We all had a nonconformist bent; Skinner more so; Eareckson moderately so; and I, mildly so. Les did not qualify as an airship pilot and transferred to the Army's Ordnance Department to become famous for inventing the recoiless rocket launcher or Bazooka. Les was a genius in his curiosity about what made things tick. Peggy and Les were our next door neighbors. When I stopped for a visit one day I saw Les flying an airship model of unconventional design on a tether among the diapers drying in their kitchen. His model was shaped like a doughnut with a rubber band motor in the central opening. While in the Ordnance at the Aberdeen Proving Ground, he continued his experimentation with jet propulsion and rocketry, often when assigned to other projects. As far as I know, Les was the only officer in the Ordnance Department who was knowledgeable on that subject when he came up with the Bazooka. That knowledge was gained through his own efforts and curiosity.

School being over for the day, we would stop at the Quartermaster Bakery to buy our bread before heading for home. That bread had a good crust and a rather coarse texture, excellent for French toast and bread pudding. In those days the Army bought only hard wheat flour for it was more nutritious. We paid three cents per loaf, the cost of the ingredients.

Our social life was confined to our friends in Belleville living close by, for everyone had a small baby. Clayton was then less than a year old. Mary and Eddie White were in the group and their son Edward H. White II became an astronaut and a victim of the Apollo disaster. My classmate Howard Davidson who had moved up from Brooks Field was still a bachelor and was dating Martha Hoppe of Belleville. They were married at the end of the course and were transferred to the Philippines.

The graduation exercise was a cross country flight to Little Rock and return, three hundred miles each way. That flight was made at night when flying conditions were stable, to arrive about dawn and returning the following night. The trip south was interesting and I enjoyed it, but the return trip was boring for I was used to cross country travel in a DH-4.

Edith and I moved back to San Antonio for I had orders to Brooks Field for another try at pilot training. We arrived during September 1926 and rented a house in the Hot Wells section convenient to Brooks Field.

Free Ballooning

The free balloon is a delightful mode of flying when one is not particularly concerned about a destination. The pilot has good vertical control, but only a very limited horizontal control. That is achieved by locating a wind stratum where the air is moving in the desired direction, a general rather than a specific direction. Vertical control is achieved by releasing ballast to rise and releasing gas to descend. The trick was to make any adjustments in small increments for the momentum of the craft would result in overcontrolling. Two instruments sufficed, the statoscope which measured very slight changes in altitude, and the altimeter which measured the height of the balloon above the surface setting.

The Army type of free balloon had been around a long time. We used hydrogen gas as the lifting agent because it's density was only one seventh that of air under the same conditions, but hydrogen is very flammable. One does not use an open flame near a balloon, it is for nonsmokers.

James Gordon Bennett an American Newspaper Proprietor had established an international trophy for balloon racing and the Army customarily had an entry. In 1906, Lieutenant Frank P. Lahm won that race when he was on duty as a military attache in Paris, that race being held at Paris. Lahm then went on to become an airplane pilot in 1909 when he was qualified by the Wright Brothers.

The Army team for the international Balloon race in 1928 included Captain William E. Kepner as pilot and Lieutenant William O. Eareckson as aide. They won that race and as it was the third consecutive win by the United States, we gained permanent possession of the Gordon Bennett Trophy.

When preparing to take off in a free balloon, the first step was the *weighoff.* That meant to balance the balloon about a foot off the ground so that it neither rose or dropped. The two elements of control were the gas and the ballast which was in sandbags hooked around the rim of the willow basket. It was customary to dribble the ballast from your hand, seldom more than a handful at any one time. Then, the pilot observed what happened. As you rose the gas expanded and lift was gained. The object was to stabilize at your selected cruising altitude.

My qualifying flight for the balloon pilot rating was an eight hour flight, and Fogelsanger, an aviation cadet, was with me. We had had no air instruction, just careful ground drill on procedure. The flight was at night so we had stable conditions and we leveled off at 800 feet with a light breeze that took us to the Northeast. While we were idly passing away the time and watching our instruments, Fogelsanger said, "I wish that I had a trumpet to blow a long blast and shout 'Lo the Angel Gabriel cometh!' to see what might happen." Since it was about three in the morning and we had no trumpet, I was pleased because people become hysterical readily.

The farmers were out at dawn doing their chores, but we were making no sound drifting along. The chickens knew that we were overhead and scurried around in great excitement causing the farmer to look up. So we said, "Good morning to you!" Our eight hours were over at dawn, so we began looking for a nice field before the sun came up. We selected one close by a school and made a soft landing as the wind was light. Fogelsanger remained with the balloon while I went to telephone for a truck to take us home.

Boy power was a great help in free ballooning and we had plenty in removing the net and folding the envelope. The entire equipment could be packed in the basket and it had a cover to fit. We emptied the sandbags and were ready by the time the truck arrived. Total distance in eight hours, about twenty miles. That was my only flight in a free balloon, a thoroughly enjoyable experience.

What does one do when conditions were not ideal as we had for that trip? We did not valve gas as we were slowly descending to our landing spot. As soon as we touched ground Fogelsanger pulled on the "Ripcord" which opened a long seam on the upper portion of the envelope which released the gas in one blast, so the wind did not drag us and the basket remained upright. With a stronger wind, we might have ripped the panel a few feet above the ground and then cut loose several bags of ballast to check the downward momentum. It was a matter of judgement, with Fogelsanger on the ripcord (or gas valve), my task was to work the ballast. It took two people to land a balloon.

There has been a resurgence of interest in free ballooning in recent years using hot air as the lifting medium. Materials for the envelope have become lighter and sturdier. The hot air is generated by a burner using liquified petroleum gas (propane or butane). In this situation, lift is controlled by adjusting the temperature of the air via the gas burner's heat. When the burner is shut off the air cools and one descends.

Brooks and Kelly Again

My third tour at Brooks Field in the flying training program placed me in an ambiguous status. I was welcomed as an "Old Timer," given a checkout ride on the Jenny and then told to fly at my own convenience to build up time and to maintain proficiency, a freelance student and handyman in the flying department. When the class began to solo and practice landings, I was placed in charge of an auxiliary field. My duties were to fly out early with a mechanic and set the wind "Tee" for the landing direction, grade student landings and handle any emergency. I used the numbers on the solo aircraft and graded them satisfactory unless the student appeared to be having problems. The students flew in the front cockpit and a sandbag was securely fastened to the rear seat of the solo aircraft. On one occasion as a handyman, I went to Seguin to return a Jenny which had been involved in a forced landing on the Fair Grounds and overturned. The aircraft had been repaired at the site and was ready to go.

While cruising around on my own just before Christmas of 1926, I had my first forced landing when the cam shaft sheared on the Hiso engine. I was near Fort Sam Houston over farming country and landed in an old corn field. It had been raining for almost a week and the field was a sea of mud. The wheels sunk to the spreader bar and I slowly turned over, not quite all the way, causing a problem in getting out as I was hanging upside down in my seat belt. I went ankle deep in the mud when I dropped out, walking to a nearby farmhouse to telephone Brooks Field. They, too, had been marooned by the mud and were just ready to leave for town, so I left the Jenny and rode in with them. Edith picked me up in town.

There was no way to prepare for a forced landing, but we did have some folklore as a guide, based on the experience of others.

The first consideration was to maintain one's speed and control. The next was to avoid a head-on collison with any immovable object, rather maneuver to cause a glancing hit so that the wings could absorb the impact. A spin was lethal because the airplane would strike the ground nose first, since control had been lost.

There being no brakes on either the Jenny or the DH-4, the tires were smooth on the wearing surface and not very thick for lightness. There were inner tubes and tires were repaired with hot or cold patches using rubber cement as with an automobile tire. I had my only flat tire on a DH-4 at Fort Clark when a one-inch cactus thorn punctured a tire and that caused little delay in patching the hole. The smooth tread was suitable for a grassy field and skidded easily in a ground loop so that the wheel did not collapse.

The landing gear on the Jenny and DH was a simple affair with a shock absorbing element between the wheel axle and the structure proper. The spreader bar was split with a central slot for the axle. At each end there was a wrapping of "Bungee" cord adequate to support the static weight of the airplane. Bungee cord was made up of a large number of elastic rubber strands encased in a woven fabric cover, about one-half inch in diameter. This arrangement worked nicely for normal landings, but could magnify the bounce when a hard landing was made.

The Air Service was seeking a replacement for the venerable Jenny and several proposed models had been sent to Brooks Field for evaluation by the instructors. The most unusual one that I flew had the LeRhone air-cooled rotary engine which had the crank and piston assembly attached to the airframe while the propeller and cylinder assembly rotated. There were separate controls for fuel and air, rather than a single throttle. The pilot's control was through the button on the stick which cutoff the spark, complicated for a student. For takeoff, the pilot set the controls, started the engine and then kept the revolutions down by "burping" the engine with the control button, making short bursts to keep it going until lined up for takeoff. Castor oil was used as a lubricant and mixed with the fuel, so the exhaust fumes were not pleasant.

When the class moved to Kelly Field in March 1927, Edith and I moved to a house on Fairplay, off South Presa Street, convenient to both Brooks and Kelly. I breezed through the observation training program this time. We worked training missions with the Infantry at Camp Bullis and with the Field Artillery at Camp Stanley. For aerial gunnery we went to Fort Crockett where we lived in tents on the parade ground near the seawall. I looked out over the Gulf one afternoon to see a half-dozen waterspouts playing around about ten miles off shore, dipping down and them moving back up into the squall line.

While I was off on other things, the Third Attack Group had been organized at Kelly Field under Major Lewis H. Brereton and were training on DH-4s at the west end of the field. They had the one and only GAX for Ground Attack Experimental airplane. It was a triplane powered with two Liberty engines, with light armor to protect the engines and crew. However, the armor was too thin to withstand small arms fire and only one was built. The Attack Group finally received the A-3 type aircraft.

Our graduation exercise at Kelly Field was a joint maneuver with Cavalry units at Fort Bliss, Texas. We flew to Biggs Field at Fort Bliss via Forts Clark and Marfa to settle down in a tent camp on the edge of Biggs Field, field operations style. All our specialties were involved. The maneuvers were held on an area East of Fort Bliss where the ground was broken with gullies and with no roads. That was my first in working with Cavalry patrols from the air and I discovered that they were difficult to locate and disappeared suddenly in that broken terrain. It was an excellent learning experience for all of us.

Fort Clark was established in 1852 at Brackettville, Texas, for the Cavalry to protect the stagecoach line from San Antonio to El Paso. During the Indian wars the line of Cavalry posts gradually extended along the Rio Grande River from Fort Brown at Brownsville to Fort Bliss, with another line of Cavalry posts branching off from Fort Davis to the Northeast. During World War One the Air Service patrolled the Rio Grande operating from numerous small fields, many adjacent to the Cavalry posts. During the Thirties, Fort Clark became the headquarters for the 1st Cavalry Brigade, Commanded by Brigadier General Hamilton S. Hawkins, whose aide Wesley W. Yale was my classmate. When flying from San Antonio to the West coast, the preferred route was via Forts Clark and Bliss, then on to Lordsburg, New Mexico, Tucson, Arizona, to land at Rockwell Field, San Diego.

It was no surprise when I received orders sending me back to Brooks Field. I was to be in the Ground School under Lieutenant Charles C. Chauncey and he told me that I would be teaching Map Reading. I then said that I did not care for the way map reading had been taught to me, and Chauncey said, "Eddie, fix it to suit yourself!"

The standard Army map reading course was based on topographic maps with a person standing on the ground. I thought that it should be taught for the pilot in a cockpit and from a cross country point of view. The Army had topographic maps but no special maps for cross country. Each pilot had to provide his own, usually Rand McNally state maps showing towns, railroads and major streams. I wrote a manual to suit the pilot's approach describing the various problems in depicting the curved surface of the earth on a flat sheet of paper. The Mercator projection was used on charts for seamen, while the polyconic projection was common for the Rand McNally maps. I also included suggestions for preparing a map similar to the one I used which was cemented to airplane cloth and varnished against the weather.

Harvey Holland was transferred from Scott Field to Brooks Field and was assigned to the Ground School staff to teach air navigation, arriving shortly after I did from Kelly. He had almost completed work on an air navigation text for which he had coined the word *Avigation.* His project had been approved by the Chief of the Air Corps to be done during off duty time. There was unfinished work on the line drawings to illustrate the text, so I did them for Harvey, also working at home or at his house. As I read the manuscript I noted several obscure statements due to his stilted style and suggested minor changes. Harvey then asked me to review the entire manuscript to fix any others that I might find. *Avigation* was published and used in the Ground School until about 1932 when I returned from Panama.

The Air Corps had opened a second primary flying school at March Field, California and Harvey was designated to visit March Field to coordinate the two schools. Harvey was an airship pilot so asked me to fly him out to March, and planned our itinerary, not the most direct route, for we toured the West coast from San Diego to San Francisco before we turned for home.

Our first overnight stop was at El Paso on our way West. When we inquired at the desk of the Hussman Hotel about the hour of the bridge closing, we met Woodward M. (Tex) Ritter at the desk and the three of us rode the street car to visit Juarez. Back at the hotel Tex got his guitar out of the cloakroom and suggested a party in his room. Since it was ten P.M. by that time, I suggested that Harvey represent us while I went to bed. Such impromptu parties were not unusual as Army aviators were warmly welcomed in Texas. Tex began his singing career on radio station KPRC in Houston during 1929.

Brooks and Kelly Fields were invited to send Army pilots to civilian airport opening celebrations in the Twenties. Benny Chidlaw and I attended the one for Meacham Field at Fort Worth in 1927. Benny won the toss and elected to fly to Fort Worth. After that celebration, it was my turn to fly the PT-1 back to Brooks and it was slow going because we had a forty mile head wind. We flew low to avoid as much of the wind as we could and stayed close to the highway. Near Georgetown I looked down to see a Model T Ford towing a trailer with a cow in it and that rig was doing better than we were. It took us seven hours to do two hundred miles with two refuelings for the PT-1 did not have a large fuel tank.

The Air Corps held a special class for celestial navigation at Wright Field, Ohio, in February of 1929, and I was selected to attend that course. It had been instigated by Albert Hegenberger after his flight with Lester Maitland from Hawaii to the West coast. Major Clyde V. (Kewp) Finter was in charge and Mr. Bradley was the principal instructor, for he had had maritime seaman experience. We used the Navy material developed for the flight of the NC-4s to the Azores several years before. In the air we used a variation of the sextant with a bubble to provide the reference instead of the horizon.

On pilotage or dead reckoning problems I paired with Eddie Langmead who had been at Kelly with me. We stayed overnight at Selfridge Field on one trip and I learned how to start the Liberty engine by hand in zero weather. The crew chief placed a hot brick in the air inlet of the carburetor, dripped some ether on the brick and then turned the engine over several times to suck in the fumes. He removed the brick and the engine kicked off sweetly on the first try. The airplane had been in a heated hangar overnight. When parked outside in such weather, one should drain the oil and keep it inside near a stove to be poured back into the crankcase in the morning. We never had to use such measures in San Antonio.

That course ended in a grand tour using a tri-motor Fokker transport which had been fitted with a plastic dome for star sights and tables for our charts. The main idea was over water and night flying, so we went to Corpus Christi to fly the first over water leg to Pensacola where we landed at the Navy station, Corry Field. Then we had a night flight to make a land fall at Cedar Key and landed at Cross City where Hegenberger knew a former Air Corps officer who ran the flying field. Miami was the point of departure for our over water leg to Charleston, South Carolina.

Again we landed at the Navy field at Charleston and put up for the night at a hotel on the waterfront in the old part of town called the Battery. Dinner over, Finter, Hegenberger, Langmead and I were strolling along to see the sights when I heard a loud cry from behind us. "Hypockets!" We had been hailed by my classmate James McDavid who was then Insurance Commissioner of South Carolina. After the introductions and greetings, he guided us on a tour of the old town.

Since I was on my way to Panama for duty, I thought that I might be called upon to teach a course in celestial navigation at France Field. But nothing happened. As a matter of fact, there was little long-range over water flying done at that time, or need for locating one's position from the stars. However, I enjoyed that experience.

My family had settled on a farm near Carrizo Springs, Texas, in 1927. There was a meadow near their place where I could land a primary trainer (PT-1) and make luncheon visits from time to time. Since Harvey Holland was on flying status and with no airships at Brooks Field at that time, he would be my passenger. While I was in Panama, Harvey was transferred to Langley Field where they were still flying airships in the Thirties.

Cross Country by Automobile

The Army provided detailed advice and instructions for officers ordered to foreign duty. Edith and I learned that we had to deliver our automobile to the Army Base in Brooklyn forty-eight hours before the transport departed in order to have it travel to Panama with us on the transport. We drove our Dodge Sedan to Brooklyn, but not by the shortest available route.

Edith's father and mother were raised in Southern Arkansas

and had moved to Port Arthur, Texas, where she was born. She had cousins at Clarksville and Texarkana, Texas. Then, there were old friends from Port Arthur days who were living in Pontiac, Michigan. Our route to Brooklyn included Pontiac, Niagara Falls and Collingswood, New Jersey, for a visit with my Aunt Nancy. The gravel roads in those days did not permit much more than three hundred miles per day, so we allowed plenty of time in our trip planning. We shipped our trunk for the transport trip to Brooklyn by express.

Our hosts in Pontiac operated the country club where we stayed several days to see the sights of Detroit, including the Ford Plant at River Rouge. From Pontiac we drove through Canada to get to Niagara Falls for an overnight stay, and to see the Falls. We visited around Philadelphia until it was time to deliver our car and then moved to the St. George Hotel in Brooklyn.

The interesting feature of that trip was the cultural change we observed by the attitude of the people along the way in servicing our car, as well as in the various hotels and restaurants. In the small towns the hotel was usually close to the railroad station, and only one. Edith noted the change as being for the worse as compared with what she was used to in her experience. I saw it as a shift to what I had been acquainted with before moving to Texas. To oversimplify, until we got to Blytheville, Arkansas, there was little change. The car was serviced with a cheerful smile or greeting. As we moved further North, services were performed only when asked for and then often grudgingly. At the hotel in Blytheville we were greeted warmly and provided a copy of the local paper. The clerk pointed out the newest arrivals on the magazine stand. At the St. George Hotel in Brooklyn the attitude was indifferent and the tall blond at the newsstand chewed her gum and eyed me like I was about to snatch a magazine and dash for the door with it.

We embarked on the Army Transport Chateau-Thierry for our first ocean trip with a full load of passengers. Edith and I were fortunate to have a cabin to ourselves with Clayton. Couples without children were doubled up; four wives in one stateroom and their spouses in another. The meals were good with several seatings due to the crowd. Since seawater came out of the showers, we learned about salt water soap.

Kitts and Jack Davies were also bound for France Field, so we became well acquainted during that trip. Jack and I would exchange reminiscences while we sat late on the deck until told to "shut up and go to bed!" Jack had taken his ground school training at the Aviation Cadet School in Austin, Texas. This was located in the former facilities of the School for the Blind and operated by the University of Texas. He had then been sent to Italy to learn to fly the Caproni Bomber as there were no twin engined airplanes in this country at that time. He served under Major Fiorello LaGuardia on the Austrian Front. During a visit to Austin in 1957, Jack showed me the dormitory in which he had lived, now long gone. In Panama, Jack flew the Keystone Bomber our replacement for the Martin Bomber used during World War One.

There was a small library aboard the Chateau-Thierry. Among the books was a text on hydraulic power which I read with interest for it explained why the alternating electric power in the Canal Zone operated on fifty cycles per second. The power plant at Gatun Dam had been designed about 1912 with the rotating element of the alternating generator directly connected to the water turbine which drove the rotator within the static pole pieces. The turbines would not rotate fast enough to do better than fifty cycles at the power output desired. The interesting point for me was that the people from the electric department did not know why the output was fifty cycles when I would quiz them at the Strangers Club.

The transport made a short stop at San Juan Puerto Rico and then on to Colon where we disembarked. That was a pleasant trip as the sea was smooth and the weather fine. Compared to a commercial liner of those days, we were all steerage class, but all of the same family, the Army.

France Field

Marge and Jim Fitzmaurice were waiting for us when we docked at Colon, and whisked us off to the Stranger's Club to celebrate our arrival. Alcoholic beverages were not legal within the Panama Canal Zone, so much of the social activity took place at the Stranger's Club or the Palace Hotel in Colon.

True friends, Marge and Jim had prepared temporary quarters for us and engaged our cook and washerwoman. There were no closures on the various building openings, just a fine meshed screen to keep out the sand flies and the screens were kept oiled as well. Both the temperature and humidity averaged about eighty, so no windows were needed and the wide overhang on the roofs kept out the rain. Due to the high humidity mildew was a problem and our quarters had heated closets for shoes and leather goods. All our clothing was washable, so a washerwoman was important. She also starched our dress uniforms of white duck. Our duty uniforms during the day were of khaki.

There were two seasons, the dry season when it rained most of the time, and the rainy season when it rained all of the time. The dry season corresponded to our winter season in Texas. The rains were showery caused by the warm moist air drifting in from the ocean and then being lifted up by the central mountain ridge to cause the rain. Generally, the mornings were clear and good for flying, so most of our missions were early in the mornings with afternoons devoted to ground duties.

Most days we were finished by four in the afternoon and there would be a random gathering at the Palace Hotel for a social hour under the open air covered patio. Our most distinguished visitor was Bernt Balchen, the famous Norwegian-American pilot who had stopped over several days at France Field on his way home from the Antarctic after Admiral Byrd's flight over the South Pole in 1929. He gave us a first-hand story of that flight, the most difficult part being the initial takeoff when they were grossly overloaded. He also told us about the flight to Paris in 1927 when they were forced to ditch off the Normandy Coast in the dark, but the breaking surf marked the surface for the ditching, and they walked away. Balchen impressed me as a complete "Stoic" who knew the limits of his ability and was willing to stake his life on that knowledge.

France Field had and old fashioned telephone system operated by the Signal Corps. The operator at the switchboard could look out the picture window close by the main gate and observe the traffic entering and leaving the post. The operators soon became acquainted with the officers and their families. It was not uncommon for me to call my quarters and have the operator tell me that Mrs. Lynch had just left the station with Mrs. Fitzmaurice.

The Panama Canal Company operated a *commissary* which was more like a department store, for they carried a wide assortment of household goods in addition to food. They purchased their goods all over the world for quality and price, many were both cheaper and better than what we had been accustomed to in the States. Frozen meat from New Zealand was preferable to our taste than fresh meat from the States. One day I picked up a bar of Ivory Soap in its familiar wrapper to read the fine print, "Made in England."

Chinese rugs were a very popular item. We could bring them home duty free provided they had been in use for a year or more. Since we were on a two year tour, and it took six months to receive an order from China, such a purchase had to be made promptly. The Post Exchange took our orders and sent them to the Fette Company with payment in gold, so we had to pay in advance and rejoiced when they arrived.

While there were several military stations on the Atlantic side, we did not mingle socially except for the Naval Station adjacent to France Field, Coco Solo, a submarine base. The ladies played bridge together and the officers would compete at softball from time to time. General mixing was at the Stranger's Club for the weekly dances. The setup there was with tables holding about six, or three couples. The popular drink was "Rum, Gum and Lime," where the club furnished a quart bottle of rum and the associated mixes, plus seltzer bottle. Gum was simple syrup and a jigger each of the rum, syrup and lime juice made a tasty cooler when mixed with ice and seltzer.

It did not take us long to learn how to have a beer party after a soft ball game. One of the beer distributors on the Atlantic Side was a reserve officer in the Army and he would sponsor, as host, impromptu parties in his warehouse because he did not have a retailer's license. On short notice we could gather at his warehouse and he would show up to roll out a keg, then disappear. The only furniture was a wooden table or two and we provided our own mugs. Hod Eller, a pursuit pilot was expert on his banjo and provided the music for a sing-song with old familiar tunes. Such parties would last an hour or so and any beer left in the keg would return to the cold room. The following day we would check on how much beer had been consumed and remit the cost at wholesale price.

There were Japanese gardeners who operated small farms in the Canal Zone. They brought us fresh vegetables daily in their push carts, plus avocadoes and papaya. Bananas and plantain were staples and our cook knew many ways of preparing and serving them. For bananas we would go to the dock when a United Fruit boat was being loaded, tip the supervisor a dollar and come home with a full stem which we would hang on the back porch to last about a week. The method of loading was interesting as the small local supply boats would tie up on one side of the dock and there would be a stream of carriers, each with a stem moving into the boat and returning empty handed.

For most Army people the Atlantic and Pacific sides were worlds apart. Aviators went back and forth freely, but ground travel was limited to the Panama Canal Railroad. One of our friends from Fort Sam Houston, a retired Cavalryman, had moved to Panama City and had acquired the Coca-Cola franchise. They had a houseparty for us and invited Marge and Jim Fitzmaurice. The ladies had a train ride across the Isthmus while Jim and I flew to Fort Clayton for that weekend. We saw more of the sights on that trip as it was our first venture into Panama City.

In contrast to the Atlantic side the Pacific coastal strip was quite dry since most of the moisture had been milked out by the trip over the central mountain ridge. The country was covered with grass, but few trees, on the arid side.

The Panama Canal Company went to great lengths to keep the mosquito under control, two major steps were drainage to keep standing water off the ground, and the use of an oil film on the water in the drainage ditches to prevent larva from hatching. There was always someone around with a back sprayer to spray a film of oil on any puddle, a regular patrol.

The climate was healthy as far as we were concerned and we had an enjoyable two-year tour. For the return trip to the States, we embarked on the *St. Mihiel,* a sister ship to the *Chateau-Thierry,* departing from the Atlantic side so that we had a ride through the canal and could see at first hand all the various lock operations. We were to debark at San Francisco.

James A. Mars

Lieutenant Colonel James A. Mars was commanding France Field, Panama, when I arrived. He had graduated from West Point in 1903 as a Cavalryman and had learned to fly airships during World War One. Mars had been Commandant of the Airship School at Scott Field, Illinois, when I was a student in 1925.

Mars had an excellent sense of humor, but quiet. On one occasion he told us that he was in command of a troop of Cavalry in 1915, camped at Texas City across the bay from Galveston. That was the year of a great hurricane and their first warning was when the flood waters began to reach their camp late at night. The bugler sounded *Boots and Saddles* for the move to higher ground in pitch black darkness, so they left everything behind. Three days elapsed before they could return to find the campsite clean, everything gone.

Mars had no problem in clearing the property records of the material they had left behind except for an eighty pound anvil which had been left in the farrier's tent. That, too, had disappeared. The higher ups could not understand why Mars could not find that anvil. The obvious answer was that it had sunk in the muck. It may still be there for someone with a good metal detector. Mars did get credit for that anvil, eventually.

We had an Infantry style parade every Saturday morning. The France Field Staff; Commanding Officer, Adjutant and Post Operations Officer would line up to take the parade at the march by. The Headquarters of the Panama Canal Department issued a directive that all officers should be mounted for such parades. We had no horses at France Field, but we did have several mules which pulled a wagon.

For the next weekly parade, the staff calmly rode into position mounted on mules. The Adjutant Major Eddie Lyon had been a Cavalryman, E. D. Jones, the Post Operations Officer had been a polo player at Kelly Field. All were saddlewise and presented a credible showing, with the mules cooperating. I was leading a platoon of the 7th Observation Squadron so I had a front seat. It was quite a surprise for me when I saw the staff riding into position from behind a hangar where they had prepared their show.

The post photographer was on hand to record the highlights of that parade which became the talk of the Atlantic side. France Field was soon exempt from the mounted requirement. everyone enjoyed watching Colonel Mars display the proper Cavalry way with his floppy-eared mule on parade.

The 7th Observation Squadron

My specialty being observation, I was assigned to the 7th Observation Squadron. Captain Samuel E. (Sammy) Skemp, was the Commanding Officer and an experienced observer. He was serious about training his pilots in ground duties. I was rotated through Mess Officer, Supply Officer and had a short term as Assistant Communications Officer before I moved up to Post Operations Officer.

Captain Skemp had his own system for keeping books on the Mess Account. The squadron received a daily ration allowance for each man on the Morning Report and supplies were drawn from the Commissary against that account. The basic idea was that each daily menu should stay within that allowance, or that a weekly average did. Sunday dinners usually cost more, so savings were made to balance such as by using leftovers. Skemp had a spread sheet for posting this data each day to eliminate surprises. I was a bookkeeper pricing each menu from the supplies drawn. There was no magic, just attention to detail. We had a good Mess Sergeant.

My contribution as Supply Officer was to clean house at the hangar because we had too many tools and spares. Because of the humidity, each item was coated with cosmoline, a sticky goo. I was well aware that a supply sergeant needs a trading stock to help out his brethren in making up shortages, so I had Sergeant Noble make a selection. I knew that he had a storeroom in a remote part of the hangar. Then, we cleaned everything out other than for a specific need. Each crew chief had his set of tools and we had kits to take along on a cross country. We just kept spares likely to be needed. Noble was not too enthusiastic at first, but we could make a count without picking anything up. He finally agreed that it made things easier for him. We had another supply room at the barracks, but that was mainly bedding and similar supplies and presented few problems.

We were equipped with the Douglas O-2 airplane, powered by a Liberty engine. I flew the same airplane at Randolph Field where it was known as the BT-1 or basic trainer. We flew many towtarget missions and had several DH-4Bs for that work, equipped with winches. These were the DHs with the fuselage made of steel tubing in place of the spruce longerons and struts. Heavier than the DHs which I had flown at Kelly Field, these landed like a brick, meaning that there was little float just before the touchdown. We also had several Loening amphibians for overwater work, new to me. This aircraft used the invented Liberty which kept the propeller high enough to clear the bull and provided better visibility for the pilot. For the Liberty engine to work upside down, it had an extra oil pump to keep the crankcase dry by pumping the oil into a separate tank, or radiator to cool the oil.

I liked to fly that amphibian for there was plenty of water around France Field. While it had an undercarriage and wheels that required 75 turns of the crank from full up to full down, we always took off and landed on the water. When taking off the first thing was to get it up on the step so that you could gain speed. With glassy smooth water it was hard to break away, so we would slow and turn to use the ripples, the wind being zero the direction of takeoff was not critical. While taxiing back to our seaplane ramp in a small inlet, the large side area of the hull would act like a sail in a cross wind. When the speed was low and the rudder had little effect, we would crank down the landing gear to create drag. We used the amphibians for familiarization flights along the Atlantic coast where there were no places to land our 0-2s, and for missions with the Coast Artillery beyond gliding distance from the shore. I had one flight to the San Blas Islands in a group with Eddie Lyon as leader. He knew enough Spanish to communicate with the chief.

Towed target missions for the Coast Artillery, both anti-aircraft guns and machine guns, were the largest group. We also towed targets for the pursuit squadron for their aerial gunnery practice, as well as for our rear gunners. All the observation pilots fired on ground and towed targets in our training missions. We flew familiarization in groups of two or three airplanes until we had seen just about every corner of Panama. The flight to David near the Costa Rica border was an overnight trip. We would ride the narrow gauge railroad to the town up on the mountain and stay at "Pop Wright's," a small hotel. There were coffee groves around David as well as orange trees. Jim Fitzmaurice and I flew together on many missions for we were well acquainted from our mapping experience. Dave Schlatter was the Operations Officer of the squadron and Bill Craigie was Engineering Officer, both from the Class of 1923, as well as Charlie Lawrence.

An unusual event came when the Coast Artillery took their 12-inch disappearing rifles out of mothballs and fired them for target practice with some problems designated for air observation. They had not been fired since their installation during World War One. I was in the observation post at Fort Amador for the first shots and, as to be expected, there were troubles. It was customary that the first round be fired with a primer operated by a long lanyard, with the following rounds fired by an electric primer. Since nothing happened another primer was tried, but the first box was faulty and another sent for. The other gun in that pair had been fired on the first attempt, but it was out of action because the breech block was struck and could not be opened for the second round. The obturator pad that sealed the backflow of the gases had stuck. To add to the problems, the long tow line on the target was so heavy that the target would dive when the tug began towing, and floats had to rigged to hold the tow line up. The guns had been silent for too long, but the wrinkles had been ironed out before our problem was scheduled.

We were to adjust fire by air observations with the target about 12 miles from the battery. For that type of fire, the observer would use the clock system with twelve o'clock at the forward end of the tow line and the angles referred to a clock face, with distance in yards from the target. We were suspicious souls and took extra care to avoid any foulups by having two teams in the air using our amphibians. Bill Craigie was the primary observer and I was the backup man. We both kept logs and made observations, but only Craigie sent the message. I was to be ready to step in at any time. Also, we had our base station at France Field log all communications. Our caution was justified.

What happened was that someone on the ground did not believe Craigie's sensing of the error and sent a different correction to the firing point and that shot went wide of the mark. At the critique, we challenged that correction and got the proverbial runaround. However, General Brown pressed them with this question, "What would have happened if they had used Craigie's data?" Then, they had to admit that the shot could have been a direct hit. Ground officers at that time had little conception of what an air observer could see, or his ability to judge distances. Craigie was about 5000 feet looking down on the target area. A ground observer with a telescope and seldom more than 50 feet above sea level was not in a good position to judge both angle and distance.

Parsimonious was descriptive of the Army's staffing in those days, just enough to get by with. All junior officers had a special duty assignment in addition to squadron duties. I was Post Ordnance Officer and in charge of the Post Theater later on. These were primarily supervisory as we had seasoned non-commissioned officers to handle the routine work. When I first walked into the Ordnance Office I noticed a dozen large bolts on the floor and inquired about them. They were for the reveille gun when it was moved to a new mounting, the present mounting being wobbly and the gun rocking back as the blank round was fired. No one knew how to set the bolts in the new mounting before the concrete was cast. The gun was about fifty years old, but I found a copy of the manual in the files and showed the non-com. how to lay out a fixture for holding the bolts from the base diagram in the manual which gave all the necessary dimensions. When the new base was ready we used a bomb hoist to move the gun and it was over in a jiffy since the bomb hoist could maneuver like a forklift. The negative side of that improvement was that the officers who lived across the inlet from the reveille gun now complained that the sound was too loud. I could testify on that point because the gun was almost pointed at my quarters. The rocking of the old base had absorbed much of the sound.

As for the theater, most everyone bought movie tickets in a book because of the discount. Each day I would receive the money from the cashier and replace the books which he had sold. I had the cash in a safe and made periodic transfers to the Department Office. With two people making daily checks there was little temptation to dip into the funds.

I attended the Cooks and Bakers School shortly after I arrived in Panama; a course designed to acquaint junior officers with what should be done in the mess hall, rather than to make cooks of them. The text was the Army's cookbook with recipes designed to feed fifty men. The amount of the dry ingredient was stated by weight, so the issue was accuracy in that step, or all steps in the recipe. We did make bread dough and sweet dough to observe how they turned out and various pastries like bear claws from the sweet dough. We were introduced to the stockpot where all edible residue was placed, including juices from canned vegetables, for no edible material should be wasted. To walk into an Army kitchen the state of the stockpot was a good measure of the quality of the mess sergeant.

We had a good group of pilots in the 7th Observation Squadron. Dave Schlatter would devise problems as operations officer for our own training. There being little doctrine other than the experiences of World War One, we could experiment and test out new ideas. In working with the other services, the Coast Artillery were most cooperative, the Field Artillery were so-so, and the Infantry had no interest in what the air observer could do for them.

Post Operations—France Field

One Saturday morning I was invited to attend the weekly staff conference in headquarters to learn that I was to be the new Post Operations Officer. Colonel Mars was leaving for the States, Major Edwin B. Lyon was moving up to be Commanding Officer, while Lieutenant E. D. Jones would be the new Adjutant.

This news was both an honor and a challenge, but while walking back to my quarters it dawned on me that I knew nothing about what went on in the Post Operations Office, although it was across the hall from the 7th Observation Squadron. That weekend I worked up my plan for action. When I told Sergeant Gray about the change on Monday morning, I told him that I needed his help to learn the job and that he should tell me what to do until I got my feet on the ground.

My plan was to read every regulation that pertained to the job and make a list of duties to be performed. I had my usual flying missions with the 7th Observation Squadron, so it took me a week or more to go through all the regulations that Sergeant Gray had marked for me to read. When my list of duties was complete, with the authority for each. I asked Gray to show me what happened for each. Everything was being done that was on my list and I felt comfortable. During World War Two Gray became a full colonel, one of the many well qualified noncommissioned officers we had during the Twenties and Thirties.

The two major functions were to certify the flight records of the individual pilots for pay purposes and such records were permanent and had to be accurate. We were also the channel for training programs and training reports between the Panama Canal Department and Washington. The three squadrons prepared their own training reports as they differed, being pursuit, bombardment and observation. We seldom had a visiting aircraft from the States. During my tenure we had but one when Major Dargue flew from Miami to France Field on a direct flight.

The training directive issued by the Panama Canal Department specified that officers would train with their troops in the morning and perform various station duties in the afternoons. Just exactly the reverse of the way we operated at France Field. It was clear that they did not know much about the training of air units, i.e. that flying came first.

I made a trip to the Department Headquarters to visit their training people but made no headway in changing the basic rules and they were not much interested. That was understandable for the directive applied to regiments of Infantry, Field Artillery and Coast Artillery, while our three squadrons would not add up to more than three companies of Infantry. They seemed willing to leave us alone. After that, I was careful to leave off any reference to morning and afternoon for the reports from France Field and we continued our usual pattern of flying in the mornings and working with the enlisted men in the afternoons.

My new status did not change my flying missions with the 7th Observation Squadron, but I was now free from special duty assignments, and could take the weekly parades with the staff.

Major General Preston Brown

Major General Preston (P.) Brown became the new Departmental Commander while I was operations officer. We thought that things were due for a change because he had a pilot-aide and had been assigned an observation type airplane, an O-19 for his official use. His aide was Lieutenant John W. Sessums. Albrook Field on the Pacific side had not been completed, so General Brown's plane was kept at the landing strip on Fort Clayton on the Pacific side. We were expecting him to visit France Field at any time.

I well recall our first meeting as I could see his airplane parked in front of my office as I walked to work. I entered the office to see General Brown sitting in the chair at my desk, and said, "Good morning, General," introducing myself. His first comment was, "How long has it been since you cleaned out your desk?" I replied that I had done so when I took over the job several weeks before. General Brown then related his experience when he had been assigned a desk in the War Department, looked in the center drawer and found a prescription bottle with a date more that twenty years before, and he thought that too long. Since I had code practice at seven every morning, I explained that fact and asked to be excused. Thereafter, it was not unusual to find him sitting in my office while waiting to attend a meeting on the Atlantic side.

There was a porch or shelter from the rain outside my office, a gathering place for pilots waiting for a flight or free for the moment. General Brown sometimes would strike up a conversation with the pilots and I could listen to them from my desk chair. All the pilots were lieutenants and flying was their business, so when General Brown got in too deeply in a flying topic, I could hear a pilot say, "I beg your pardon General, but that is not the way it is!" and that would open up the topic further. It was rumored that General Brown was having Sessums teach him to fly the O-19 and that would not have surprised me.

In contrast to his easy conversations with the pilots at France Field, I learned that many Army ground officers were apprehensive in his presence for he had the reputation of being a martinet and being unpredictable. I knew of one instance that supported that view. General Brown called for all the officers of Fort Amador to meet him in his office at nine in the morning. When he walked in at about nine fifteen, he said, "Gentlemen, I have just finished an inspection of Fort Amador. There was not one office where the personnel on duty knew where their superior was that morning." He went on to say that in one office, when he asked an enlisted man about his duties, the answer was, "I listen for the telephone to ring." General Brown shot right back with, "Who answers it?" and the reply was, "That man over there!" As to be expected, General Brown gave them a lecture on their responsibilities. On several occasions he took me along with Sessums when he was visiting a station on the Atlantic side. I noted that he was perceptive and asked sharp questions and to the point.

The word came through the grapevine that General Brown was planning a field exercise for the Panama Canal Air Force. Our stated mission called on us to defend the Canal from France Field. As a consequence, we had only garrison equipment, no tentage or the usual field equipment. The staff got together and we worked up a speech detailing why we should not engage in such an exercise, ready for the meeting.

That conference was in General Brown's office and began with the reading by the Chief of Staff of a very brief plan for the exercise. General Brown then turned to us and said, "Gentlemen, I know that the mission of the Panama Canal Air Force does not call for an exercise of this nature, but I think that it will be good for you, and you're going to do it!" To which, Major Eddie Lyon our Commanding Officer replied, "Yes Sir!" to end the matter. General Brown then went on to say that we would have a free hand to work out the details in our own way. He authorized all the field equipment that we would need and extra trucks to haul our baggage. The general plan was that we would go by rail to the Pacific side and then march in easy stages to Rio Hato where we would camp for a few days before our return march. Since we were given a free hand, the exercise was taken as a challenge and we decided to show General Brown what we could do in the way of improvising.

A major difficulty was that few of our enlisted men had had any experience in making camp Infantry style. We needed a simple plan which was a model campsite with a street for each of our three squadrons, plus the mess tents and other tents for the officers and offices. On the squadron streets, each enlisted man would have his designated spot to pitch his tent. The streets were to be marked out with ropes and stakes, while tent locations were marked on the ropes with colored cloth ties. When the tentage arrived, we pitched camp several times until it was done to our satisfaction, and an aerial photograph was taken for use as a template. A special team laid out the camp sites adjacent to landing strips which we had been using for various exercises before and were adjacent to the highway to Rio Hato. This team and all its gear was moved in one of our Keystone bombers as a unit, and the men did not have to march as compensation.

The entire operation of making and breaking camp had been broken down into work units with a team for each unit. The teams were headed by noncommissioned officers while various officers coordinated the separate teams. Everyone had been involved in working out the details and we had practiced several Saturdays before the exercise began. Since we were short of aircraft at that time, the few airplanes we had were used for courier or emergency duties and most of the pilots marched with the troops.

The daily procedure for the march was that the individual packs and other baggage would be loaded on the trucks by the loading detail and the trucks would move out to be unloaded at the next campsite. The remainder of the troops would begin their march. As soon as the trucks were unloaded, they returned to the head of the column and loaded up with men who were taken to camp. This shuttle continued until all men were in camp. As soon as a man arrived in camp, he located his pack, took it to his tent marker and went about his assigned task. The camp grew by increments.

Striking camp was a swarm of activity with each team concentrating on their task. Individual packs were taken to the designated spot for loading. The campsite had to be cleaned up, and the column began to march. Few men walked more that five miles and the order of march was changed each day. As we gained experience, it took about thirty minutes to break camp and begin the march.

It was General Brown's habit to fly over the camp early in the morning and then visit us at the new camp that afternoon after we had settled down. By the third day, much to his surprise, we were on the road when he flew over as he told us that afternoon.

Air Corps noncommissioned officers were more accustomed to doing things themselves rather than to direct the work of enlisted men. We in the 7th Observation Squadron understood this and made a special effort to coach our noncoms to see to it that every man did his share and that the work moved smoothly.

General Brown was correct in his thinking that the field exercise would be good for us. Everyone was involved in the planning, both officers and enlisted men. This cooperative effort brought them together on a common task to gain experience. The men liked being *soldiers* and away from garrison routine. All had the can-do attitude and were bent on showing General Brown what the Air Corps could do.

Major Adam E. Potts

Towing targets was an excellent method for building flying time because one would spend an entire morning cruising back and forth on a designated course. The 7th Observation Squadron did all the towing for the ground force units, a major part of their work, and all the pilots took their turn. We had trained winch operators so there seldom was any problem with equipment. For the three-inch antiaircraft guns, we towed a long narrow flag type target at ten thousand feet and about one thousand feet behind the airplane. The target for machine gun firing was a tube similar to a wind sock, usually towed at an altitude of one thousand feet. Before landing, we would drop the target either on France Field or at the battery position, the winch operator sending a device down the cable to trip the catch. I had no problems the first season, but did observe that we would be on course at the designated time and the ground crew would not be ready to fire. There was one case where the pilot had been on course for thirty minutes before the ground crew climbed out of their trucks, and the battery commander complained that the pilot had left the course early.

Before the next season began I had a call from Major Adam E. Potts, Coast Artillery, who told me that he was a recent arrival and would be in charge of all their antiaircraft firing during the coming season. Further, he planned to come to France Field to visit me and obtain the Air Corps point of view before working up his plan.

Major Potts had been my French instructor at West Point and knew me, but a major should not call on a second lieutenant. I suggested that I interview all our pilots who had towed targets and collect suggestions from them to bring to his office at Fort Amador.

We met as planned and I had all the suggestions written out in detail. They boiled down to two major items; should the courses be laid out on prominent landmarks, it would be easier for the pilot to maintain a steady course. The year before they had been designated as compass headings. The second item was that the battery should be ready at the time the pilot arrived on course because of our limited fuel supply. Potts had dozens of batteries to schedule through the firing point, for they all used the same firing range. His plan would determine our towing schedule.

Major Potts sent me a copy of his plan and I noted that he had injected a new idea, the battery commander was now responsible for notifying the pilot thirty minutes in advance of the time he expected to be ready to fire. When the pilot was on call at France field, the usual procedure, it would take him about thirty minutes to take off and climb to ten thousand feet while crossing the Isthmus to get on course. Further, Potts had laid out the courses on landmarks.

We also had a working arrangement for that season, Major Potts would talk to the battery commander on his view of the day's mission, while I would talk to the pilot who had flown that day. Later on that day we would exchange that information. At first there would be a few details to straighten out, but it was not long before a battery commander would ask Potts to pass the word to the pilot on an excellent flying mission. It became a game to have their first rounds in the air as soon as the target entered the firing zone. I had that experience on several missions that I towed.

The end result of the improved coordination and daily feedback was that their firing program was completed in about one third less time, and with a positive improvement in the scores over the previous year. Everyone was on his toes and the spirit was high. From our point of view it took much less flying time and the pilots liked to see the puffs behind them to know that it was useful flying.

With Pistol and Rifle

Target shooting with the pistol and rifle were sporting events in the Army and the Panama Canal Department held annual competitions. There had been no France Field teams entered before my arrival in 1929, no doubt because we were small frogs in a large pond. When the announcement was circulated a group of officers at France Field decided that we should enter a team in both competitions, that the goal should be to win, and that this fact should come as a complete surprise.

As cadets at West Point we had a detailed course in musketry under Major Paul Newgarden, top shot in the Army with the Springfield rifle. Sidney Hinds, an upperclassman in my company went on to earn a Gold Medal in the 1924 Olympics, so the goal was feasible. This group set up a rigorous training program of muscle building, breathing control, aiming and squeezing. They worked in the hangar during the afternoons out of the rain and coaching each other. Those intending to use the Colt regulation pistol carried a piece of metal rod comparable to the grip on the pistol, but weighing about twice that of a pistol. They carried this weight during the day and flexed their muscles for holding and aiming. The Springfield rifles came out of the stock in the Ordnance supply at France Field. There was no shooting on the range until the very last when they checked their weapons and shot to see who would start with each team.

The France Field teams won hands down in their competitions, a matter of considerable pride for everyone. Air Corps officers were equipped with the Colt pistol, so that was not much of a surprise. However, the Infantry officers were not happy about being shot out of first place and filed a complaint to have the France Field team disqualified on the basis that the rifle was not their authorized weapon. General Brown ruled against them so the record stood.

Talking Pictures

Our movie theaters were the basic form of entertainment and well attended. They were operated by the Army's Motion Picture Service and overseas stations had priority in the conversion from silent to the new *Talking Pictures.* Within the Panama Canal Department, France Field stood seventh in priority based on the size of the population. Lieutenant Malcolm Stewart who was Communications Officer of the 7th Observation Squadron lobbied hard to use the trained radio repairmen in the squadron to expedite the conversion at France Field. I urged him on expecting to tag along and learn something in the process.

We did get permission to install our new equipment and it had been delivered. But, Stewart was ordered to the Cooks and Bakers School at Fort Clayton on the Pacific side. I was left to handle the project and he left with these comforting words, "Eddie, I know that you can handle this job!"

There were two types of talking pictures in the early days, one had the sound on a large record, while the second type had the sound on a special strip beside the picture on the film. The projection heads had to be changed because the silent film ran at 16 frames per second while both sound films ran at 24 frames per second. The projection heads were changed by the motion picture technicians. The new projection head included an electric eye to scan the sound track and convert the sound track to an audio sound for amplification to drive the large speakers that went behind a perforated screen. For the platters or records, we had a heavy duty turntable with a magnetic pickup that fed the signals to the amplifier.

The major problem for me was that the Army Motion Picture Service had purchased the various components from different sources and the terminals were not coded the same, some with numerals and others with letters. I had to work out a Master Wiring Diagram with wire ends coded to match the various components. That was done on the dining room table in our quarters where there was room to work things out. The installation was straightforward electric work, drilling holes in concrete, installing conduit for the wiring and my part which was the interconnections. When the new projection heads were installed, we were ready to check things out.

The theater auditorium was open air, with the top quarter of the side walls screened, so the movies were shown after dark. We checked out the equipment in the afternoon and it was weird to listen to the sound track without being able to see the picture. The speakers were hung from a pipe frame stand with light rope so that they could be pointed in any forward direction. We aimed them at the audience with the perforated screen out of the way with several observers to check the volume. Since people absorb sound, we checked it again during the show and made further adjustments until everyone was satisfied.

The radio mechanics enjoyed doing something different and earned passes to the movies for the remainder of their tour. It was not long before we had our first emergency when the turntable did not work. A quick check showed that there was an *open* resistor in the speed control and a replacement was not available in Panama. I knew that light bulbs could be used as resistors, so we rigged up several lamp sockets and tried various combinations until we were back to the correct speed with the stroboscope. The humidity had caused corrosion at the terminal of the resistor and eaten away the resistance wire. I suggested to the Motion Picture mechanics that they should cover such terminals with a rosin-beeswax mixture that we used on our aircraft radio parts to keep out moisture, not to mention having spare parts of that type which were not commercial sizes.

My hobby activity in Panama had been to convert our acoustic phonograph to play records through a magnetic reproducer with an amplifier to boost the sound for a loud speaker. The necessary parts were obtained from a mail order house in the States. Since the power for the Panama Canal was fifty cycle alternating current rather than the sixty cycle standard for the States, I had to build my own power transformers using formulae provided by my brother Walter from his reference books. I had enough experience to cope with the various problems in working with the talking pictures.

Ferry Trip to Kelly Field

The highlight of my Panama tour was a ferry trip to Kelly Field to exchange our 0-2 Douglas Observation aircraft for the new 0-19 type, destined for the 7th Observation Squadron. We used the land route pioneered by Pan American Airways; their refueling facilities and communications. The trip would not have been possible without that assistance. Their headquarters were in Miami and they occupied one hangar at France Field at the remote end, so we did not see much of their local crew.

Their route followed the Pacific Coast of Central America from Panama to Tehuantepec in Mexico and then across the isthmus to Vera Cruz. The trip was early in 1931 during the dry season. We had four aircraft in the flight north with eight pilots to return eight of the O-19s. Captain Albert Guidera who was Commanding the Pursuit Squadron was my passenger to Kelly for the entire trip. I carried my chamois filter to keep any water and dirt out of the fuel tank. The Pan American fuel pumps all measured in liters and new to me, so I had to convert to check my fuel consumption, there being no gauge on the O-2.

Our trip was in easy stages and we flew in the mornings when conditions were good. The first day we went to San Jose, Costa Rica then on to Quatemala City, the next. We were able to sightsee and spent our afternoons looking around. At Quatemala the military attache, Lieutenant James H. Walker, Cavalry, took us in hand to show us the Quatemala Military Academy as well as the city. Ten years later, Jimmie was my boss in the War Department General Staff. At Managua, Nicaragua, we landed at the Marine Base and flying field, staying with them. On our way to Vera Cruz from Guatemala we refueled at Tapachula, the most primitive stop along the way the the Chief came out to greet us with his badge of office hanging from his neck. We did visit the market to learn that their meat was slaughtered very early in the morning, purchased and in the pot for the noon meal, there being no refrigeration.

There was nothing to see on the ground across the Isthmus of Tehuantepec due to the rain forest. Our navigation was simple for we flew a compass course knowing that we would reach the Bay of Campeche and then follow the coast to Vera Cruz. Other than at Managua we stayed in the downtown hotels. The Latin taxi drivers were a revelation as they drove at top speed to impress the aviators and tooted their horns all the time, despite the fact that there was no place to go. The majority of traffic was on foot or horse draw carts.

On the way to Vera Cruz I had noted that all the hotels used telephone equipment of German manufacture. While in the hotel there I had an opportunity to talk to the manager and asked him about the German monopoly of that equipment. He told me that the Stateside manufactures were only interested in unloading their surplus, or standard types of telephone equipment. Whereas, the Germans would build a system to their specification in all particular details. That appeared to be the general attitude toward marketing our products in Central America.

From Vera Cruz to Brownsville we followed the East coast of Mexico with an overnight stop at Tampico. We cleared customs at Brownsville, spent another night with a trip across the border and then on into Kelly with the first poor weather of the trip, some low clouds and rain around Alice, Texas.

We spent several days at Kelly Field to get acquainted with the O-19, powered with the Wasp engine which had a little more power than the Liberty. We practiced landings and made local flights to see how it handled before we began the return trip which was the reverse of our trip North. Again, we flew in the mornings and were able to do more sightseeing on that trip as well. It was an enjoyable flight and I had seen much new country both from the air and on foot.

Back to San Antonio

We embarked on the St. Mihiel at Colon for our return trip to San Antonio by way of San Francisco. During the transit of the Canal we were able to get a close view of Culebra Cut where there were slides from time to time to block traffic. I was surprised to learn that the so-called slide was horizontal. The water from the canal permeated the ground under the small hill at Culebra where the cut had been made. Eventually, the weight of the hill squeezed the mud out into the channel and it had to be removed by dredging. That hill was slowly losing height.

On our way north we stopped off the coast of Nicaragua to pick up several passengers. There was no port, so the transport anchored offshore and the passengers came out on a lighter. I recognized Sid Williamson, a Marine Corps pilot on duty at Managua when we stopped on our ferry trip several months before. I greeted him at the gangplank and he told me to join him in his room at four that afternoon. He was bringing aboard a foot locker with great care. There were four Marines in that stateroom and in the center was the footlocker containing six gallons of Bacardi Rum amongst old laundry, so we had a tot before dinner. Williamson was circumspect, but every afternoon we had a quiet get-together in the late afternoon to swap flying stories, about six aviators.

We decked at Fort Mason which was adjacent to the Presidio, close to the Golden Gate Bridge. Friends from Brooks Field days were on duty there and we stayed with them a few days to see the sights and to get the car ready for our trip to Texas. For one thing, the battery was dead on arrival so I had to jump start it to drive to Sears and buy a new one.

We headed south on Route 101 to stop at Saratoga for a visit with cousins of my mother. They had been in the grocery business in San Francisco during the earthquake when everything tumbled to the floor. They had then moved some forty miles south to open a general store near Saratoga. We did not stay more than a few hours to get acquainted and them moved on to Glendale.

Pauline Palmer, one of Edith's close friends in San Antonio, had moved to the West Coast about 1923 thinking that she could make a career in the movies, but married instead. Her husband operated a dry cleaning business in Glendale. At that time, Los Angeles was a cluster of small villages with fields and open spaces between them. They showed us the sights including a trip to the ocean at Wilmington, much in the open at that time. We also went to Pasadena to view the famous "Blue Boy" painting and to have lunch with my newfound cousin the son of the Smith's who operated the grocery at Saratoga.

From then on we kept pushing for San Antonio, again making about 35 miles per hour on largely gravel roads. Again there were many detours and much summer construction. We crossed the Coolidge Dam, for out of Phoenix we took the shortest route to El Paso via Globe. In El Paso we put up at the Hussman Hotel where I had met Tex Ritter in 1927, but we did not cross the border. Though the trip was made in May, it was hot and slow, about three hundred miles per day.

Eventually we arrived in San Antonio and rented a house close to Brooks Field. We knew that a move to Randolph Field was pending so that we did not really settle down. That move came in October, four months later.

Randolph Field

My five years at Randolph Field were wonderful, living the good life in brand new facilities rather than those left over from World War One, and my office in the Ground School was but a short walk from my quarters at Number 46 Main Circle. While the Great Depression was on for the country, we suffered only minor difficulties. The Army added its *Mite* in several ways. Our flying time was reduced to four hours per month, the minimum requirement for flying pay. We all had a fifteen percent cut in our pay, and there was a freeze on promotions to save money. I became a first lieutenant seventeen days before that freeze was effective.

This was the first Army flying station designed by aviators. An area, square in shape and one mile on each side, it was actually two flying fields arranged back to back. The west side was devoted to primary flying and the east side was for basic training. The common facilities were in the center with each field having separate hangars and barracks for the training squadrons. The officer quarters were arranged in concentric circles around the club at the center. The Administration Building and common facilities were at the north end of the building area, while the Ground School and the Aviation Cadet facilities were at the south. Large grassy areas were on all four sides.

It was designed to be the Headquarters of the Army's Flying

Training Wing, with one of the flying schools at Randolph and the other at March Field, California. The first commander was Brigadier General Frank P. Lahm who had been qualified to fly by the Wright Brothers in 1909. He was also a balloon pilot and had won the Gordon Bennett International Balloon Race when it was held in Paris in 1906. The Flying School was commanded by Colonel Fred Martin. Facilities were also provided for the School of Aviation Medicine adjacent to the Station Hospital.

The Army recognized during World War One that aviators and flying presented some special needs. An Army doctor at Fort Sam Houston Hospital, about 1919, had treated pilots with stomach upsets, such as heartburn. The conventional wisdom was that smoking and drinking were the cause among aviators. But his patients neither smoked nor drank. He determined that anxiety was the problem for it interfered with the normal stomach secretions and advised his patients to refrain from eating solid foods until after their flying was over for that day. His study had the euphonious title of, "The Aviator's Belly."

A School of Aviation Medicine was established at Mitchel Field on Long Island generally known as The Flight Surgeon's School. In addition to training specialists in Aviation Medicine, their mission was to conduct research on the medical problems of flying personnel and to improve the selection of candidates for flying training with the idea of reducing the failure rate. The school was moved to Brooks Field in 1927 and then moved to Randolph in 1931.

One topic was that of *Fear of Flying*. It was first considered to be a personality defect, the lack of an adequate male image. It soon became apparent to the flight surgeons that anxiety was the issue, or ability to deal with stressful situations. While the problem was studied when I was at Randolph, I do not believe that their prediction improved, however, they were alert to the symptoms.

Major Keith Simpson, whom I had met at Scott Field, and a specialist in opthamology was doing research on modifying the standard goggle to install bifocal segments for those who needed them, since the usual eye glasses did not work in an open cockpit. He was also active in the study of *vertigo* and the practical aspects of instrument flying. He turned an old dental chair into a rotational chair to prove to the pilots that they could not depend on their sensations for orientation. I went with him to give a demonstration for a luncheon club in Seguin as his guinea pig.

The flight surgeons were on flying status and habitually flew with various pilots to observe conditions from the rear seat, or to check out ideas. On some occasions a cross country flight would be organized to fly to Laredo or Piedras Negras to have lunch and see the country.

When the Volstead Act was repealed and liquor became legal, the senior flight surgeon, Major David Grant, assembled all the pilots in the Post Theater and gave us a lecture on alcohol and its effects, making it clear that it was a poison and a depressant. His theme was moderation and how to handle it for your protection as to health, acknowledging that abstinence was unlikely. For one thing, he stressed the point that, as a depressant it interfered with the normal stomach functions in digestion, so no more than two cocktails were the norm. The consequence of going beyond two was that the food would not digest, but sour and would result in a "hangover," a condition you would create.

Being some twenty miles from downtown San Antonio, Randolph Field was a self-sufficient community. For the officers, the social center was their club and swimming pool. Weekend dances were formal, officers in their dress uniforms and the ladies in their long gowns. It was not uncommon to dance the early part of the evening at Randolph and then move to Fort Sam Houston or Kelly Field, to keep in touch with whatever was going on. Much depended upon the band playing.

During the week social activity was quiet, a model of sobriety with bridge a popular pastime. Such parties ran from seven until nine followed by cake and coffee, or perhaps ice cream. One could not fly all morning, starting at six in the summer, and party all night. Small dinner parties were popular. Anita Daniel had taught Edith and me to make her special spaghetti sauce from scratch and made the day before. Also, how to make ravioli. We would have Italian dinners on our patio after the sun went down, doing them in style with colored lights, and red checkered table cloths.

Edith and I were faced with the problem of new draperies since our quarters were bare of everything when we moved in. After we priced custom made and ready-made draperies, we decided to make them ourselves. I took a close look at those on display at Joskes in San Antonio and made a pattern. Edith selected material which we could buy at a wholesale house through the Post Exchange, but only in bolt lots with a bolt of unbleached muslin for the linings. We selected rods which matched the Spanish style of the building.

That pleasant life came to an end when I received orders for the Air Corps Tactical School, a step upward in my career. Edith enjoyed our tour at Randolph for her parents were living in San Antonio and her brother and his family were in Corpus Christi. She was an active member in the chapel choir and played a good hand of bridge. Every summer we would take Clayton for a visit with his grandmother at Carrizo Springs, while we had a short vacation, usually about two weeks. I could make luncheon visits for there was a meadow close by the farm where I could land a PT-3.

"Daddy" Baker

Major Cadmus J. Baker, Medical Corps, a very early Flight Surgeon, earned the affectionate sobriquet of "Daddy" when he was the sole physician at Chanute Field and delivered the numerous postwar babies. He was their family doctor before the days of gynecologists and pediatricians.

Graduated from the University of Arkansas Medical School at Little Rock, he became the physician for Pulaski County to look after prisoners in the jail and the residents of the poor farm. He noticed that many of the residents were badly nourished and that many of those had few or no teeth. He pulped the fresh vegetables from the farm and fed that pulp to them by the spoonful, with some resistance. To his surprise, their bleeding gums and mouth sores also improved, for he had rediscovered Scurvy, a disease not covered in his medical school classes since it was seldom seen at that time.

Another lesson he learned in his work with the county was that physical activity after surgery could be beneficial. One sturdy black prisoner developed appendicitis and Doctor Baker operated early one morning at the jail hospital. The prisoner was put to bed to recover with his leg irons on but no special guard otherwise. Late that afternoon the prisoner was observed hopping into the underbrush along the river. Ten days elapsed before the prisoner was recaptured and then only because he was found drunk and asleep in the river bottom several miles distant. When Daddy examined the incision he said that, "It had healed beautifully!" But, he did not fully realize the implications of that experience until much later.

During World War One Baker became a battalion surgeon, serving overseas. After Chanute Field duty he switched to the new specialty of Aviation Medicine. The School of Aviation Medicine was first at Mitchel Field, Long Island, and he moved to Brooks Field in 1927. Edith and I had met Gussie (Augusta) and Daddy Baker soon after their arrival at a party given by Ruth and Arnold Rich. The Riches had been on duty at Chanute Field and Daddy had delivered their first child.

Daddy's generation of doctors held to the belief that Nature was the healer and the function of the doctor was to assist Nature by keeping the patient comfortable during that process. Where surgery was indicated, the attitude was the the risk of *not* doing surgery exceeded the surgical risk, for there was always risk. They were chary in their interventions, including medication. For normal aches and pains including the common cold, they prescribed tablets of aspirin, phenacitin and caffeine (APCs). For a sore throat, a gargle with Dobell's Solution was effective for the phenol deadened the soreness. A cough called for Terpin Hydrate, although a mixture of half honey and half whiskey would do as well. When Clayton was young and fretful as a baby, we would feed him a half teaspoonful of sugar saturated with whiskey. Doctor Baker considered alcohol a proper depressant or tranquilizer, because the metabolism of alcohol in the body was well understood. The doctors at that time had great respect for the human body as a chemical factory which converted the food eaten into diverse forms to be absorbed through the blood stream, often in mysterious and wondrous ways. Major Keith Simpson who had graduated from the University of Texas Medical School in 1915, held the same views.

Major Baker was the Attending Surgeon at Randolph Field, seldom separated from his black "Doctor's" bag, for he took it home at night and carried it during the day. Edith came home one afternoon to find our maid stretched out on her bed in an hysteric trance with her eyeballs rolled back, so she called Major Baker. He and I arrived at the front door about the same time, so I followed the procession to the maid's room. Daddy took a look and said in a quiet way, "I could splash water on her, but that would wet the bed; I could slap her face and shock her out of it; I suggest that we go to the living room and have a drink while she recovers by herself." We followed his prescription and the maid showed up about twenty minutes later with a sheepish expression. She had had an argument with her boyfriend that afternoon to precipitate her condition.

While Edith and I were visiting at Fort Crockett the Summer of 1934, the Davasher's organized a Beach Party to be held at North Beach, Corpus Christi, about eight couples including Gussie and Daddy Baker. The Davasher's had rented enough cottages which were available at that time. While swimming that evening, Dave cut his foot badly walking on the beach. Daddy took a look at the wound, opened his black bag and treated it on the spot. The next morning he said to Dave, "It was a good thing that you were well lubricated with Scotch last night. Had you been sober the medicine I used would have burned hell out of you!"

Edith and I were visiting Nathalie and Harold Conway who were stationed at Fort Crockett. They were renting a large home at the west end of Galveston proper, near that fort located right on the beach. There was much social activity during our stay for the battleship *Wyoming* arrived with the midshipmen from The United States Naval Academy at Annapolis who were on their summer cruise. Conway was acquainted with Captain Rufus King the skipper and several of the staff for his elder brother had graduated from the Naval Academy and several of his brother's classmates were aboard. Also, there was a British cruiser in port for a short visit; the *Wyoming* being tied up at the dock while the cruiser was anchored off the channel. The town people had arranged a series of activities for the middies, including a dance. The Conway's had a party at their home with their friends of the staff. The main entree was a large fish we had caught that afternoon at the end of the jetties and then baked.

Ground School

Back at my old stomping ground in the Ground School of the Air Corps Primary Flying School after my tour in Panama, I found a few changes. Major Clyde V. (Kewp) Finter had replaced Charles Chauncey as Director. We were well acquainted from the navigation course I had taken at Wright Field in 1929, so we worked well together. I was the Assistant Director, while no formal duties were set up, I took care of all routine administrative detail in the office, leaving Finter free for policy and planning. Our offices had a communicating door so we could consult at any time.

Planning for the move to Randolph was quite simple. We had all new furniture in our building, so all we had to move were the records and school supplies. Since the Technical Library then at Brooks Field was to be housed in the Ground School Building, it came under our jurisdiction at the time of the move.

I was back to teaching map reading, air navigation and meteorology. We were still using the mimeographed manual prepared by Harvey Holland and based on his textbook *Avigation,* and I had assisted in its preparation. The stock of manuals was almost depleted and I had some ideas for a revision, so I obtained approval to go ahead with that project. In Holland's text he had included alternate methods for solving several type problems and I thought that they were more confusing than helpful to the student. I selected solutions for the new manual which were progressive steps in the graphic solutions, one built on another so to speak. Also, I added some practical hints on how to get a good start on a cross country flight through trial and error in determining the drift. I had a hunch that pilots who determined that they were lost after an hour's flight had been lost from the very beginning. With our training aircraft a ten knot wind directly on the beam called for five degrees of correction for drift as the maximum, so an estimation between zero and ten degrees depending on the relation of the wind to the desired ground track, could be made at the start and then adjusted after a half-hour or so of flight. The issue was not to fly a precise line but to know where you were at all times in relation to your desired path over the ground.

For map reading I was using the manual which I had prepared and saw no reason to change it based on my experience. Meteorology was then taught with a standard textbook written by Millen, and based on the Weather Bureau's system of forecasting. Shortly after the move to Randolph we were joined by Lieutenant Anthony Q. Mustoe who took over that course. Mustoe had just returned from Europe where he had taken a course under Vilhelm Bjerknes at the University of Oslo based on his "Polar Front Theory" of cyclones. The basic point in Bjerknes theory was the clash of cold polar air meeting warm moist air, also referred to as Frontal Theory or Air Mass analysis. Bjerknes changed the entire concept of forecasting and we were teaching it at Randolph some years before it was adopted by the Weather Bureau. Mustoe was later our Weather Officer for the Eighth Air Force in England during World War Two.

The ground school operated on the flying training schedule which called for one half the class to be flying while the other half was in ground school. The sections would reverse at mid-morning. I taught two sections each day and, in the summer my first class began at six in the morning. Since I lived a block away, I would have a cup of coffee and wait until after class for my breakfast.

The Technical Library was something new for me, although I had used the one at France Field. There was little traffic for the ground school location, and the noncommissioned officer in charge came up with the idea of buying surplus books from Joske's lending library. We were able to obtain some non-appropriated funds from the Post Exchange and introduced popular fiction to boost circulation, and it created a new problem, the repair of our books. We bought a repair kit from a supply house and our library staff became proficient repairmen.

We produced our training manuals through the mimeograph process and there was only one secretary in the ground school, so she cut the stencils and I proofed them. Later on the Army purchased an offset machine which copied typewritten pages and produced line drawings quite like printing. Since that machine could reproduce printed money hard to detect, The Treasury Department checked out all our operators for security purposes. That machine was in headquarters, but we had full access to it for our manuals.

We had a large basement room listed as a laboratory adjacent to the room where the radio code equipment was installed. It became a social room for the radio operators and several were knowledgeable about repairing receivers for their buddies in barracks. Since I was supervising the radio code training, I spent quite a bit of time in that room and it was not long before I was teaching radio theory and various circuits for the men who were planning to take the Air Mechanic's Examination to qualify as a radio mechanic in addition to being a radio operator. The Air Mechanic rating paralleled the noncommissioned officer grade pay scale to provide increased pay for technicians. To qualify, a man had to pass a written examination and also demonstrate his proficiency on the job.

Carl Crane, one of our ground school instructors, was interested in instrument flying and had designed a folding hood for the front seat of our basic trainer. This hood had been installed on several of our aircraft and we were able to practice instrument flying using the radio beam. A popular flight was from San Antonio to Corpus Christi as there was little air traffic at that time. Two pilots would team up, one to fly and the other as a safety observer or lookout, switching seats for the return trip.

When things had settled down after our move, I had some time on my hands in the afternoons and a nice office in which to work, so I enrolled in an Army correspondence course, as much out of curiosity as anything. Then I learned that Lieutenant Howard A. (Pinky) Craig was enrolled in the Command and General Staff School series, so I switched to them. Those courses proved very beneficial in my work at the Air Corps Tactical School, primarily because I had learned the form and symbols used in such problems.

Except for the period when we were restricted to four hours per month during the depression, I preferred to meet my flying time requirements by flying cross country for I could practice pilotage and see the weather first hand. The word soon got around that I was available to fly any enlisted man working with the ground school to a field near his home in Texas when he went on furlough.

So, I became well acquainted with Texas flying fields. I had one ferry trip where I rode the train to the Middleton Air Depot near Harrisburg, Pennsylvania, to return a PT-3 which had been repaired at that depot. Since the normal route from Scott Field to Muskogee had hops too long for the fuel supply in the PT-3, I flew south from Scott Field to Memphis and then on to Texas through Shreveport.

The Morse Code

The Morse Code using dots and dashes was, and is, a basic language for communicating information because it can work with radio, light or sound. The Navy used blinker lights between ships at close range, and prisoners have talked via tapping sounds. It should be no surprise that candidates for the pilot rating should have had to attain a speed of twelve words per minute in that code as part of their program. There were occasions when voice communications would not be intelligible and one had to drop back to code.

Our new facilities were an improvement over what I had used at Brooks Field when I took the code course. The instructor sat on an elevated platform with a switchboard so that he could communicate with all students, or just with one. The students had cubicles with a key and headset. The classroom held three similar sections for three instructors, so we could run slow, medium or fast sections. The instructor used a hand key of his choice, usually a *bug* or one that made dots with a vibrating reed. We considered that hand keying was more realistic than the mechanical sending from tapes, using the standard Signal Corps Training Manual with its groups of numbers and letters.

I had observed very early that the last few weeks of the code course were hectic trying to push the slowpokes over the twelve word goal. There would be extra instruction, often at night, so I began my supervision looking for a better way, to isolate students having problems early when they needed help the most.

Every Friday there was a progress test to determine the student's top speed. Such tests were in our filing cabinets and went back quite a few years, so I made a plot of the weekly progress for one class, average score against weekly progress. But, that did not tell me much.

Miller, one of our enlisted instructors, was older than the other instructors and somewhat of a "loner" in mixing with them in their activities. He complained to me often about this and that leading me to believe that he was unhappy about something, but I could not put my finger on it. Thinking that if Miller were busy it would take his mind off his troubles, I suggested to him that a scatter plot of all the student scores for one class would be more revealing in working up a standard of progress. He liked the idea and I got him a large sheet of cross-section paper. When he had plotted one class he moved on to another and soon the sheet was covered with fly-specks, some scattered and some closely grouped. We studied the pattern and it was clear that we could draw in by hand a line to separate the upper one-quarter and the lower one-quarter, with the middle fifty percent representing those having no problems. We now had identified the lower limit where those below needed extra instruction. What to do about the students who were in the upper one-quarter? The final solution was that every student took the weekly test on Friday, those above the top line were excused until the class caught up with them. Those below the minimum began extra instruction which continued until they had moved up to the class minimum. The goals were published for each week beforehand and a list of students excused for the following week was published. A little more paperwork but it reduced the night sessions and hustle and bustle at the end of the course. In the case of one student who held a commercial radio operator license, we put him to work as an extra instructor, for it helped him keep his code speed up.

I helped Miller write the story of this project and saw that he got a commendation from the Wing Commander, General Lahm, for he had done the tedious work. The most interesting feature for me was the way Miller "perked up" and his attitude improved in all aspects as a result of this effort. It had boosted his self-esteem.

I freely admit that my first purpose had been to get Miller off my back. When he became enthusiastic about the project, I encouraged him. That was a learning experience for me.

Participation

To obtain cooperative effort with all shoulders to the wheel from a group of people was no easy task, and greatly complicated when there was a radical change in routine involved.

We were short of basic training aircraft with a full class of students in 1935. There were enough aircraft to provide the flying hours for the students, but not enough to permit doing fifty-hour inspections during the day while flying was going on. The obvious answer was to do the scheduled maintenance at night, but it had never been done that way before, at least since the war.

Colonel Henry W. Harms, the base commander, prepared the way by having a meeting of all the officers and noncommissioned officers in the squadrons supporting the basic training. He explained the necessity for the plan he presented, solicited their cooperation and promised a ten-day pass for everyone on the east side involved in the effort.

There were benefits from working at night because it was cooler, but the lights attracted the insects. This change created some stir and Colonel Harms could be seen in the maintenance hangars rather often. Others were curious to see what was going on, and I made several visits myself. The job was done according to plan and everyone got their pass as promised.

The final tally did not come for a month or so when all the indicators were in. The basic training squadrons had produced better than normal performance in all measures; flying hours were up for their aircraft, the disciplinary rate was down. Their spirit had been high because the task was taken as a challenge. Harms developed teamwork by having everyone involved well before the action was taken. Colonel Harms was a Brigadier General commanding Fort Douglas at Salt Lake City the next time I met him in 1940 while on a visit to a reception center under his command.

Post Operations — Randolph Field

As part of the Army's program to strengthen the Air Corps, it had been authorized temporary promotions to a grade appropriate to the position an officer occupied. Since I was eligible for promotion to captain, I was transferred to duty calling for a captain's rank and became Post Operations Officer in 1935, having been a lieutenant for thirteen years. My new office was in the Administration Building, so I now had a nice walk to work from my quarters on the south side.

Sergeant Holmes, the senior noncom in Operations was well-qualified as in the case of Gray at France Field, and I knew what was supposed to be done. This was a larger office with six clerks as we had considerable transient traffic, visitors or just passing through. We took care of visitors and filed their flight plans, the Weather Office being next door. My first problem was to get acquainted with my six helpers, so I asked Sergeant Holmes to have each man write down what he actually did every day, weekly or at a longer interval. My first idea was to look for gaps or overlaps, but when I laid out the six offerings I decided that I had something more useful. I rewrote them in a more polished version so that they could be placed under the plate glass each man had on his desk. The list would not only serve as a reminder to him, but also be a basis for training his replacement, or to assist a temporary replacement, since it avoided oral instructions. As before, our major function was to certify the flying records for pay purposes.

Our office had several aircraft on call for running errands, basic trainers of the BT-2 type with Wasp radial engines and I was free to fly at my own volition when duties permitted. When I knew that a cold front was on the way from the weather office next door, I could fly out to take a look at it. In one case it was interesting to see that the dust cloud was five thousand feet deep and flat on top.* When the Guadalupe River went on a rampage in 1935, I flew Major Simpson over that area to view the damage. His wife Linda was the health counselor for Camp Mystic which sat high on a bluff beside the river. Those at the camp were safe, but Simpson's air-cooled Franklin was parked close to the river and ended up filled with silt.

We seldom encountered icing conditions in Texas. On one flight home from a weekend visit to Barksdale Field, I had a solid overcast ceiling at one thousand feet with temperature above thirty-four degrees. I was comfortable in my sheepskin flying suit, with gloves and face mask for the open cockpit. As I flew up close under the cloud level, or into it, the wings would ice up. When I dropped to fifty feet or so below the clouds the ice would disappear, quite critical. By the time I was almost home it turned colder and I

* That dust was coming from the Texas Panhandle, part of the *Dust Bowl.*

began to form ice at lower levels with about a quarter inch when I landed at Randolph. Since I had used up most of my fuel, the extra weight posed no problems. When the temperature was lower than thirty-eight degrees, one had to use carburetor heat to avoid the carburetor icing up and causing an excessively lean mixture.

Our first replacement for the reliable BT-2 was a BT-8, a low wing monoplane with a fixed landing gear and plastic canopy. It felt strange to fly around with no upper wing as a reference to the horizon. Being a monoplane, I knew that the flying characteristics would be quite different from those of a biplane, so I took it up to ten thousand feet before doing any experimenting. When I slowed it down in a straight glide to its stalling speed, it did not squash or settle, but snapped into a spin with no notice. It flew nicely with more speed than the BT-2. It was not long before I had an extended cross country approved to take the BT-8 to Philadelphia and return in a long looping route. I ran into heavy rain near Baltimore and landed at Phillips Field located on Aberdeen Proving Ground, so I spent the night with Peggy and Les Skinner to catch up on the news since we had been at Scott Field ten years before.

He did not talk much about his assignment at the Proving Ground, but I had the impression that his ideas for developing an anti-tank weapon did not conform to those of his superior. I learned later on that it came to a showdown at a demonstration before a group of distinguished visitors when the recoiless rocket launcher did the job. That was no way to earn brownie points, but Les could be very obstinate in the support of his convictions. He finally came *home* and was a member of the U.S. Air Force at the end of his military career in 1951.

As Post Operations Officer I was a permanent member of the accident investigation board, and the recorder as well. We only investigated two accidents during my tenure. One was a P-26 which crashed in the center of Taylor, Texas, about noontime due to engine failure and the pilot spun in when trying to glide out of town. Not so long ago, one of my ham radio friends, still living in Taylor, reminded me that he had skipped school to take a look at the accident.

Another accident was near Columbus, Texas, and at night when a pilot lost his orientation and spun in from about one thousand feet. One witness was a German lady who did not speak English and her five-year-old grandson translated for her. He was quite knowledgeable about airplanes, too.

The telephone system at Randolph Field was an automatic dial system which operated as a satellite of Fort Sam Houston which performed all repairs. As part of my office and as a special duty, I collected the monthly telephone bills and then turned them over to the Signal Officer, no arduous task.

The Army Signal Corps used homing pigeons for carrying messages, and had a pigeon company at Fort Sam Houston which I had learned about through indirection in 1923. An enlisted man had failed to salute Colonel Tommy Tompkins who was in command of Camp Stanley, north of San Antonio. When Tompkins asked the man the name of his outfit, he replied that he was a "pigeoneer." Tompkins thought that he was being ridiculed and put the young man in the stockade because he did not know about a pigeon company in the Army. That was true of others, including myself.

Homing pigeons had been used by the French during the Siege of Paris in 1870, and the Army had used them on the Western Front in World War One. There was one pigeon which flew twenty-four miles with a message at the rate of one mile a minute, to arrive at the loft wounded. The pigeon company operated a trailer which served as the home loft and near a headquarters at the rear. The pigeons were carried to the front in a wicker basket, the message being written on tissue paper and enclosed in a metal tube fastened to the pigeon's leg. The Signal Corps had a breeding program to improve the speed and quality of the homing pigeon and worked with enthusiasts interested in pigeon racing. That program continued until after World War Two.

A courier delivered a pair of breeding pigeons to Post Operations at Randolph with instructions to deliver them promptly to Congressman Thomas L. Blanton's son in Abilene. I left early the next morning and turned the pigeons over to him before lunchtime. After lunch at his home, Blanton showed me his loft and arrangements for pigeon racing, his major interest as a hobby. He was a beneficiary of the Army's program since he was a breeder. Congressman Blanton represented the 17th Congressional District for many years and was on the Military Affairs Committee.

Maxwell Field

Living at Maxwell Field, Montgomery, Alabama, was a contrast to that of Randolph. For one thing, the Officer's Club was crowded with both student officers and permanent party. Students were transients and would move on after their nine-month course at the Air Corps Tactical School. School was serious business for them.

Edith and I were fortunate to have quarters on the station. We tended to socialize with old friends from Brooks and Kelly who lived in our vicinity; Zoe and Earl Deford, Ruth and Arnold Rich, plus Marie and E. D. Jones. For weekends we often congregated at Narrow Lane Inn several miles south of Montgomery because we could have a private room and there was dancing in an open-air pavilion. The Inn was operated by Mr. Sargent who aged his own steaks and served country fried chicken. We went to the club on Friday nights because they served excellent seafood flown in by commercial air from New England, lobster and other choice items.

Ruth Rich was the oldest of the three daughters of the Moncure family of Richmond, Virginia. She had married before World War One and her two sisters followed her, Frances the middle sister married Stowe Sutton an Infantryman. They met when Frances was visiting Ruth at Brooks Field. Marge the youngest had met and married Jim Fitzmaurice when Ruth and Arnold were at Chanute Field. The Moncures made the rounds visiting their three daughters. Since Mr. Moncure was the senior engineer on the Richmond, Fredericksburg and Potomac Railroad, they had no problems in getting around and were well known in Air Corps circles. They had visited Ruth and Arnold in San Antonio during the Christmas Season of 1927 and gave a "going away" party at the Menger Hotel in the Old Coach House behind the hotel in the stable yard, prohibition being in effect. Mrs. Moncure had some minor argument with her husband and he disappeared, still missing when Edith and I arrived to help Ruth with her brunch. Mr. Moncure reported in shortly to say that he had spent the night at the Menger, would we pick him up? When Arnold and I arrived on a bright Sunday morning, he was standing on the curb a very dapper gentleman in white tie and tails, quite unconcerned about the stir he had made.

Julian Haddon who had been a checkout instructor at Brooks Field was the Post Exchange Officer at Maxwell Field. He had lost the sight of one eye due to an aircraft accident and had been grounded. His father-in-law, a Montgomery native and amateur archaeologist, was interested in the Indian villages which had been along the Alabama River between Montgomery and Selma. The only remaining evidence of such villages was through the "Midden" or dump where the foliage was more luxurient than elsewhere in that vicinity. Such villages were located at bends along the river and there were quite a few. Julian thought that aerial photographs might disclose such middens through their foliage and proposed that I fly him to take such pictures, which I did. Since there was at least one qualified photographic officer on Maxwell Field, I considered his request a compliment.

Clayton attended a private school in Montgomery as did most of the children on Maxwell Field. The school had small classes and an assembly every morning with designated students giving a five-minute talk on a subject of their choosing to give them self-confidence. When complaining about the difficulty of selecting a topic, I said, "Tell them about what you have done, or about things that you have seen on your travels. I bet few have been to San Francisco, or driven across Coolidge Dam." That was the last I heard about topics.

During our stay at Maxwell we hired a *houseboy* who cleaned the house and looked after Clayton when he came home from school, for Edith preferred to do her own cooking. William also served the drinks when we had guests. Coming home from the school in the late afternoon, I would find William in his immaculate white coat sitting in the shady back yard with Clayton and other children of the neighborhood. When I looked around the house with care, it was spotless, so I asked William about his method. He cleaned one room every day including the windows, the rest of the house he "redded up." He carried all his tools in a tray and did the living room last just before the weekend. He had worked that system out on his own. Edith began teaching him to cook simple breakfast items like scrambled eggs, and how to serve at table with the idea that he could upgrade when he left us.

The photographic officer at Maxwell Field, J. G. Pratt, had been a student in my class at Kelly Field in 1927. He had gone on to the Photographic School at Chanute and then to Marshall Field at Fort riley where he had met Roslie Kulmus and they were married. I met her on the dance floor of the Officer's Club, and when we were introduced she said, "I know that you will not remember me, but we met at a picnic at your home in Sharon Hill about twenty years ago!" She was about six years in age at that time and I did remember the occasion. She brought me up to date on her parents who were then living in Leavenworth, Kansas.

I saw my first frog farm east of Montgomery while we were out looking for paper shell pecans. The frogs were raised in a large pond and harvested with a gig to be dressed and shipped by express to New Orleans, via the Southern Railroad. They were the largest frogs that I had seen with legs as large as those on a spring chicken.

Since we were to have a long leave the summer the class ended, my sister Mariann joined us for an auto trip to Philadelphia. On our trip north along the East Coast we found that the best accomodations were in "Tourist Homes" so marked by signs, but now called bed and breakfasts. They were usually in large old homes of the two-story type and operated by widows or elderly couples. When we got to Philadelphia my sister went to Sharon Hill to stay with her friends. Clayton stayed with my Aunt Nancy, while Edith and I went on north to visit West Point. On our return we spent a day or so in New York, at the Astor this time as we had been in Brooklyn on our way to Panama.

The remainder of that summer was spent in San Antonio and Clayton could have his visit with his grandmother. Edith's mother became ill during the summer and she decided to stay on a week or two while Clayton and I headed for Fort Leavenworth to get settled in our quarters before the new course began. Edith joined us making the trip by train.

The Tactical School

The Air Corps Tactical School was designed for officers qualified at the squadron level and to acquaint them with the larger aspects of the Air Corps mission in the support of the ground forces.

We had a mixed group for the students included the Infantry, Signal Corps, Chemical Warfare Service and the Marine Corps, both air and ground officers.

This course had the reputation of generating stress for the student as it was an important step upwards in one's career. Further, many students had been out of the habit of serious study for some years. One of the introductory lectures was by the flight surgeon, a cautionary talk on the benefits of adequate diet and a good night's sleep.

We were concerned with the employment of the larger elements, groups and wings, of bombardment, observation, pursuit and attack, and the material came from the Army Field Manuals. The base was the experience from World War One with little change. Captain Hoyt Vandenberg was our instructor for the pursuit section. He had been a cadet in "A" Company with me at West Point and was destined to become the second Chief of the Air Force as a separate service. The regular instructor for "Maps" was not available, so I taught that course. The subject matter was how to deal with maps as used in the map problems, heavy on symbols.

The lectures on "Strategic Bombardment" presented by Laurence Kuter and Haywood (Possum) Hansell, included new ideas for me. These young lieutenants, all proteges of Colonel Hap Arnold at March Field, reflected his views on the subject, I felt certain. Their theme was that bombardment aviation could be an instrument of national policy through defeating the will of the enemy to resist. Their approach was in contrast to the Army Doctrine that the defeat of the enemy ground forces came first, with bombardment supporting that effort. General Douhet in his book *The Command of The Air* had used the term Strategic Bombardment to mean the destruction of the enemy's industrial base in order to demoralize the people and their will to resist. I could not accept this notion because I thought that would be just as likely to solidify resistance and the will to fight.

The school did not endorse Douhet's view, rather that Strategic Bombardment could be an instrument of national policy related to reducing the will of the enemy to resist, a vague and plausible theory closer to Admiral Mahan's work, *The Influence of Sea Power upon History*. Mahan described the role of the British Navy in protecting their trade routes around the globe which he considered an instrument of foreign policy. England's position as a World

Power during the nineteenth century was sustained by importing raw materials, processing such materials and shipping finished goods around the globe.

However, I noticed that very little was said about the limitations of strategic bombardment in relation to air power and there were two; first, it was intermittent due to refueling and rearming, not to exclude the influence of the weather; and second, air power cannot hold possession of territory, an Infantryman was needed for that task. From what I had learned about armed conflicts, their purpose was to gain or retain territory deemed essential to the survival of a particular social entity, willing to fight for its rights.

Events over the past fifty years have not changed my thinking. Interestingly, we lost the battle of wills with the Vietnamese and they had no air power, nor industrial base. In Douhet's thinking it should have been a pushover.

The British experience in the Falklands illustrates my view on territory. Argentina seized British territory and England reacted. The Argentine Air Force, despite their Exocet missles, was unable to influence the outcome, which was settled when the British placed five thousand foot soldiers ashore.

Pat Booker, one of the students in our class who had been with us at Randolph, had the misfortune of dying in an aircraft accident while he was night flying. His memorial was the highway leading from Interstate 35 to Randolph Field, The Pat Booker Road.

All pilots were required to have a certain minimum of night flying hours per year. There was no night flying at France Field although we could have made do in an emergency by lining up automobiles to shine their lights on a landing area. At Brooks and Randolph I often chaperoned several students on the basic stage for their night flight. We would land at Waco before dark, have a sandwich and take off as soon as it was dark. A thunderstorm came up one of those evenings and we were forced to spend the night at the Kyle Hotel. I was in my flying suit and had no pocketbook, so made my duty call on the manager to establish credit for my stay so that I could leave him a check. During the Thirties we began to get landing lights on the basic trainers. The Federal Aeronautics Administration began building lighted airways with a green flashing beacon for an emergency landing field. Night flying soon became routine.

From my point of view a beneficial aspect of the Tactical

School was the acquaintances made. Captain John Dahlquist, Infantry, and I were to work together on a project to update the Army's Classification System which had been dormant since World War One. Tom Rives the Signal Corps student was to bring a group of scientists to Alaska for a study connected with the Distant Early Warning Network. Vernon Magee, Marine Corps, was stationed at their base at Quantico and I could have lunch with him when flying from Langley Field to Washington. He went on to become Commander, Fleet Wing Pacific before retiring.

Fort Leavenworth

Fort Leavenworth and the Command and General Staff School were an expanded version of the Air Corps Tactical School, more students, a bigger station, but with a subtle difference in atmosphere. General Honeycutt, the Assistant Commandant, held a reception for the new students early in September. Our invitation said that the reception would begin "At five pm precisely," the one and only time I have seen the time so stated. However, "precisely" applied to the way Fort Leavenworth and the school were operated, and the student was the pivot. Francis W. Honeycutt, West Point 1904, was a member of the U.S. Fencing Team for the 1920 Olympics at Antwerp and won a Bronze Medal.

Edith and I were assigned quarters in a former enlisted men's barrack converted into eight apartments, spacious and comfortable, but not fancy. My temporary rank as captain was beneficial for lower ranking students were housed in a large apartment building termed the *Beehive* with many small children. There were two other Air Corps families in our building, Ann and Wally Whitson and Marion and Donald Fritch. There were two Infantrymen, a Field Artilleryman and a Cavalryman, as I recall. Our group was congenial and not too serious about the study activities. Several times the ladies would get together and we would have a "potluck supper" during the week. Sidney Hinds, one of the Infantrymen, was our celebrity for he had won a Gold Medal for his shooting at the

1924 Olympics. Sid had been a cadet in "A" Company as an upperclassman, graduating in 1920.

Our household goods had been stored at Maxwell Field during the summer and shipped to Fort Leavenworth, so we had to be on hand at the designated time to receive them. Ann and Wally Whitson looked after Clayton and me during the unloading process. Since the movers could not eat at the local cafeteria, Clayton and I took them to town to eat at a homestyle restaurant like a boarding house. I selected the "plain steak" to find that it was a delicious piece of tenderloin, a new name for that cut.

In the hustle and bustle of getting settled I met Fred Westervelt, a major in the Medical Corps, who was an amateur radio operator and seeking help to put up his antenna at his quarters. The majors were quartered in duplex units somewhat distant from the old enlisted barracks. Also, he was uncertain about operating as a student. He felt reassured when I told him that I had operated while a student at Maxwell Field and that I intended to continue operating at Fort Leavenworth. He planned to put up a new type, an off-center fed antenna called the Windom for Loren Windom, W8GZ. It posed no problem and I showed him how to tune it up using a flashlight bulb to indicate the current. Once tuned the light bulb was removed. In my case I installed the antenna in the huge attic space as we were on the second floor. The roof material was slate and did not affect the radio signals. Elizabeth and Fred Westervelt, plus baby Ann, were close friends that year. Several Saturdays we drove to Kansas City to visit the radio stores and view any new equipment.

My cousin Arnold Lynch, who was a professional church organist, had moved to Topeka, Kansas, to play for the First Presbyterian Church and direct their choir. Edith and I visited him one weekend soon after her arrival as it was about fifty miles to Topeka, also meeting his future wife, Margaret.

The Officer's Club was the center of general social activity, confined to Friday and Saturday evenings. Tradition called for weekly parties sponsored by students to get everyone acquainted. Due to the large number of students and limited number of weekends during the course, it was customary for four couples to sponsor one party. That created a new problem. With the same guests, the same servers at the Club, much the same food and drinks, one had to take the invitation along to peek at before thanking the proper sponsors at the end of the evening.

Fort Leavenworth had been established during the Indian fighting period and before Kansas became a state, so the reservation was not under state jurisdiction. There was a bridge crossing the Missouri River into that state and we could drive to Kansas City, Missouri, without getting into Kansas. We were able to buy liquor in that city in case lots through a friendly wholesaler.

Our new feature was the Hunt Club operated as a semi-private club on the Western part of the reservation, and popular among the Cavalrymen. The club had several packs of fox hounds and the members would turn out in their regalia of pink coats, the ladies riding sidesaddle, everything quite formal. For those who wished to follow the hunt but were unable to ride, there was an old horse-drawn ambulance with glass sides, for them to use. That ambulance dated from about 1875. Edith and I were invited to a hunt breakfast by our Cavalryman neighbor, but passed up the hunt, driving out in our car. The breakfast served at eleven after a morning's hard ride was substantial, more of a brunch, and with cocktails.

Edith and I visited Rosalie Pratt's folks who lived in Leavenworth. Mr. Kulmus was employed in the Federal Prison as a Deputy Warden in charge of sanitation. He had been a Cavalryman serving in the Philippines and later on in charge of the remount depot at Fort Sam Houston during World War One, the site of Dodd Field. He was the first person to tell me that drug offenders were sick people, for he could see them come and go, as through a revolving door. While there was a rehabilitation center operated by the Federal Government in Kentucky, he took a pessimistic view of its effectiveness judging that less than two percent were really cured of the drug habit. Edith and I visited them several times during our year at Fort Leavenworth as he had many interesting tales of his days in the Cavalry and about his work with drug offenders.

Major John W. Monahan was one of our Air Corps students who had recently returned from a tour of duty as a military attache in Europe. He had returned with an Alpha Romeo racing car which sat so close to the ground that he could not drive it cross country, so it arrived at Fort Leavenworth on a trailer. He had been a dirt track driver before World War One with Eddie Rickenbacker and Cord who later designed and manufactured the first front wheel drive automobile. Monahan had one of the last models of the Cord with a special racing suspension. He gave me a demonstration ride one Sunday morning on a straight stretch of concrete highway west of Fort Leavenworth. I believe that it had a supercharger as well, for we were cruising along at ninety miles per hour and there was marked reserve power for acceleration when he stepped on the pedal. The remarkable thing about the suspension on his car was that one had the sensation of *squatting* as the speed increased. Almost every passenger car I have driven began to float at high speeds and lose contact with the pavement.

At the end of the course we had orders to the General Headquarters Air Force at Langley Field with a month's leave en route, so we promptly headed for San Antonio to spend much of that month with Edith's folks and give Clayton a visit to the farm near Carrizo Springs. We left San Antonio with a six-week-old setter pup named "Rusty" by Clayton. Every time the car stopped Clayton took Rusty outside the car. By the time we reached Langley Field, Rusty was housebroken. When we stopped overnight at Montgomery, we paid a visit to Mr. Sargent at Narrow Lane Inn and he was glad to see us again, treating us to a meal on the house.

The Command and General Staff School

My course at this school was intended to prepare me for staff duty in large army units, based on integrating the various arms and services into a fighting unit, the Infantry division which had about twenty-five thousand men at that time.

We were instructed in Army Doctrine, the Army's way of coping with certain combat situations. Doctrine for the Infantry came from the Infantry Board and that for the Field Artillery from their board. When approved, their proposals were published in Army Field Manuals. We received the material in lectures backed by reading assignments in the manuals or other sources. Friday afternoons were devoted to solving map problems or terrain exercises.

A map problem was built up around the application of one particular aspect of doctrine. It was presented in story form, printed in a leaflet of six pages or more, plus a special map with an overprint of details in the leaflet. Our problems were centered on the Gettysburg area in Pennsylvania because of the excellent maps. The topic could be on anything we had studied in prior weeks. The story was carefully drawn to illustrate one point with red herrings and material injected to perplex the student and stimulate analysis. To illustrate, the air observer would report a column of infantry and artillery on the march with the head and tail of the column located by map coordinates. The student had to convert the column length to yards from the coordinates and then estimate the composition from the length. Each student had a data book which provided normal marching lengths for various units. There were clues hidden away for analysis.

While working correspondence courses at Randolph Field I had discerned the general structure of a map problem, that the problem was designed around a particular idea. I was able to scan a map problem and look for the general nature of the problem and then concentrate my analysis on that problem, or learn quickly that I was on the wrong track.

We had one map problem that I have never forgotten and that dealt with crossing a river where the Army doctrine called for making the crossing during darkness. The details of the approach march had been set up so that there was not enough time to prepare for the crossing before dark of that day. The school solution would call for waiting twenty-four hours until the next period of darkness. The teaser in that problem was that no enemy forces capable of serious interference were within a marching distance of twelve hours, and the wait was thirty-six hours. My professional judgement got the better of me for I considered the risk of waiting to be far greater than the risk of a daylight crossing the next morning. As a consequence, I received and Unsatisfactory for that problem. Two years later when the German Army invaded France, they consistently made daylight crossings so I felt vindicated.

We were mounted for one terrain exercise. I was a sight to behold in my Bedford cord breeches, booted and spurred, with a strange horse and a clipboard under my arm. The horses had been led to the locality of the exercise that morning while we rode out in our buses that afternoon. All the aviators did well in their horsemanship. The horses were available for recreational riding, but I used my free time for proficiency flying. That was the last time that I was on the back of a horse.

Early in our course we went to Fort Riley to view a Cavalry demonstration, for many Army officers had never seen a Cavalry regiment mounted up and ready to go. Fort Riley near Manhattan, Kansas, was a major Cavalry post similar to Fort Bliss. While I enjoyed sitting in the stands and watching the demonstration, I thought that my experiences in the maneuvers at Fort Bliss were more interesting. However, sitting in the rear seat of an observation airplane does not provide the larger picture. Within a few years the Cavalry would be converted to armor and ride around in tanks.

It was at Fort Leavenworth that I understood why a Negro trooper would address a bird colonel as *Sergeant,* or anyone of high officer rank. The reason was that a sergeant was the highest rank they ever encountered in their daily lives. The reenlistment rate in the Negro Cavalry units was high and it took thirty years to make sergeant. Those I saw at Fort Leavenworth all had grizzly hair. They were the last of the Negro troopers who had been enlisted in the Army after the Civil War to fight the Indians. The Comanches called them *Buffalo Soldiers* as a title of respect from a tribe of fierce warriors. The Comanche were referring to their hair which resembled buffalo wool.

Our instructor for Air Corps topics was Lieutenant Colonel Lewis H. Brereton, who had commanded the Third Attack Group at Kelly Field. He followed the standard doctrine and made no mention of strategic bombardment in his lectures. Edith and I knew the Brereton's from Kelly Field days and on one occasion Edith accompanied Mrs. Brereton on a trip to San Antonio to help with the driving, and to visit her mother who was not well.

Fort Leavenworth sat on a bluff above the Missouri River and the landing strip was along the river. We had a variety of aircraft to maintain our flying proficiency and to qualify for flying pay. I got acquainted with the P-12 pursuit type and enjoyed flying it whenever I could. There being no Army fields other than Marshall Field at Fort Riley, I generally flew a triangular pattern that would take four hours at least, and then shift around the compass to see new territory on the next flight. For the Spring break I was authorized a P-12 and a cross country to El Paso. When I landed at Carlsbad, New Mexico, to refuel, I learned that there was none at the field and that it would have to come from town, a wait of perhaps an hour. I decided to go on to the F.A.A. emergency field at Delaware Springs, near Guadalupe Peak in West Texas, for I knew there was fuel in tin cans stored at each emergency field.

The only buildings at Delaware Springs were the pumping station on the pipeline and a bunkhouse, so I walked to the pumping station to locate the caretaker of the field, and learned that he had left for Pecos with the keys. Since Pecos was seventy-five miles distant and the caretaker had arranged for someone to milk his cow, I spent the night at the bunkhouse in very comfortable surroundings, using the telephone line into El Paso to report my arrival to Biggs Field. The next morning I got enough fuel to get me to Midland and then returned to Fort Leavenworth.

I graduated in the upper part of the class, was designated a member of the General Staff Corps, and assigned to the General Headquarters Air Force at Langley Field, Virginia.

Langley Field

Edith and I were fortunate to have large and comfortable quarters at eight Wright Avenue, one half of a duplex with Bess and Art Thomas living in the other side. They had been with us at Randolph Field where Art was General Lahm's Adjutant. Marge and Jim Fitzmaurice were there as well as Gussie and Daddy Baker, plus other old friends. Daddy was in command of the station hospital.

As the case at Randolph, the Officer's Club was the social center for there were no suitable places for entertaining in Hampton or Newport News. The club had an excellent seafood bar on Friday evenings with clams and oysters on the halfshell for we were at the source, Chesapeake Bay and its surrounding waters. Edith and I attended an oyster roast at the Hampton Yacht Club by invitation which was new to us. Several bushels of oysters had been piled on a huge steel plate over a wood fire. We stood around until the oysters began to sizzle as they opened due to the heat. Then we would take several on our plate to eat with various condiments.

It was a nice walk from our quarters to my office and I could have lunch at home. I varied my route sometimes to pass through the maintenance shop to observe on the job training in sheet metal work. Mr. Fox, a civilian sheet metal worker, had them working on various projects as in apprentice training. From my point of view it appeared to be the same as that of a tin smith, so I asked Mr. Fox what the difference was, if any. His answer was quite to the point for he said, "One sixteenth of an inch!" I had met Mr. Fox's brother at Scott Field and had noted the resemblance. His brother also worked in the maintenance shop there. Mr. Fox was a skilled man himself and had the knack to teach his trainees, the gist of on the job training.

Shortly after our arrival I had a telephone call from Harold Gibbs who had been First Sergeant of my father's company in World War One and had seen the notice in the local paper. Gibbs became a frequent visitor for Sunday dinner and brought us up to date on the old timers. Gibbs was then working for the Veterans Facility at Kecoughtan in Hampton, but moved back to Chester to take a position with the Atlantic Steel Castings Company.

For the first and only time, Edith and I attended an Army-Navy football game at Philadelphia in the fall of 1938. Leaving Thursday for an overnight stay with friends at Bolling Field, we woke up to see four inches of fresh snow on Friday morning. It was slow going for we had no chains, they were not needed in Texas. We were able to buy a set at West Chester and then made better progress. The plan was to leave Clayton with my cousins near Norristown before going to the hotel in downtown Philadelphia, a ninety mile trip which took all day.

Despite my sheepskin lined flying suit and all the clothes underneath, I became chilled by the fourth quarter. The traffic was heavy and we were due for dinner in Lansdowne with Edith's friends from Port Arthur who had moved to Philadelphia with the Gulf Oil Company in the Thirties. From being chilled to being extra warm, I could hardly keep my eyes open during dinner. Most of the snow was gone for our trip home in clear weather. The next fall, Edith and I had little enthusiasm for a repeat performance.

While the Coast Artillery School was close by at Fort Monroe, we had little social exchange unless invited as their Officer's Club was small and crowded. Brigadier General Frederick H. Smith was commanding and when his son, Freddie Junior and his wife came for a visit, Edith and I as well as Marge and Jim Fitzmaurice were invited to the Smith's for their party.

We lost no time in taking in all the historic sights for the area was new to Edith and me, and it was an opportunity for Clayton to learn some history on the ground, the Yorktown Battlefield and Jamestown Island. Progress had been made in the restoration of Williamsburg and the Governor's Palace was complete. Edith and I subscribed to a concert series arranged by Richard Kirkpatrick to present replicas, in costume, of concerts which had been performed at the Palace when the Governor was in residence. Since there was no electricity in the Palace, the concerts were performed with candle light. The mirrored walls bounced the candlelight around to magnify the illumination.

Clayton completed his elementary education in Hampton, but Edith was not happy about the high schools. Jane Clement, Chief Nurse, had a son attending Greenbriar Military School at Lewisburg, West Virginia, so Edith paid a visit with Jane to look the school over. We decided to enroll Clayton for his high school work because the classes were small and there was stress on the basics. Jane and Edith would take turns driving to Lewisburg and I went along on several trips to see the country. There was an historic inn at Lewisburg where we stayed on our visits, and an academy for girls at Lewisburg which had joint social programs with the cadets at Greenbriar.

Norfolk was just across Hampton Roads and the direct route was to take the ferry at Old Point Comfort and ride to Willoughby Spit for the drive into town. The main attraction was the beach on the Atlantic south of Cape Henry, an all day trip. Richmond, about eighty miles inland, was the only suitable place for serious shopping, another all day jaunt. Several times we went with Marge and Jim Fitzmaurice and ended the day with tea at Marge's home with her parents, the Moncures.

Our familiar Mexican food in San Antonio was unheard of in Virginia. Edith persuaded Captain Ward Davies, the Post Exchange Officer, to order one case of El Paso brand canned tortillas for we knew about them having been to the restaurant in El Paso where they originated. When the first case was placed on the shelves it sold out the first day and Edith never got a can. Mexican food became popular and the Post Exchange soon carried a complete line.

The one and only B-15 was stationed at Langley, an experimental model to test the wing section which was used on the B-17. The interior was only partially finished with a seating ledge along both sides. Major Caleb Haynes and Captain Curtis Lemay were the regular crew and made frequent trips to England to transport our observers for a first hand look at hostilities. Major Robert Williams who commanded the Forty-ninth Bombardment Squadron was wounded in London during the Blitz.

A number of the officers had motorboats at Langley, Dache Reeves and Charlie Caldwell of our friends, and we sometimes went out to the flats at low tide to dig for clams. One soon learned that the clams could dig faster than you could dig, it was fun, but not up to eating them served at the Club. There was much work required to keep up a boat with a wooden hull. Each spring it had to be scraped and repainted, perhaps recaulked. There were still a few old time Chesapeake Bay boats which had been made with a dugout bottom and built-up sides, but the huge trees required had gone. Such boats used a one cylinder engine, perhaps fifty years in age, which made a characteristic banging sound, recognizable and distinct.

Rusty enjoyed growing up at Langley for the base veterinarian, Colonel Mallan, lived across the street. He had his personal horse on the station and rode every Sunday morning, taking Rusty for a run on the reservation. On meat inspection days, Dr. Mallan would treat Rusty with a fresh bone.

The General Headquarters Air Force

The Congress, in 1935, had created the General Headquarters Air Force to group all Air Corps tactical units for operations and training under the Operations Division of the War Department General Staff, with administration and maintenance the responsibility of the station commander. The Air Force had three wings: the First at Mitchel Field, the Second at Langley Field and the Third Wing at March Field. The permanent home was to be Scott Field, a central location, so Langley Field was a temporary location.

Major General Frank Andrews was commanding when I arrived. His senior staff, all colonels in the General Staff Corps were: Chief of Staff, Walter Frank; G-1 Personnel Ralph Cousins; G-2 Intelligence James Hodges; G-3 Operations Earl Naiden; and, G-4 Logistics Hume Peabody. during my tenure, General Andrews was replaced by Delos Emmons and Colonel Frank By Clinton Russell. I had been designated General Staff Corps after graduating from the Command and General Staff School. Further, my arrival was timed for an expansion in the number of tactical units in the Air Corps.

My first assignment was to the G-2 Intelligence Section which dealt with war plans. As they were new to me I took a look at them and noticed that it was rather unrealistic for logistic details had been omitted. Thinking that I would have to revise them, I decided to visit the War Plans Division of the General Staff to obtain information. That Division was housed in the State, War and Navy Building, now the Executive Office Building. Colonel St. Clair Streett was the Air Corps member and he introduced me around. I met Colonel Lewis Hershey who was working on the Selective Service System and the draft law which had not yet been passed by the Congress. I learned on that trip that no one was interested in the old plans because there were more important issues brewing.

Colonel Hodges took me on a trip to March Field to get acquainted, as copilot on a B-18 which we used for a staff airplane. As it had bomb bay fuel tanks, Hodges planned a dawn to dusk flight across the country with one refueling stop at Fort Sill, Oklahoma. That was my checkout flight on the B-18, the first two-engine airplane that I had flown since the Martin Bomber at Kelly Field. I was the navigator and we used the automatic pilot all the way and the weather was good. It was actually full dark when we left Langley and the sun had not set at March field.

The Chief of Staff decided that I was needed in the G-1 Section because most of the work in the expansion was in personnel. I was in charge of enlisted personnel planning while Major Dache Reeves looked after officer personnel. Colonel Cousins had graduated from West Point in 1915 just in time to learn to fly the JN-2 type Curtiss in the Punitive Expedition. His basic policy for the expansion was that every enlisted man then in the Air Force would have an equal opportunity competing for the promotions bound to come from the expansion, and that included our base personnel. Since we were doubling the tactical units, the existing experienced men would be divided in half and the two new units built up with graduates of the Air Corps Technical Schools and men direct from the replacement training centers to be trained on the job. In the case of noncommissioned officers there were complications because we had too many of certain types such as photographers not needed in the new setup of units. My first task was to arrange for their retraining at the Technical Schools, a waiver of the usual requirements for a student and to assure that we would get them back. The point was that surplus noncoms could volunteer for such retraining to improve their chances. Good ideas sometimes create other problems. I arrived at Lowry Field, Denver, Colorado, on one trip to find Colonel Rudolph, the Commander, pondering what to do with one of our men who was failing in his chosen new field. He wanted to be a bombsight mechanic but could not keep up with the other students in that course. He had only been an average student in the photo course some fifteen years before. Colonel Rudolph's problem was to counsel that man to switch his goal without damage to his self-esteem.

The first G-1 in 1935, Colonel Harvey Burwell, had found considerable imbalance in the distribution of experience among the units when the GHQ Air Force was formed. He instituted a program to classify all enlisted men using part of the Classification and Assignment procedure which had been developed in World War One to put the right man in the right place. We had a firm base from which to start and charting the program was no great problem. Colonel Cousins visited all the stations to explain our plan and ask for comment. On his return he told General Andrews that the plan must be good because, "No one liked it!' Dache had prepared the officer part except that he used rank and years of service as the basis for distribution of experience.

It was quite apparent that we could not afford to use pilots in administrative positions for they were needed in the cockpit. The War Department approved a plan to assign reserve officers for such positions on a voluntary basis. Many came from ROTC graduates who had commissions in the other arms and services. For instance, Harry Robinson who was assigned to the Second Bombardment Group as their Communications Officer had a Signal Corps appointment. He was an electrical engineer for police communications at Asheville, North Carolina. My foster brother, Samuel F. Langley, a Texas A&M graduate had been called to active duty under his Field Artillery commission and was on duty at Fort Sill. He volunteered, attended a supply school and was on duty at Hickam Field when the Japanese attacked. He then moved South across the Pacific setting up supply bases for the Air Force moves, and did not return to the States until February 1945.

A plan or program will not work without supervision and control to cope with the actual events. I made frequent visits to the Office of the Chief of the Air Corps and to the G-1 Division of the War Department General Staff in working out details. I had two important contacts, one being Major Herbert Holdridge of the Adjutant General's Department who had been a fellow student at the Command and General Staff School. He introduced me around his office until I became better acquainted. My General Staff Corps insignia was a great help when looking for information. The other was Major John Dahlquist in the G-1 Division of the War Department General Staff who had been with me at the Air Corps Tactical School. The G-1 was Colonel Wade Haslip at that time.

Major Dahlquist had the project to bring the Army's Classification and Assignment System up to date after it had been dormant since 1919. He gave me a copy of the final report made in 1919 and asked me to study it, for he planned to organize a conference of all the original members of the 1917 Committee. That conference was held at the Army War College for two days to determine whether there was new information that should be included in the revision. The only significant suggestion was that we needed a new Army General Classification Test to replace the old Alpha and Beta Tests. The Adjutant General established a working group under Doctor Marion Richardson of the Civil Service Commission and the new Army General Classification Test was ready by August 1940. The Adjutant General then issued orders that all enlisted men be classified by January 1941 and the data entered on their records.

A school for training personnel specialists was established under Colonel Holdridge, first at Fort Myers and then moved to Fort Washington. I lectured the students on what we had been doing in the GHQ Air Force to show the practical purpose.

The new Army General Classification Test was standardized by testing the enlisted men at various stations. Doctor Richardson's group had an interesting anomaly arise at a camp in South Carolina. There was a five-part picture panel depicting four vegetables and one fruit, a banana. The test was to distinguish the one fruit from the four vegetables, but the tests from that camp were not valid. A team was sent to look over the shoulders of the men taking the test and when the panel was marked wrongly, ask the young man why? The men being tested said that the banana was *okra* and hence all five items were vegetable to them. These men had never seen a banana but there was plenty of okra grown. That panel had to be revised to use a fruit that they did recognize in South Carolina.

There were many activities calling for staff visits. Joe Smith of the G-3 Operations Section and I flew a number of them; to visit potential sites for flying fields, to inspect the facilities at Jackson Barracks, New Orleans as a replacement training center and an air mechanics school at New Orleans. The Air National Guard squadrons had been called to active duty and were participating in the Louisiana Maneuvers of 1940. On that trip we had the Assistant Secretary of War, F. Trubee Davison with us on the inspection team.

The GHQ Air Force never got to its permanent home at Scott field Because the decision was made to move it to a temporary building at Bolling Field in 1941 to be closer to the Chief of the Air Corps and General Staff.

There was one interesting conference which cleared the air for the future. Major General Walter Weaver was exploring his idea that a flight crew should be waiting and ready to fly away an airplane as it came off the production line, plus other direct support in personnel. While training time varied among the varied specialties, we all agreed that we had the knowledge to schedule the flow of personnel to meet a specific date. That idea ran into a stone wall because no one knew, at that time, when an airplane would be delivered, nor could anyone guess. The consequence was that all training went full blast and limited by the training facilities. When bottlenecks developed, as they did, that problem would be resolved as appropriate.

A flight of Russian bombardment aircraft landed at Bolling Field in 1941. They had brought senior military officials to a hush-hush conference in Washington. While the aircraft were guarded and there was no publicity, our pilots were invited to look their aircraft over. The heavy bombardment aircraft were technically similar to our Keystone bombers which came out in the Twenties.

I was particularly interested in the selective treatment of parts in the construction of the fuselage which was box-like and fabric covered. Steel tubing was used with aluminum castings to connect the vertical and horizontal members. Steel wire tensioned with turnbuckles gave the fuselage its strength and rigidity. Where the tubing fitted into the casting, the boring was excellent, but there had been no attempt to smooth the outer surface of the casting. It was our practice to polish such castings, perhaps to observe flaws or reduce weight, but mainly for cosmetic reasons I suspect. It was clear that the Russians did only that work required from a functional point of view. Their construction might be classed as crude, but it was utilitarian with no frills.

I was working in the basement of my home when I heard the news of the Japanese attack on Pearl Harbor on the radio. It came as a complete surprise for I had been engrossed in my routine work and had paid little attention to the international scene. I put my uniform on and went to my office to find the place empty and dark. A few others straggled in to see if there was any news. The telephone was quiet and there was nothing to do, so we drifted off for home.

I had received my promotion to Lieutenant Colonel in October 1941. When Robin Day left early in 1942 to assume command of a new air base at Santa Maria, California, I moved up to G-1 and was soon promoted to colonel before moving to the War Department General Staff in March 1942.

Dache M. Reeves

My partner in the G-1 Section, Colonel Dache M. (Dash Madly) Reeves and I had worked together at Kelly Field when I was engaged with the mapping project using the Bagley Camera. He had been most helpful to me in making up a small reference library before I left for Pope Field.

His nickname was appropriate for he had a keen and restless

mind, jumping from one idea to another, easily. He was an excellent researcher in devising a plan, but sought perfection rather than utility and kept improving his study. Colonel Cousins understood Dache's temperament and would call a halt to further study when it came time for action. We sat side by side at our desks, so we could easily share ideas. One that we worked over from time to time was that of efficiency reports. Dache considered the existing form encouraged conformance and that led to mediocrity in his view, but he was unable to identify suitable nonconformity. I was then a member of the General Staff Corps and wore a distinctive insigne. Dache would tease me by saying that the Corps was, "A self-perpetuating admiration society" because you were selected by those already in the Corps. He had a point, but a paradox because the Corps was criticized as an elite group.

While Dache worked primarily with officer problems and I with those of the enlisted men, we had two long-range studies where we worked together to pool ideas. In 1939, the typical aviation cadet started his flying training after high school, and was commissioned a Reserve Officer in the Army when he graduated from the flying school. He was then called to active duty and assigned to a tactical unit. That was Dache's supply of new officers. While there was no agreement for tenure, his active duty tour continued on a year to year basis depending upon the number the Air Corps was authorized under the appropriation bill. Since we were short about twenty percent in manning tactical units, that imposed no immediate problem. The reserve officers on active duty could compete for Regular Army vacancies each year as they became available, not many.

I had observed from the Tables of Organizations for the tactical units that the pilot seats were predominately lieutenants and captains with no possibility that normal attrition in peace time would provide promotion as the years passed. The issue was what to do about over-age pilots. The Flight Surgeon told us that the typical pilot peaked in performance from a physical point of view at about the age of thirty-five. We worked up a study with a plan calling for a fifteen-year contract to clarify and stabilize what career the Army had to offer. At the end of that contract the typical reserve officer would be about thirty-five years of age and young enough to begin a new career. We included severance pay rather than retirement when the reserve officer reverted to inactive status.

During those years they could still compete for Regular Army vacancies. At that time, all regular officers in the Air Corps were required to hold an aeronautical rating. Our officer losses were small as the airlines preferred to hire their pilots from the civilian pilot training schools, as they considered military pilots reckless, no pun intended. The China Trading Company began hiring a few pilots for employment with Chiang Kai-shek's fledgling air force to train his pilots and we had been authorized to release them when they wanted to go to China.

In contrast, the civilian airlines had been actively recruiting our enlisted mechanics and the increased pay through the air mechanic rating plan had been designed to slow that attrition. As a consequence, the Air Corps had a hodgepodge pay system with about fourteen grades. There were the seven typical Army grades from private to master sergeant, plus a parallel set of grades for air mechanics. Broadly speaking there was a channel for command and a channel for technical work. Dache had been working on a plan to integrate the various pay grades into seven categories, the seven-grade plan, in essence a separate pay play for the Air Corps. The chevrons were to be similar to the standard Army type with a symbol indicating line or technical status. We already had one such symbol in the first sergeant's chevron, a diamond. I took over that study and continued to polish it, for it had considerable support, discussing it with various senior officers on my staff rounds to collect comments, pro and con. I did not find much support in my visits to G-1 of the War Department Staff, too much change for them.

Both studies were overtaken by events as they did not deal with current problems. In the postwar period, the Air Force faced the same problem as we had anticipated and they chose twenty-year retirement in Public Law 810 (1948) as their solution. That has generated problems for them. The numbers were there in 1938 and again in 1948, but no one paid attention to the long-range implications. In 1938, we thought that early retirement was too expensive a solution.

When the GHQ Air Force was dissolved in 1942, Dache was assigned to command the Air Force Base at Columbia, South Carolina, where he got himself into difficulties through his penchant for changing his mind about things. He did not understand the inertia in an organization of that size, that it takes time for a change to soak in and operate smoothly, the need for stability.

In personnel assignments, a colonel was a colonel was a colonel, meaning that any colonel could do any other colonel's work. While Dache was a colonel, his talents did not fit the stereotype of a "universalist" colonel, he was a square peg that needed a square hole.

STAFFING STUDY

In 1940, I summed up the officer positions for each grade called for in our attack, bombardment, fighter and observation units according to the GHQ Air Force tables of organization. No support activities were included. We were then on manning tables for budget reasons and such authorizations were about twenty percent lower than the T/Os. By personnel count we were about twenty percent under our manning table authorization. The idea was to make a long range study to analyze peacetime opportunities for promotion. The Army published a register of officers for each year. Among other detail it listed the number of officers, by grade, who were lost during that year by death, retirement or resignation. I derived an average attrition rate by going back ten years and averaging the losses. I also derived an estimate of time in grade.

The data were presented on the following chart which had thirty years of service for the vertical axis and a year level for promotion to each grade, that for major being 17 years. The bottom horizontal line length represented the total number of second lieutenants, that for the majors was the line G to H.

It was clear that up to the grade of captain there was no apparent problem. On the next step to major there was a surplus of captains. The dashed line F to L shows the effect of attrition on the number of captains at F, thus the surplus at H to I continues to grow.

This led to the conclusion that we should recommend a fifteen year contract for the Air Corps reserve officers who were filling the cockpit seats, with generous severance pay (the rate then was $500 per year of active duty). While the Navy had a precedent of a twenty year retirement plan, we deemed that it would not cope with the surplus early enough and would be too expensive, not to overlook swelling the retired list which was paid from current appropriations.

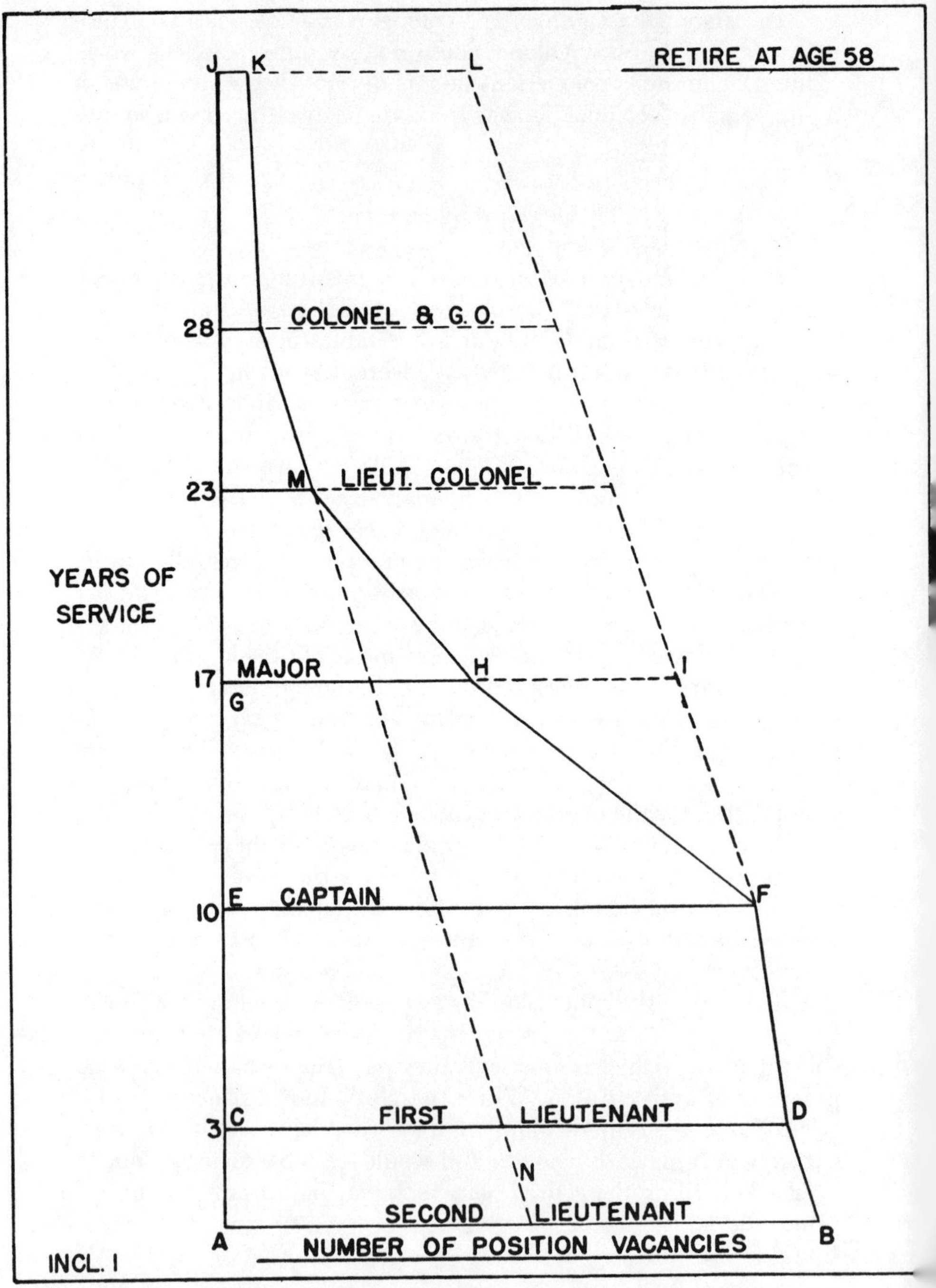

RETIRE AT AGE 58
J
K
L
COLONEL & G.O.
28
M
LIEUT. COLONEL
23
YEARS OF SERVICE
MAJOR
H
I
17
G
E
CAPTAIN
F
10
C
FIRST
LIEUTENANT
D
3
N
SECOND
LIEUTENANT
A
NUMBER OF POSITION VACANCIES
B
INCL. I

Alfred Kessler dressed for riding.

Gordon Armes dressed for class.

Paschal Strong dressed for hiking.

Our alarm clock, universal in the Army.

Old style sentry box at summer camp 1919.

North Guard House where flags designated the uniform of the day.

The summer camp area was on the N.E. area of the plain.

My first ride in a Jenny — Camp Dix 1921.

A campsite on the march from Camp Dix to West Point, 1921.

The Cadet Regimental Staff, 1920–1921.

Take a look at our feet (Hensey's sister).

A cadet lieutenant in Company "A," 1921.

In full dress whites for the last time.

My last parade, 1922.

Benjamin (Bennie) Chidlaw, 1922.

Bachelor Officer Quarters, Brooks Field, 1922.

The Jenny Hospital plane, 1922; the rear cockpit reworked for a litter.

Waiting to fly; a cadet, Bill Goddard and Bill Lawton, 1923.

Gunnery practice on a hangar roof; Capt. Hale in background. The camera gun was mounted on a Lewis Machine Gun.

Refueling the Jenny was primitive.

Pauline Palmer, Marie Miles and Edith Hightower (L–R), 1923.

The Model T coupe, 1923.

Cadet J. B. Stowe and I made a bad landing at Smithville, Texas, April 1923.

The Ground Attack Experimental Airplane, Kelly Field, 1923. Only one was made.

The son of Mr. King, Morristown, Tennessee, 1925. His task was to clear the pasture of cows for us to land.

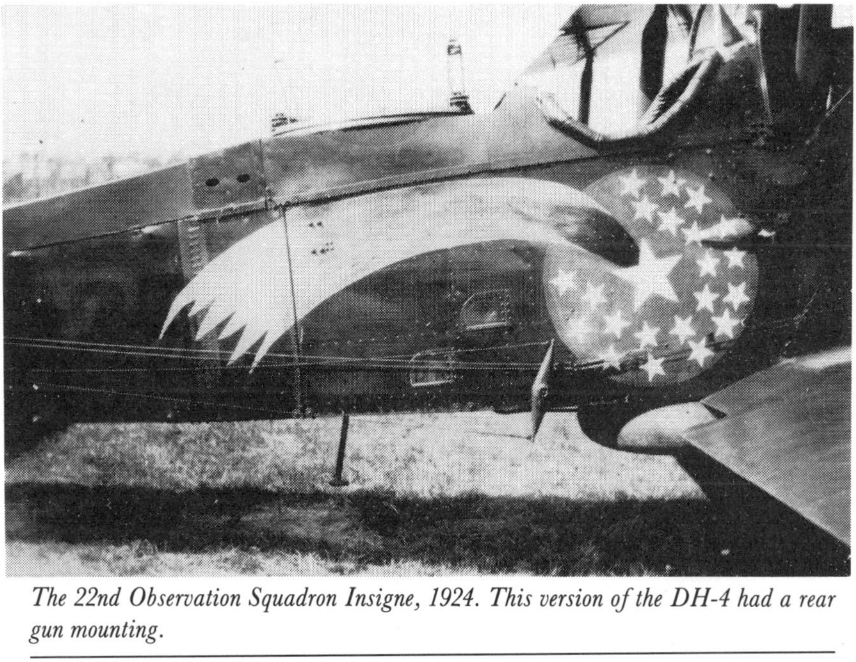

The 22nd Observation Squadron Insigne, 1924. This version of the DH-4 had a rear gun mounting.

"Old 97" was the photographic version of the DH-4, 1925. The marking was non-regulation.

Edmund C. Lynch, Jr. at the age of nine weeks, August 1925.

James A. Mars, 1929

Skippy Davies and Bill Blaufuss, two bachelors and accomplished pianists who led our sing-songs at Randolph Field, 1933.

My class at Scott Field, spring 1926. Howard Davidson and Robert Selway were not in the picture.

My first star, 1945.

(L–R) Colonels Patient, 11th Air Force, and Detwiler, Commander, APO 980; Captain DeWolfe, Navy Facilities and Colonel Selzer, 11th Air Force, 1945.

The uniform for touring Aleutian Bases, 1945–1947. The trout were Dolly Varden.

Averill (Tex) Holman, my pilot aide, 1945–1947.

Mr. Fletcher, U.S. Commissioner at Dutch Harbor, 1947.

Simeon Oliver, Superintendent of the Indian School at Atka, 1947.

Colonel Aldridge Beattie and his wife Myrtle, loyal helpers at three posts, Alaska 1947.

General Eisenhower, Mrs. Frank G. Jamison and Colonel Jamison, my Deputy Commander, APO 980, 1947.

Dr. John Hannah, Assistant Secretary of Defense, presenting the Legion of Merit as I depart for Austin, Texas, July 1953.

— Official U.S. Army photo

Mr. Lovett, Secretary of Defense, joined members of the Requirements Division in singing Happy Birthday to Anna Rosenberg, 1952.

Performance Appraisal

In my early years of service, I gave little thought to efficiency reports, I did my assigned tasks to the best of my ability for that was the way I had been raised. Eventually, I reached the stage when I had to make such reports and quickly learned that it required hard thought. I concentrated on the way the person's work was performed and their value to the organization, universal factors as I later came to find out.

The psychologist Walter Dill Scott devised the Army's first scale for selecting captains at the Second Officers Training Camp in 1917. It was an interview procedure based on his *Man to Man Rating* interview which he had developed for selecting and rating salesmen. The interviewer selected men known to him as standard for a certain trait in each of five dimensions, poor to excellent. Scott, working with the Army, selected the traits of: personality, intelligence, physical, leadership and general value to the service. The interviewer concentrated on each trait, one at a time, to increase the accuracy of his judgement. Scott's technique would work both in selecting and rating salesmen. However, with five traits and five dimensions, the interviewer needed twenty-five models, though some could duplicate. It worked well for limited purposes, rather than in general use. The technique is still basic in merit rating.

I was president of a board with four other officers to screen candidates for promotion, to select one hundred best qualified from a stack of four hundred folders. We used a series of screenings, the first for obvious disqualifications by agreement on criteria. Each screening became tighter and tighter until we ended up with one hundred. The four officers paired on the early screening while I checked. Everyone worked every folder on the final screenings. Selection was a matter of *rejection*. On the efficiency reports, I thought that the most significant entry was to the question, "Would you *ask* for this officer to serve with you again?"

My usual approach was to set some standard in any screening process, so I was surprised and interested by an experience in GHQ Air Force Headquarters. The expansion had created vacancies in the higher noncommissioned officer grades and we were to recommend staff sergeants for promotion to technical sergeants.

Our Headquarters Squadron operated as two separate units, one clerical in the office and the other in support, maintaining the aircraft, supply and the like. It was unlikely that an officer would be personally aware of the performance of every noncom in the squadron. However, it was decided that every officer and senior noncom would rank order the list of candidates and turn their list over to me. I had the task of integrating the various lists into a headquarter's listing. It was a most interesting exercise for the only criterion was "Value to the organization." Among the top ten on the final list for each grade, every name was high on every list submitted. Picking the top ten was easy and showed that there was a consensus. That converted me to the rank ordering method.

While on the War Department General Staff I had occasion to look over the Adjutant General's file on efficiency reports, several inches thick, and thumbed back over the years. It was clear that the War Department took a realistic view. In theory, the reports should present a normal distribution curve, and they usually do in a new system. But, the curve becomes squewed over time with too many high ratings. The Army's solution was a new report to get matters back on track. My recollection was that a peacetime revision occurred about every ten years.

One paper in the file showed that the search goes on for a "magic number" as a substitute for hard thinking. This proposal suggested a numerical scoring for certain items, with the total score to indicate the individual's value to the service.

There is no easy way, someone must pass judgement. Fear of favoritism is the bug-a-boo of any system, a sensitive issue. The system must not only *be* fair, but it must *appear* fair to the people being rated.

My view from the perspective of the War Department General Staff was that command concern should concentrate on the top five to ten percent of the officer group because that portion included the future leadership and should be nurtured. This would entail identification by name at an early stage. It was my observation that an outstanding second lieutenant usually continued to be outstanding throughout his career. Their duty assignments should be monitored to enhance their growth and experience. Conversely, the lowest five to ten percent should be brought up to an acceptable minimum performance level. Otherwise, they are not worth keeping. The central eighty percent should be left alone to get the work done and not be unduly stimulated.

Ham Radio in the Thirties

After we had settled down after our move to Randolph Field, I decided to broaden my hobby and look into Amateur radio, generally known as *Ham* Radio, a contraction of amateur English style. I became a member of the American Radio Relay League in 1932 for the reason that their journal *QST* published excellent technical articles. While in Panama I had observed the radiomen of the 7th Observation Squadron operating their amateur station with the call of K5FR.

My family had settled on a farm near Carrizo Springs, Texas, in 1927. My brother Walter suggested that we set up our private telegraph circuit using the amateur radio frequencies. His problem was that there was no commercial power at the farm and he would have to operate with battery power. He built a wind charger by modifying a Ford Model T generator since there was usually a good breeze. I designed the impeller using an airfoil cross section to minimize the drag or air resistance. A description of that project was published in *QST* for April 1935.

I took the Federal Communications Commission examination in San Antonio during the fall of 1934 and obtained my Amateur Radio Operator and Station License with the call sign, W5EQD. I had been building my receiver and transmitter with not much urgency because I enjoyed building as much as using the gear. Unfortunately, my brother died before we ever got to the point of operating. I began operating it after we settled down at Maxwell Field in our quarters. The Army encouraged such operation, but we needed permission from the Post Signal Officer. My practice was to operate for about thirty minutes before bedtime, for my studies came first. I followed much the same routine while a student at the Command and General Staff School.

Ham radio operators have a natural affinity for getting together. Shortly after I arrived at Fort Leavenworth I met another student, Major Frederick B. Westervelt of the Army Medical Corps. He was inquiring about operating his gear from his quarters on station. I helped him with his approval and also in putting up his antenna. He was more of an operator than a technician. We went around together that year visiting radio stores in Kansas City and became lifelong friends.

Langley Field brought another view of amateur radio for I joined the Peninsular Amateur Radio Club in Newport News. This club cooperated with the American Red Cross and provided emergency communications. The club met in the Red Cross offices. Activities included classes in Morse code and theory for those seeking their licenses. There were social activities such as picnics at Jamestown Island while testing emergency gear which operated free of the regular power lines.

The members were a mixed group both as to age and occupation. We had engineers from the National Advisory Committee on Aeronautics at Langley, an instructor from Hampton Institute, a variety of employees from the Newport News Shipyard, and military personnel from Langley Field and Fort Monroe. There were active nets in Virginia on both Morse code and radio telephone for handling messages or social chit-chat.

Norfolk also had an active radio club and the two clubs got together to sponsor the Roanoke Division Convention of the American Radio Relay League. That area included Virginia, West Virginia and the two Carolinas. I was on the Executive Committee for that convention in 1940 and learned a lot about organizing such an affair with about four hundred in attendance. Our key speaker was John Reinartz, W3IBS, an applications engineer with RCA. He was well known through the *Reinartz Tuner* which he had invented. John and his wife were our house guests for the convention period.

The amateur radio operators pioneered in the use of the higher frequencies, that is above the broadcast band. Fenton Priest, W3EMM, of Norfolk was the primary source in the States for direct communication with Admiral Byrd's Expedition to the Antarctic of 1929. Fenton operated his equipment on the 14 MHZ amateur band and used directional antennas oriented on the great circle route to the South Pole. The frequencies used by the U.S. Navy required that any messages be relayed between the South Pole and the States.

When a bombardment group moved to Borinquen Field in Puerto Rico, the dependents were left behind at Langley or Hampton. The amateurs on Langley organized a direct message service to Borinquen Field to handle family messages with regular schedules during the evening hours when radio conditions on the 7 MHZ band were good. All messages were sent by Morse code. There were plenty of volunteers for this service, but I did handle one shift when I was needed to help out.

As the war in Europe began to build up, the Federal Communications Commission tightened up on amateur operations. We had to provide proof of citizenship and register our equipment. The General Headquarters Air Force moved to Bolling Field, Washington, D.C., and for all practical purposes, my activity ceased until after World War Two.

My hobby activities during the period 1938 to 1941 while serving at Langley Field were most enjoyable. I made many new friends both on the air and person to person. My other hobby was photography and Edith and I went to Roanoke for one weekend to visit with the local camera club and talk about aerial photography. That visit came about because one of my ham radio friends was in the camera club.

Shortly after I moved to the War Department General Staff in March 1942, we had a request from the Eitel-McCullough Company of San Bruno, California, for the deferment of their radio engineers as necessary in the war effort. No one could understand why all their engineers were under the age of thirty-five. At that time, the company was the sole manufacturer of transmitting tubes (Eimac) for very high frequency usage for their market had been built on supplying amateur radio operators. Further, their engineers were all amateurs.

I was able to explain that the typical amateur radio operator had acquired his license at the age of fourteen and was knowledgeable before he entered college to graduate as an electrical engineer. Before 1930, most amateur radio activity was below 28 MHZ. From that date to 1940, activity expanded in the 28 and 56 MHZ bands which called for vacuum tubes of a special design with low distributed capacities. The Eitel-McCullough Company was the major source of such knowledge. The founders were William W. Eitel, W6UF and Jack A. McCullough, W6CHE.

The War Department General Staff

When the War Department was completely reorganized in March 1942, I moved to the G-1 Division, Personnel, of The War Department General Staff. I was an aviator and a full colonel at the pinnacle of the Army Command structure. I wore a distinguishing badge on the left breast pocket of my uniform to show that status. I felt quite at home in my new surroundings and well prepared through my three years work with the GHQ Air Force. Further, I was acquainted with about half my peers.

The reorganization was designed to speed up action in the conduct of the war. Under the War Department were three major commands: the Army Ground Forces to control the training of combat units; the Army Air Forces to take over the work of the Air Corps; and, the Army Service Forces in which the various services, Medical, Quartermaster, Ordnance and Signal Corps were consolidated, and also responsible for training service units. The Headquarters of the Army Service Forces also included a Military Personnel Division which was the manpower procurement agency. The War Department General Staff was a planning and policy agency while the operations were carried out close to the scene of activity. The concept had been developed in a doctoral thesis submitted by Colonel Otto L. Nelson, Jr., for his degree in political science, Harvard University 1940.

In March 1942, the G-1 was Major General John H. Hilldring, a former Infantryman. The Officer Branch included Colonels Donald Wilson, Air Corps, and Reuben Jenkins, Infantry. I was in the Enlisted Branch and my boss was Colonel James H. Walker, Cavalry, whom I had met in Guatemala. We were the developers and interpreters of policy relating to Army personnel as individuals. Policy comes before action and states the governing principal in that action. There were already on-going policies in effect, so we each had our policy files to include the latest ones that had been issued.

The Adjutant General's Department was our action agency for administration. It comprised the Adjutant General and several officer assistants who were designated Adjutants General and could sign off on papers prepared in that department. The staff were career civilian employees. That department was sometimes criticized for undue official routine (red tape). However, in my experience they did a very good job.

To illustrate; the wife of an enlisted man with a complaint wrote six letters to the following addresses: Eleanor Roosevelt, the senator and representative in Congress who represented her, the Secretary of War (Mr. Stimson), the Army Chief of Staff (General Marshall) and to the service chief concerned. Outside complaints had been sent to the War Department for "information on which to base a reply." I read the six replies in the files of the Adjutant General. They all gave the same answer, but were written in different styles. suitable for the addressees; signed by different Adjutant Generals.

The basic plan was the Troop Basis which listed all combat and service units needed to fight the war, with a time schedule for their activation. This established the flow of personnel through the system, individual training and then unit training in preparation for movement overseas. The Military Personnel Division prepared the monthly increments and passed them on to the Selective Service System, which, in turn, broke down the allotments to be filled by the local boards.

My major responsibility was with manpower procurement and I worked closely with Colonel Charles Collier of the Military Personnel Division. We were like the Siamese Twins at various conferences, he for operations and I for policy. We could settle most operational problems on the spot, for if a course of action was satisfactory to Charlie, I could back him up. On some policy issues I might have to consult with General Hershey and my boss. We sought to identify problems before they arose, or catch them promptly, to keep things moving smoothly.

The Selective Service System was the creation of General Hershey alone. He had made a study of all the Army's procurement procedures for war, back though the Revolution in George Washington's day. His two major contributions were that men were drafted for the duration of the war, rather than for any stated period. His second innovation was the unpaid local board which he envisioned as "The Conscience of the Community" to decide who would go and who would stay, exercising value judgements to recognize the local view. He considered the local board the democratic approach, and an exercise of social responsibility, similar to the tribal council or council of elders in tribal societies. Nationwide rules and regulations would not consider the uniqueness of local area problems in operation. Consequently, there was little disstisfaction with the operation of the Selective Service System. Hershey, himself, was the major trouble shooter when problems arose. Lotteries or objective type selections, computer operated perhaps, do not provide social responsibility, they abdicate such responsibility.

As a sample problem, the Navajo Indians were playing games with the system. After induction, they were provided train tickets and meal tickets to get them to Fort Sheridan near Chicago where they arrived unable, or unwilling, to speak anything but Navajo. We needed someone from the Bureau of Indian Affairs who understood Navajo to keep them in line. Charlie and I went to see the head of that bureau and quickly got a man to strengthen them out. During World War One, the Army used Navajo Indians to communicate over the field telephone lines because the Germans could not learn what was going on. They were better than a coding or scrambling device.

We held a conference of all the regional workers in manpower procurement in Chicago twice yearly to review operations and procedures, looking for improvement. That was when Charlie and I could deal with operation problems and anticipate trouble. We became acquainted with the people in the field and they felt free to call us at any time to discuss matters. The main purpose of such conferences was to establish a free exchange of ideas about the workings of the manpower procurement system. They were not intended to solve problems.

There was a new and popular musical show playing in Chicago during one conference. We could not get tickets at the hotel and were assured that the show was sold out. Charlie and I had dinner with one of the conferees at a restaurant several blocks from that theater and took a stroll after dinner to see a line at the ticket booth. We selected Charlie as the one most likely to get a sympathetic greeting at the booth should there be any tickets available. As luck would have it the man in line ahead of Charlie had three tickets and we saw that show. All was not work at the conference.

The Four-F category of draft deferments was for physical disability. It was a catch-all category including a wide variety of disabilities. We had suggestions that this group be screened with the idea that some men could be used for limited service work in the States, though not fit for combat duty. I made a study of that group to develop a policy. The Woman's Army Auxiliary Corps were already filling many of such positions and we had no pressing need. The main objection was that it would create a special class which would have to be identified for limited duty assignments, an added administrative burden. However, I noted that there was a considerable number of hernias as the basis for rejection and consulted the Surgeon General. I was told that surgical repair was a routine procedure and that it was successful in nine out of ten cases, or better. With the Surgeon General concurring, I worked up a recommendation that selected volunteers could have their hernias repaired before they were assigned to basic training, subject to their agreement beforehand. The proposal was shot down by the legal counsel. I had no illusion that we would pick up many volunteers for some of those then deferred would fear surgery more than the status quo, or prefer the status quo. My point was that it would provide some men a choice and such men would be likely to have quality. Further, it would show affirmative action on the Army's part.

My secretary, Mrs. Hill, was a wonderful aide, more of an administrative assistant. A native of Columbus, Georgia, she had worked for the Infantry Board before moving to Washington to join the G-1 Personnel Division several years before the war. She knew where to find things. Our chief clerk was also an old timer and a source of knowledge. One had to ask the right questions for the G-1 Division had an archaic filing system where papers were numbered serially and there was no cross reference. One could work back from the Adjutant General's files, but the Chief Clerk could remember and was close at hand.

We started out in the Munitions Building and then moved to the Pentagon in October of 1942. Returning to my office one day I saw Mrs. Hill talking to a tall, lanky Brigadier General who turned out to be Omar Bradley calling to see how she was getting along.

She had worked for him at the Infantry Board.

We had some changes early on because Don Wilson and Jimmie Walker had been in G-1 before the organization was changed. Wilson was replaced by Colonel Richard Nugent, Air Corps, and Reuben became Chief of the Officer Branch. When Walker left, I moved up to the head position. General Hilldring was replaced by Miller White who had come up through the Georgia National Guard.

I enjoyed knowing and working with Reuben Jenkins for he was a sound person, later to command the Eighth Army in Korea. The Army was using temporary promotions by March 1942 and Reuben wanted G-2 Intelligence, to take a block of vacancies and provide promotions to officers serving under G-2 around the world, flying instructors, military attaches and advisors, to maintain them in step with their peers on the regular list. G-2 refused on the basis that it was not his responsibility, and Reuben did not care for that approach.

Several months later, I met Hugh A. (Lefty) Parker when heading for the cafeteria. Lefty had married Janet, Gussie and Daddy Baker's daughter and they had been in Argentina. Janet had returned several months before and was living with the Bakers at Mitchel Field. Lefty had lunch with me and I learned that he was on his way to Army Air Forces Headquarters to protest his lack of promotion. I suggested to Lefty that he stop by my office on his way to Air Force headquarters. When we got there, I told Lefty to tell his story to Reuben as he was interested in his case, too. Reuben did not blink an eye or comment when Lefty told his story. He asked Lefty, "What is your serial number?" The he picked up the telephone and dialed a number. Reuben then said, "Grotenrath, take down this name and serial number and promote Captain Parker to a Lieutenant Colonel. When can he pick up his orders?" Then he turned to Lefty and said, "I am sorry that I cannot promote you more than two grades without the approval of my boss!" I felt certain that Reuben would do something for Lefty as he felt strongly that G-2 should have taken action. You should have seen the expression on Lefty's face when he realized that he had jumped to a lieutenant colonel in less than fifteen minutes.

Shortly after I joined G-1 we were processing a paper that would increase the Army's strength several million. I noted that Reuben got busy with a scratch pad making some calculations.

Then I heard him talking to the commander of the Officer Candidate School at Fort Benning, for our desks were jammed together in the Munitions Building. After the greeting Reuben said, "We are going to need more Infantry officers and I believe that your quota is going to increase [naming a figure]." He did the same for all the combat arms. Anyone checking the output against the authorization would have discovered that the officers were coming out of the program before the authorization was received. Reuben well knew that any increase should be phased in for an orderly increase. The school commandants knew Reuben and had confidence in his integrity.

When Oveta Culp Hobby arrived to start up the Women's Army Auxiliary Corps we were not involved as it was to be separate from the Army, however we did sit in on the initial conferences when she was working up the details to provide advice. At one meeting someone brought up the subject of re-writing the Army Regulations to accommodate the women. Mrs. Hobby disagreed vigorously saying that the women should be treated the same as the men, and that obvious differences should be settled on an individual basis. I thought that to be quite a sensible approach. Their training center was at Fort Des Moines, Iowa, and I flew out to take a look at what they were doing when they had settled down.

I met General Benjamin O. Davis, Sr., at a conference called by Mr. John J. McCloy, the Assistant Secretary of War to discuss the state of morale in the Army. I was an observer for General White the G-1 who was out of town and I was sitting at the low end of the table when General Davis came in to sit beside me, introducing himself. We chatted a few minutes before the conference began. The topic had not been clearly defined but related to the perceived low status of the Infantry. The various speakers did little to define the problem or to offer solutions. When it came to General Davis he said, "I was in the Army for forty years before I heard of a morale problem and I don't know but what we have talked ourselves into it!" That conference did spark interest in the idea for the *Combat Infantryman's Badge*

General Davis had been called out of retirement for duty with the Army's Inspector General's Office and was a member of the team that inspected combat units before they moved overseas. Also, he held the complaint sessions which were part of such inspections. Since he had had much duty with troops, he understood the typical enlisted man and could respond to their complaints in terms which they could understand and accept. Benjamin O. Davis, Jr., graduated from West Point in 1936, completed flying training and commanded the 332nd Fighter Group in the Fifteenth Air Force during World War Two.

I was fortunate in being able to visit Army stations along the Eastern Seaboard between Fort Bragg, North Carolina, and Springfield, Massachusetts, while doing proficiency flying and learn what was going on at the station level. Colonel Clyde (Kewp) Finter was commanding at Windsor Locks, Connecticut. On a visit to Pope Field at Fort Bragg, Colonel Glenn Salisbury asked me about some personnel problem and I told him that he would find the answer in a recent War Department Circular for I had just written it, but that circular had not yet arrived. I sat in his office and copied down the dates other circulars had arrived to learn that it took three weeks for the word to get from my office to Pope Field. That told me that I had to allow for that lag in my calendar. For instance, the policy was that the training system would operate through the Thanksgiving-Christmas season at the fifty percent level or above. Individual leaves could be granted for one or the other holiday, but not both. The instructions for that policy had to leave our office about October first. I also used that knowledge to convince General White not to react in one situation because our action would arrive too late to be effective.

My counterpart in the G-3 or Operations Division was Colonel Thomas T. Stevenson, an actuarian in civil life. G-3 was concerned with men in units rather than as individuals, so there was much overlap and we coordinated on most papers to arrive at a common policy. When I originated a paper I would write the final draft double spaced so that he could edit it to fit the G-3 policy and I would sit down with him in his office while he checked it. When he had made his contribution, I would have the paper typed in final form and take it to him. He would initial the paper and walk it to his front office for the executive to initial and then return it to me. There few papers that we did not clear in the same day. He followed the same pattern and we got along well together.

Steve's major concern was with skills and one of his projects was to assemble a radio teletype unit for General MacArthur's headquarters at Brisbane. He was working with the Signal Corps at Fort Momouth, New Jersey, and having some problems. I corresponded on a personal basis with several of my amateur radio friends made while I was on duty at Langley Field. One of them had been called to active duty as a member of a Coast Artillery unit as he was in the communications section, and that was about 1939. He had written me about his experience: that he was now a master sergeant in charge of the Radio Operators School at Fort Monroe, that he had a qualified replacement trained and was now interested in going some place where there was more action. I handed that letter to Steve and said, "Here is a man who can run one of your teletype units for I have known him for five years." Sergeant William Kiblinger was on his way to Fort Momouth within a day or so.

When I moved up to Branch Chief my assistant was Colonel Logan C. Berry who had been G-1 of the 20th Armored Division. He had done considerable work in that unit to place the so-called "Undesirables" where they could be effective, through interviews in depth. This special board included the Division Surgeon and several senior officers with troop experience. Typically, these men got drunk on weekends, had a fight with the military police and ended up in the stockade. One of these men was diagnosed as a true claustrophobic and reassigned from a tank crew to the armored Infantry who ride around in a truck open to the sky. Another was a logger from the Northwest accustomed to hard work and did not find enough work to do in the Army so he worked off excess energy on weekends. Berry had each unit nominate their number one problem soldier and reassigned nine out of ten successfully through this interview. The logger went to the Engineer Troop since he was qualified as a rigger and became a technical sergeant in about six months.

The Army used individual replacement for combat losses rather than unit replacement as in World War One. An Infantry company had a built-in combat reserve of about twenty percent. The G-3 Division had been tracking the movement of combat trained replacements during the fighting on the Italian mainland and determined that the numbers reaching the front were much too low, that some had been diverted along the way, but where? To find out we sent a team of three, Colonel Berry with one from G-3 and another from Army Ground Forces to follow a batch of replacements, the team being incognito. They discovered and plugged the holes to solve that problem making it clear that any commander caught diverting a combat trained replacement would be in dire trouble. Members of the War Department General Staff went wherever required to deal with a problem.

General White met regularly with the Chief of Navy Personnel (BUPERS) to maintain similar policies for our mutual problems. When the War Manpower Commission complained that our recruiting of women interfered with their efforts to recruit women for industry, a joint committee was set up and I was the chairman. We saw no problem because we were recruiting women from the rural areas outside of the industrial areas. We decided to play it cool and find out what the real problem was for we knew that industrial employment was on the decline. After several friendly meetings, their representatives proposed that they recruit for us in their areas which was agreeable to us. That was a peaceful solution through procrastination.

In June 1944 Major General Westside T. Larson asked for my release to assume command of the Third Tactical Air Division. I was awarded the Legion of Merit for my work while on the War Department General Staff.

Manpower Control

Counting people in the Army was like carrying water in a leaky bucket, there was no single precise number. Our tabulations were after the fact with people scattered all over the globe, plus those in the *pipeline*, moving from one place to another.

The Adjutant Generals Office (AGO) was the action agency for personnel accounting and their records were kept on punch cards. For various staff studies we used a sampling technique rather than to count all the cards, several million. The accuracy depended upon the size of the sample, which one had to know in using such figures. One of their statisticians was Lieutenant Bonus who had a doctoral degree in statistics. G-1 planning called for future estimates rather than past summaries.

The Troop Basis listed all units needed by the Army for the war with a schedule of activation running about two years. To establish the training facilities for individual and unit training, we had borrowed the authorizations from the tail end units to provide staffing. The idea was that when it came time to activate such units, the training establishment would consume itself through filling up such units. The plan had logic, but it required intervention.

The Military Personnel Division of Army Service Forces had a control unit under Lieutenant Colonel Hal P. Crane which monitored the activation of units. As the time drew near to activate the tail end units, he was unable to locate enough people. For various reasons, the stations could not give up any men for that purpose, despite the reduced training load on the books. Since Crane was dealing with commanding generals, he did not have much leverage, only persuasion.

General Brehon B. Somervell, the commander, was an Army engineer and kept a close rein on the activation schedule. When Crane reported the difficulty in prying loose people, Somervell asked Crane how many men he needed. After a few minutes with a scratch pad, General Somervell said, "Cut everyone ten percent and tell them where to send the people." A command decision settled the matter in minutes and General Somervell would tolerate no argument about his decisions. Crane had come up through the National Guard and considered himself the best bass fisherman on the Potomac River, for he spent much of his spare time on that river.

During the Louisiana Maneuvers in 1940, I visited the air squadrons in the field. The squadron commanders could tell me in a flash how many mechanics of various types they were short, but when it came to the number of men they had training on the job, or a total figure, or their total strength, the figures became vague. In the GHQ Air Force I had adopted the principle of "Parsimony" in staffing the units in our buildup, to keep them somewhat under strength for control. It was easier to hand out a few more than to retrieve men.

There were conditions where too many factors were at work and plans were affected in a way such that we were unable to control the outcome. During the early days in G-1 we had closed off the leaks due to the local discharge of the so-called undesirables, death and physical disability were the only exits.

During the summer of 1943, Congress was debating whether to draft fathers or not. The local boards were not about to get caught in the middle while Congress was deliberating, so they stopped drafting fathers anyway. That resulted in our monthly shipments being lower than planned. We saw no point in increasing the monthly allotments because we knew why the local boards were acting. General Hershey toured the country to urge the local boards to fill their quotas with little success. Then we discovered that certain discharge policies had been changed without our knowledge, and we were losing men by discharge, so we shut off that leak.

By that fall, everything came together: Congress made up its mind, General Hershey's pleas had been heard, the local boards were not only filling their quotas but were overshipping to make up for the earlier short shipments. Due to the inertia in the system, that continued for a month or two and, by January we were one hundred thousand men over strength. We now had the problem of finding beds for the surplus and they were scattered around the available barrack space until they could be absorbed in the training system. Once it started we were unable to stem the flow. To cap everything off, we found that the Machine Records Unit had mislaid a tray of cards, so the final score was ten thousand greater than we thought it was the day before.

The typical unit commander in the Army liked to stockpile manpower as a cushion against the unknown, not realizing that he was causing potential trouble for himself. The old saw that the Devil finds work for idle hands to do, held in the Army. My view has been that it is better to have too much work and too few people than too many people and too little work.

General George C. Marshall

General George C. Marshall was the Army's Chief of Staff when I moved to the General Staff in March 1942. I was aware of certain policies that he had instituted from his experience and knowledge of World War One when he had been aide to General Pershing.

One was that he reinstituted the Education and Recreation Branch which had been under the War Plans Division during that war. This program was intended to make every member of the

Army aware of why we were fighting the war, that it was a just war and that the individual should understand his part in bringing it to a successful conclusion. As I observed this program, the stress was more on recreation than education. However, recreation does serve to relieve mental tension and was beneficial. When I was out in the field on staff visits I would question various people about how their work fitted into the larger picture. Staff car drivers were predominately members of the Women's Army Auxiliary Corps. Their purpose was to get the war over sooner because their boyfriend or family member was also involved. Such knowledge is fundamental to morale or zest in performance.

There were a variety of suggestions that came to the War Department and were designed to involve the Army in social change, primarily as to integration. The basic policy was that the mission of the Army was to win the war and that it was not an instrument for social change.

As a practical matter, we on the staff understood that there were variations in culture throughout the country because it complicated our menu plan and providing food. We had met them in standardizing the Army's General Classification Test, and had to accommodate to them. During that war men from all parts of the country were intermingled under circumstances where individuals could be judged on their own merit, so some change was inevitable. The issue was social experimentation which would divert attention from our primary task.

I had only one occasion to meet General Marshall in his office and that was to brief him on the subject of the Four-F classification of draft deferments. General Marshall planned his schedule of daily briefings two weeks ahead of the time he expected to need the information. His long-time male secretary would hand-carry the notes to the various Gs. Since my boss Miller White was to be out of town, he turned the briefing over to me. The existing policy was that we could get along without them for the time being, admitting that some men could be used for limited duty in the United States, but not overseas.

I had two weeks to prepare for a fifteen minute briefing, including questions. The issue was whether the policy should be changed. There was no formality to that briefing. At the scheduled time I was ushered into his office and quietly sat down in the designated chair, waiting until General Marshall looked up and said, "Good Morning," my cue to begin. When I finished, he dictated a memorandum to the Secretary of War while I listened. That done, he asked, "Is that correct?" and his "Thank you" ended that briefing. His memorandum to Secretary Stimson recommended no change in current policy.

Joseph T. McNarney was General Marshall's Deputy with Major General Miller White next in line as the G-1 for Personnel. Should General White not be available, I was free to consult General McNarney on any urgent matter. In the early days, Air Corps officers held about half of the policy positions.

My tour of duty on General Marshall's staff was a pleasant experience working with a group of highly competent people dedicated to freeing General Marshall and Secretary Stimson from routine matters so that they could concentrate on the larger aspects of winning the war. Those with whom I worked at the policy level were of the *Generalist,* rather than *Specialist* type, knowledgeable about the Army from the grassroots up.

Henry H. Arnold — Five Star General

By a strange coincidence, the first airplane and the first pilot that I met at first hand involved Lieutenant Henry H. (Hap) Arnold in 1916. He had flown one of the Army's new seaplanes built by Curtis to Philadelphia, landing on the Delaware River and bringing it to a dock at Essington, near the present Philadelphia Airport. He was on a visit to his family in Ardmore.

I entered the picture as a passenger in the automobile with a group to see him off on his return trip to Washington, his brother Clifford and my father. The airplane was of the type where the pilot sat out in front, exposed to all the breeze. Lieutenant Arnold wore a long leather coat, scarf and goggles. His helmet interested me as it was of moulded sole leather to fit his head, the segments being sewed together. The departure was without incident, the craft skipping along for a considerable distance before becoming airborne.

Arnold's brother was a medical doctor, then a battalion surgeon with the Sixth Pennsylvania Infantry and my father was Captain of "B" Company. They were good friends and had just returned from El Paso, Texas, where they had been in training on the border. I kept in touch with Dr. Arnold over the years. After World War One he returned to Ardmore to practice and was recalled to active duty for World War Two when he was on duty at Fort McNair in Washington.

Surprisingly, I never had a face to face talk with General Arnold after that meeting at Essington. While I was on duty in Texas, he was commanding March field. When he became Chief of the Army Air Corps we would meet at receptions and large gatherings, to pass down a receiving line. We were in different orbits and our paths did not cross. I'll never know if he recalled our first meeting.

General Arnold was unique, the right man in the right place and at the right time. His great energy, personal drive and firm conviction about the role of air power in war, were the driving force behind the Air Force effort.

He was a pioneer in military aviation and an ardent supporter of the independent role of air power in war. The Army bought its first Wright Aircraft in 1909 and Lieutenant Arnold learned to fly at Dayton, Ohio, in 1911. Frank P. Lahm and Fredric E. Humphreyes were the first two Army aviators qualified by the Wright Brothers in 1909. Lieutenant Thomas E. Selfridge was killed in an air accident at Fort Myers, Virginia, in September 1908, during the Army acceptance tests of the Wright airplane. He had the dubious distinction of being the first person in the world to die in an air crash.

I classify the pioneering phase of Army aviation to be from 1909 until 1915, when the First Aero Squadron was formed, a tactical unit for observation. It proved itself during the Punitive Expedition in 1916, by scouting for the ground troops. The First Aero Squadron used Curtis JN-2 aircraft. When activated at San Diego, it had 16 officers, 77 enlisted men and 8 aircraft.

There were a number of West Point graduates involved in this early period. Frank P. Lahm of the Class of 1901 heads the list. He had won the Gordon Bennett International Balloon Race in Paris in 1906 when he was military attache. Lahm and Frederic Humphreys of 1906 were both qualified by the Wright Brothers in 1909. Thomas Selfridge of 1903 was an early candidate, but died in an accident when testing a Wright aircraft. The Class of 1907 provided Henry H. (Hap) Arnold and Lewis C. Rockwell who died in an aircraft accident in 1912. John F. Curry and Thomas D. Milling represented the Class of 1908. Curry participated in the Punitive Expedition and Milling trained at Dayton, Ohio, with Hap Arnold. He became a flight instructor at College Park, Maryland. The commanding Officer of the First Aero Squadron was Herbert A. Dargue of 1911 and his classmate Leo G. Hefferman was one of his pilots. Byron Q. (B. Q.) Jones had the distinction of executing the first tail spin and recovering from that spin in 1915. Jones, Millard F. Harmon and Edgar S. Gorrell were all members of the First Aero Squadron and of the Class of 1912. Gorrell later served on the Baker Board which made recommendations to Congress on strengthening the Air Corps in the Thirties. The list ends with Ralph Royce of 1914 and Ralph P. Cousins of 1915 who also participated in the Punitive Expedition.

World War One created a huge expansion from the base of 35 pilots and 1087 enlisted men in the Aviation Section of the Signal Corps. I count 69 graduates of the classes 1901 to 1916, including those named above. Oscar Westover, Infantry, 1906, became Executive Officer for the Chief Signal Officer. In 1932 he became Assistant Chief of the Air Corps, moving up to Chief in 1935. Horace M. Hickan, 1908, participated in the Punitive Expedition as a Cavalryman and switched to the Air Service in 1917. William J. Fitzmaurice, 1908 and brother of James M. Fitzmaurice, 1923, was active in the training establishment. I served with many of them over the years.

I had the sad experience of attending the funeral service for General Arnold in January 1950, held in the Ampitheater at Arlington Cemetery. It was a cold and bitter day, fitting to the occasion.

Wartime Washington

Before our move from Langley Field to Washington, Edith and Ellen Mustoe drove to Washington to locate houses to rent. They were old friends from Randolph days, and as to be expected, found adjacent houses near Bolling Field. They were located on Westover Drive, a circular drive at the top of a knoll on the south side of Pennsylvania Avenue, in the Anacostia section. It was an enclave with a single narrow road leading up to Westover Drive. It was a good location for Rusty as there was park and wooded area all around the hill, where he could roam.

Catherine and Roland Birnn lived across the drive, not quite opposite, and they had been with us at Maxwell Field. Next to them were Mildred and Jim Goddard who worked in the Army Map Service for he was a topographic engineer now on active duty. Also across the drive were the Johnsons and he was a master plumber, president of the local chapter of the Izaak Walton League. His idea of an enjoyable frosty October evening was to take his coon hounds out into the woods and listen to their talk. Much of our social activity was at home on the top of that hill.

Harriett and Robin Day, who was then the G-1 of the GHQ Air Force, lived about a half-mile away from us. The Days had been at Brooks Field in my early days there. The Reuben Kyles, Air Corps, were also close by. Among new friends were the Kessenichs. He was a patent attorney in the Ordnance Department, then on active duty. He had been researching old patents for the Ordnance Department looking for military uses based on up to date knowledge. An impractical idea fifty years earlier could be reworked and put to use.

The war brought many moves and our social activity was often a going away party, several held at the Wardman Park or Willard Hotels, if not at home. The Days went to Santa Maria in California where Robin became Base Commander of a new air base. Tony Mustoe became Weather Officer for the Eighth Air Force and left for England. When Tony and I were flying a B-18 on a staff trip, I felt better about the weather when he was at my side. Such moves broke up our car pool and I turned to public transportation.

The going away party for Reuben Kyle was at the Wardman Park and we were the only full colonels in the dining room. We felt strangely alone when we looked around to see no one higher than a major in rank.

Our gasoline coupons under rationing were adequate for Edith's use in her travel around town. While I could have easily justified extra coupons based on my position in the War Department, I decided to stay with public transportation. On downtown going away parties, we would meet at the Willard, so I only had to ride to the downtown area, and then ride home with Edith after the party. The normal pattern was that I caught a bus on Pennsylvania Avenue which took me to the trolley across the Anacostia River. After I got downtown, I transferred to the bus for the Pentagon. Passengers were always packed like sardines, and standing room only. My goal was to get through the door before it closed. I could avoid the peak crowds by going early to work and staying late.

Clayton came to Washington when he finished his program at Greenbriar and got a job at a nearby Amoco service station, for he was not yet eighteen. As a learner he was number three on the staff. He was promoted automatically when the two above him were drafted, so he became station manager and learned a lot about the real world, mainly that handling ration coupons was more difficult than money.

When he became eighteen, he enlisted and applied for the West Point Preparatory School and was sent to Cornell University. I was able to visit him over one weekend, landing my basic trainer in a little field at the south end of Lake Cayuga. Unfortunately, he was disqualified due to a chronic sinus condition and transferred to South Plains Air Force Base at Lubbock, Texas, where he was a crew chief on a C-47 used in training glider pilots.

Edith had no problems with our food rationing coupons, for there was much swapping going on. The distribution being arbitrary and based on general patterns, did not match individual preferences. Our weekly cleaning woman had a sweet tooth, and we used little sugar, so we traded our sugar stamps for her meat stamps. Then, there was an old fashioned butcher shop where she traded. It was located in a housing project where families had numerous children. They had surplus stamps and turned them over to the butcher before they expired for him to use as he saw fit. One day Edith was admiring a standing rib roast, but she did not have the coupons. He told her never mind the coupons for he would cover them. From that time on we had a standing rib roast with no concern for coupons.

While we had a private location at the top of the hill, there was one time when we had to walk up the long road from Pennsylvania Avenue. We had been to a party at Bolling Field on the Saturday before Palm Sunday in 1944. It had begun to snow at the time of our arrival. When we came out of the club about midnight, there was four inches of snow on the ground and we did not have enough traction to get up the hill without chains. Fortunately, we had our galoshes on for the trudge in the snow. by the time we went to rescue the car late the next afternoon, the snow was gone for all practical purposes.

June 6, 1944, a Monday, was a great day, Clayton left for Sheppard Field at Wichita Falls, Texas, while I left for Meridian, Mississippi. Lightning struck our house and knocked slates off the roof but no fire. Our troops landed in Normandy. Edith was left behind to clear the house, put our household goods in storage and prepare for her drive to Meridian with Rusty. We had decided to rent a furnished house or apartment.

The Third Tactical Air Division

The Third Tactical Air Division was my first major command. Since it called for the grade of a brigadier general, I knew that I was slated for promotion eventually. Back in my specialty of observation, I learned that it had changed drastically since my training at Kelly Field and work in the 7th Observation Squadron in Panama. The British had learned early in their campaign against the Germans in North Africa that the two-seater observation aircraft was a sitting duck for fighter aircraft. They had taken the obvious course and used fighter pilots as observers.

While the function was the same, it called for new procedures, and the name had been changed to Tactical Reconnaissance or Tac-Recon for short. The new procedure called for a Tactical Control Group on the ground to direct the pilot to his target by radio. Another change was to have a Ground Liaison Officer specially trained to instruct the pilot before take-off and to interrogate him after the mission. The pilot flew at treetop level to obtain information and to attack ground targets of opportunity. The Tac-Recon aircraft had a fixed camera which the pilot could use as required. We had adopted the British System.

We had the one and only Ground Liaison Officers School at Key Field and all the instructors were British, experienced in the North African Campaign. The students were ground intelligence officers and the course was designed to acquaint them with the problems of a pilot flying at treetop levels, and possibly fighting off enemy aircraft; the need to see the problem from the pilot's point of view, especially the need for patience in eliciting information after an exciting mission. I watched one instructor role play the part of a returned pilot. Jack London was dressed in a pilot's regalia with his parachute still on, who wanted to tell everyone about the dogfight he had on his way back to base. The student GLO could not get a word in edgewise.

Our task was to train fighter pilots in the Tac-Recon techniques using the P-51 airplane with a fixed camera. The Base Commander who was responsible for administration and maintenance reported directly to Third Air Force; I through the Third Tactical Reconnaissance Command. We solved mutual problems by consultation as a general rule, for I was responsible for training and there was overlap. Coffeyville, Kansas, and Key Field at Meridian, were the two major stations training on the P-51s. Will Rogers Field at Oklahoma City had P-38s for night reconnaissance and night photography. When I arrived we had several Liaison Squadrons in training for messenger work along the China-Burma Road. They were using the L-5 version of the Piper Cub, which had flaps to assist in jump takeoffs and short landings. They were field units to live in tents and operate under primitive conditions. We had two at Statesboro, Georgia, one at Demopolis, Alabama, and one at Camp Wolters at Mineral Wells, Texas. At Fort Bliss and Biggs Field, there was a radio controlled target squadron working with the antiaircraft artillery.

We had several B-25 (North American) aircraft for staff purposes, so I lost no time in visiting all stations to get acquainted. Before World War Two the Air National Guard units were observation type, and they had provided the nucleus for Tac-Recon training with experience in depth. My staff surgeon, Major Ramsey Thomas had come on active duty with the Maryland Squadron in 1939. When I left Coffeyville for El Paso I stopped overnight at South Plains to visit Clayton and then went on to Camp Wolters, before turning back for Key Field at El Paso. While in El Paso I had dinner at the Mexican Restaurant which had started canning the Old El Paso brand to learn that all his machinery had been stored during the war because he could not get tin cans, too low on priority. He did plan to resume when the war was over.

My superior was Brigadier General Hume Peabody, commanding the Third Tactical Reconnaissance Command, headquartered at Barksdale Field. General Peabody had been G-4, Logistics, on the staff of the GHQ Air Force when I was in the G-1 Section. He asked me to represent him on a conference to be held at Fort Riley about reconnaissance. It was an all Cavalry conference and I was the only Air Force officer present. I kept quiet and listened to learn that their interest was in "knowing what was on the other side of the hill just ahead." They were dissatisfied with the Tac-Recon assistance that they were getting from the Air Force, and attributed that to the emphasis on heavy bombardment. It was clear to me that they wanted closer control *or* their own aircraft. I so reported to General Peabody, commenting that if the Air Force did not act to improve matters, the Army would have their own aircraft. That did come some twenty years later.

While visiting Colonel Frederick E. Calhoun at Will Rogers Field, he told me an interesting story. Several of the enlisted men of the Negro service squadron petitioned him to authorize a truck for them to attend Wednesday evening prayer service at a church in town, which he did. Then, word trickled back that this privilege was being abused by men who professed an interest in the prayer meeting, but sought a free ride to town. The following Wednesday there was an officer in charge of the three trucks, with a noncom on each truck. When the convoy arrived at the church the officer marched them into the church and sat through the service. When church was over they were loaded on the trucks and went back to Will Rogers. That continued until the free riders were shaken out, then only a noncom supervised the trip. Those who really wanted to go to church had pleasure from the discomfiture of those who thought they were getting a free ride, who had no basis for complaint. They knew that they had been "Had." The story here is that Calhoun did not complicate matters, he just saw to it that his authorization worked as intended.

The Base Commander at Key Field was Colonel Harold G. Peterson, the only regular officer other than myself on Key Field. Late in 1944 he could foresee trouble as Key Field was getting increased drafts for aircraft mechanics for units destined for the Pacific. The fifty-hour inspections had already been arranged in a production line sequence to reduce the need for mechanics, the aircraft stopping at each stage for a specific part of the maintenance procedure. The only asset he had was on the job training for men in the Negro service squadron. Also, he knew that several of the young men had been hanging around the flight line. He bounced his plan off me for comment since no Negroes had been working on the line. I had talked several times with the First Sergeant whose name was Williams and he had impressed me as a level-headed and intelligent man.

The first step in the maintenance process was to thoroughly clean the airplane, requiring work but little skill. His plan was to place two of the young men in that crew as a starter and see what happened, the incremental approach. After a few days, add another Negro to the crew until they were the entire crew. When the other mechanics had an opportunity to see their work, Pete planned to suggest to one mechanic who he had selected, that a *helper* would be beneficial for running errands to the stock room for parts and handing him tools as needed, getting his pick of the wash crew and a promise that he could go overseas when his replacement was trained. Soon, other mechanics wanted a helper and the wash crew was the source, to be replenished by Sergeant Williams. I did not see the end of Pete's program, but it was sound. It was a big deal to be working hands on an airplane for those young men.

I knew that Colonel Frederick W. Evans, Air Corps, on duty in the G-3 Division of the War Department General Staff had worked up a policy for the induction of Negroes, simply put, to draft them in their proportion of the total military manpower pool and distribute them evenly among all units, total integration. A color blind approach, where each man would rise or fall on his own merit. He had asked me to review that plan and I favored it from the G-1 point of view. It was shot down by Judge Hastie who was advisor to Mr. McCloy the Assistant Secretary of War who was concerned about such matters. Hastie thought that the Negro would end up in all the menial jobs. That may have been partially true, but the ultimate test was how one did his work. When an Infantryman can lob a grenade with distance and control, the color of the man throwing the grenade has no bearing. We had unused talent in the Negro service squadrons.

I tried my hand at some personnel work, having noted that the driver of my staff car spent much time reading comic books. He had been a driver working out of a warehouse before he came into the Air Corps. I asked him if they had any records or paperwork at his warehouse, suggesting that he might get a better job after the war was over if he improved his skills suitable for what he could recall from the warehouse. I did get him to learn to operate the mimeograph machine in headquarters, but filing papers scared him. By that time I moved on to the Third Air Force Headquarters. I had put out several technical manuals, but he never had the curiosity to browse the contents.

My staff Chaplain Major Hewlett was excellent, truly concerned about pastoral care and interested in the welfare of the men. He spent little time in his office, but was out on the flight line or moving around where he could be seen. He encouraged hobby clubs, such as photography or model building for leisure activity. We had a basic policy that the chaplain served the entire station and that any person could see the chaplain of his choice when several were available, for his concern was with individuals. One of the chaplains at Key Field suggested to Hewlett that the base units should be divided up, two congregations in effect, and he wanted to know how to handle the matter as we did not control the base. I spotted the problem which was that one chaplain was more popular than the other and was getting all the business, to which Hewlett agreed. Since each had a receptionist, I suggested that he reduce them to one. The single receptionist could query for preference and shunt those with no preference to the shorter line. That would serve the applicant by reducing waiting time. I also suggested that he tell them to practice a little Brotherly Love in working out mutual problems. I could see from the gleam in Hewlett's eye that he would enjoy passing that along.

Our trainees were at Key Field for twelve weeks and then moved on to Hunter Field, Savannah, Georgia, for assignment overseas. While we had no unusual problems with them, I thought that it would be nice to check their religious preference when they checked in and then pass that on to the local churches so that they could be invited to get acquainted. I knew that some of the young men did look up their local church. Hewlett thought well of that idea for it was for the benefit of the trainee. But, the two local chaplains were opposed. Need I say more?

After six months I was transferred to headquarters Third Air Force for duty at Chief of Staff. The tour with the Third TAD was a pleasant interlude for it was a well run outfit, a pleasurc to work with competent people and helpful in my new assignment.

Family Affairs

Edith bore the brunt of clearing our rented house in Washington. By the time that she arrived in Meridian, I had rented a furnished house south of town and on a ridge east of Key Field. My next door neighbor was Major Ramsey Thomas, my staff surgeon. We could look down a gully and see the Scattergoods' house on a small lake on the flat below, close to the river, but there was no direct access. Colonel Scattergood later became Chief of Staff when Johnny Bodle took command of Will Rogers Field. Rusty lost no time in discovering the lake for he liked to swim, and the Scattergoods had two boys to play with. Rusty spent most of his days at the lake in good weather, coming home to eat and sleep. When we moved to The Embassy Apartment in Tampa, we left Rusty with the Scattergoods.

We had little contact with the civilian community in Meridian, but there was plenty of social activity on base. After Edith arrived we had a formal reception at the Officer's Club to get acquainted. Then we were invited to a dance at the Noncommissioned Officer's Club where Edith and I led in the Grand March, another type of reception, where we met the senior noncoms and their ladies, including Sergeant Williams and his wife, since he was the First Sergeant of the Negro service squadron. The ladies were dressed in their finest and quite a match for those at the Officer's Club. We danced down the seniority line, Edith with the men and I with the corresponding lady.

The British instructors with the Ground Officer Liaison School were charming people and fun to have on any type party. Jack London who had been a journalist with the London *Times*, and wrote plays for an avocation, had a standard approach which he used on me by asking whether I believed in *reciprocity*. That opened the way for his topic, since the Americans had taught him to drink his Scotch with ice in it, he felt compelled to teach Americans to drink warm beer. One day at Mobile, during their field exercise, he showed me his beer which was buried to the neck in the dirt outside the building, at least eighty degrees. At one party at the Beatties, when Myrtle announced breakfast, Jack merely groaned, "Just bring me a warm beer!"

When General Larson told me that I was to be transferred to

Third Air Force Headquarters as his Chief of Staff, I flew to Tampa to locate an apartment, my first stop being the Embassy, for I knew that Harriett and Robin Day were living there. I was informed that they had no vacancies and a long waiting list. When I saw Robin later he said, "Let me handle it!" My predecessor, Thomas D. White had just moved out of an apartment on the ninth floor and the Days were negotiating to move to that apartment, which they did and we moved into the Days' apartment on the seventh floor. It was quite comfortable for two people with Murphy Beds which folded up and were hidden during the day. The space behind the beds was one long, narrow walk-in closet with built-in cabinets. The apartments were next to the auditorium, not far from downtown. The American Legion sponsored boxing matches there on a regular basis. Edith and I visited the auditorium once for a performance of *La Traviata* with Licia Albanese in the leading role. She was a close friend of the lady heading the local group interested in opera.

Tampa was well known for its hand made cigars, one being the Hava Tampa Brand. The cigar trade had moved from Cuba to the Tampa area before World War One. On one of our staff visits to McDill Field, Joe Smith and I had toured a cigar factory. It was in a huge open loft with at least one hundred cigar makers working at their individual stands, arranged in orderly rows. The "filler" for the cigar was brought to them on the lower half of the trays where they had been shaped and pressed. The workers were rolling the binder and wrapper covers in a spiral fashion. In the center, on a pedestal, was one who read stories to the workers in Spanish instead of canned music.

Edith and I had several friends in the Tampa area, including Sweetie and Charlie Skow who had been with us at Langley Field. Charlie had been caught in a purge of World War One officers directed by General Arnold when he took over as Chief of the Air Corps in 1938, and Charlie was unhappy about it. When Edith and I next visited the Skows in 1956, Charlie was a changed man in his attitude toward life for he had found an engrossing hobby in researching the geneology of Sweetie's family.

When Helen and Carl Pyle came to Tampa for duty with the Third Air Force, they had an apartment in The Embassy. Helen did not go out much, so we played many hands of four-handed cribbage. Edith played a lot of bridge and had no problem in arranging a bridge game. It was usually six before I got home in the evening.

When we ate out, the Columbia was a favorite place for Spanish food and there was an excellent Chinese restaurant close by.

Edith's father came by train to live with us and we were fortunate to get him a small apartment on the ground floor. He enjoyed that for he could sit on the veranda and watch the crowd go by, and swap stories with other guests.

The big event at The Embassy was when Emma Jane, the Day's daughter had her wedding in Tampa. She married Preston King, an Air Corps pilot. He got out of the service after the war and they settled in his home town, San Marcos, Texas.

On weekends when the weather was good we cruised the area, usually to the Gulf Beaches, and often with Peg and Dave Davasher who had rented a house in St. Petersburg. Ruth and Kewp Sharon who had been with us at Randolph Field were living at Clearwater where he had retired in 1939 for physical disability; he had a bad heart. Kewp had a motor boat and was active in the Coast Guard Auxiliary. He had met his wife in England during World War One, she being on duty as a nurse at the hospital where they met. From time to time the Davashers would have a houseparty and we would all go to the beaches for a swim.

I was transferred to Alaska in October 1945, but Edith and her father stayed on for a while at The Embassy, waiting for someone who was to travel west to Texas so that they would have company on the trip. When she arrived safely in San Antonio, she rented a house in the Olmos Park section. Clayton was released from the service the next Spring and she was busy helping him enroll in Trinity University, remaining in San Antonio until late in 1946, when she could join me on Adak. She traveled by Transport from Seattle with the first contingent of dependents.

The Third Air Force

I was honored to be selected by Major General Westside T. Larson to be his Chief of Staff for it indicated that he had confidence in my judgement. I knew that, as his principal assistant, he expected me to conduct the day to day activities of the Third Air

Force through his staff, freeing him for the larger problems. I anticipated an enjoyable learning experience for I had great respect for his capabilities. He had been my flying instructor at Kelly Field and we had worked together in the GHQ Air Force Headquarters where he was in the G-3 Operations Section. His wife Gertrude and Edith were close friends. While General Larson always called me "Eddie," I used the formal style of address during duty hours.

General Larson was a firm believer in delegation and knew how to make it work properly. He was careful in selecting his base commanders who were expected to make operating decisions on the scene. Larson construed that his function was to free them from interference, either from his own staff or from outsiders. The Third Air Force Staff could approve any reasonable request from a base commander when resources were available. Only one man in the Third Air Force could say *No* to a base commander and that was General Larson. When the Staff recommended that a request be denied, and Larson was convinced, he called that base commander on the phone right away to tell him of the decision and the reason.

When we had a conference of base commanders, General Larson would open the meeting with a few remarks and then turn it over to me. At my first conference I looked around at twenty-three colonels and thought to myself, "What a gathering of high priced talent we have here," and wondered whether anything useful would result. Base commanders had the floor by seniority, and when it came to a new base commander, he placed a bulging briefcase on the table and said, "I came here loaded, but find that my problems are the same as everyone else's here, so I have nothing more to add." That was a clear answer to my question. He now understood that he had to do the best he could with the means at hand.

When the GHQ Air Force disappeared in the Army reorganization of March 1942, it reappeared as the Continental Air Forces responsible for the training of combat units and combat air crews for replacement. The First Air Force was headquartered at Mitchel Field; the Second at Peterson Field, Colorado Springs, and the Third Air Force at Tampa. We had twenty-three stations with an aggregate strength of two hundred thousand, half military and half civilian. Subordinate commands were the bomber command, fighter command and reconaissance command. Hunter Field at Savannah, Georgia, was a staging base for movement overseas. That was commanded by Jim Fitzmaurice, now a brigadier general.

Brigadier General Thomas W. (Tommy) Blackburn who commanded the Fighter Command was a veteran fighter pilot from World War One, head of pursuit training when I was at Kelly Field and a dedicated fighter pilot. There were few better qualified to pass on their wisdom to the combat crew trainees.

Continental Air Forces had a number of special programs with one or more staff officers concerned. When we received a telegram asking for the name of our designated staff officer for that program, the answer was always, Major General Westside T. Larson. He did not want any staff officers wandering around telling his base commanders what to do without his permission. When the Conservation Program came along and was something new, I teased General Larson by handing him the request for a name. After he cooled down I handed him the reply which I had ready. I thought that it would help him remember the new program better. As a consequence of pushing decisions down to the scene of action, we had few regulations and they were of a policy nature, the *What* rather than the *How* to do it.

We had a large chart room with a chart for every operating activity: aircraft hours flown, aircraft out of commission, motor vehicles out of commission, and the like. Data for all three air forces were displayed, and the Third Air Force stood at the top or close to it, among the various trends. General Larson understood the inertia of large organizations and his strategy was to look for soft spots and then give them a *nudge* upwards.

On Monday morning, General Larson would stop by and say, "Let us go and pick something for me to worry about." We would adjourn to the chart room and make the round studying each carefully, discussing the past week and possibilities for action. I may have had comments from staff members to add, or he had ideas. By the end of the round, he had selected a topic, and we would return to the front office. I then would visit the proper staff section and tell them to brief General Larson on his selected topic, and he would spend most of Monday wringing them out for details. Tuesday, he would give me his itinerary and say that he was off to get someone to help him worry.

He did not stand on ceremony and his pilot would send a radio ahead before his arrival on the topic of that visit. In the case of motor maintenance, the Base Commander and the Maintenance

Officer would meet the plane, and they would visit the Maintenance Shops. When they got out of the staff car, Larson would ask, "What is your one biggest problem?" He already knew what the answer should be from his briefing, at least from the staff's point of view. There were only three possible answers in general, the drivers abuse the vehicles, spare parts were not available and a shortage of mechanics. Should Larson get a confused answer, he would say, "Don't you think you ought to know?" That was his message, and with the base commander standing beside him, he knew that enough had been said. Then, they would tour the facility and he would be off to the next station on his list, to visit all twenty-three stations. He spent much of his time out in the field.

General Larson took flying safety seriously and carefully studied every accident report. He spotted the problem of an engine failure at one fighter station, that the pilot had taken off without warming up the engine. The clue was in the wind direction. Normally, on that field, the pilot had a long way to taxi before reaching the takeoff point and the engine would be well warmed in the normal taxi time. In the accident case, the wind was from the opposite direction causing a short taxi time. We were using Allison liquid cooled engines, and the preventive measure was that the chocks were not to be pulled until the pilot signaled the crew chief that the temperature was up to the orange zone before beginning the taxi in *either* direction.

By the spring of 1945 it was clear that General MacArthur was making good progress in the Pacific and General Larson thought that it was time that we should consider going out of business. The first step was to rank order all our stations on the basis of the ones we wanted to keep the longest, and those we could well do without. We were receiving drafts for people to fill up units destined for the Pacific, and his idea was to deplete one station and place it on a caretaker basis. Any personnel coming into the command from overseas would go to the stations we wished to keep, and maintain their effectiveness in training.

Staff sections made their recommendations and then the lists were consolidated and he had approved it.

The next step was to work up a plan for using Drew Field as a demobilization base, for it had adequate facilities, with rail transportation at Tampa. That was a special project with Major Dartman in charge. Harking back to World War One, we began with the policy that an individual should be processed and on his way home within twenty-four hours, the station would work on three shifts. We assumed that it would be responsible for returnees with homes in Florida and adjoining states. As to numbers, we assumed a trainload expecting the bulk to arrive by rail. Instead of one gigantic establishment, we had units designed to handle several hundred grouped together for a convenient flow pattern. Should the first one become loaded, we could activate a second, and so on. The idea was flexibility. Each unit had a staffing table, a flow chart and details for the operational plan, ready by September 1945.

Shortly afterwards, we had a call from Continental Air Forces to attend a conference on demobilization planning. I was confident that nothing had been done at Continental Air Forces on that subject. General Larson had left for an assignment in Germany and Lieutenant General Brereton had not yet arrived, so I was to head the delegation. While a conference was all right for exchanging information it was very poor for problem solving and we wanted to protect our plan for Drew Field. Before we left Tampa I got my team together and we all agreed that I would be the only spokesman and that we would not reveal that we had a plan until I thought the time appropriate. However, we were to be helpful in sharing any ideas that were circulated. As I suspected, with thirty people on hand, many topics and unknowns, nothing happened the first day, other than to set up working committees. The next morning there was little more clarification and people were getting irritated and touchy by afternoon. I called on Major Dartman to present our thinking, as he had flip charts ready and other details. The conference took our plan with little change for the people at the conference could find little to fault.

When I left for Alaska in October, Colonel G. L. Davasher took over as Chief of Staff moving up from Director of Administration and Personnel. He told me that the plan was used for Drew Field and the only modification was that men were processed on their accumulated release points, those with the greater number moved to the head of the line. Men were processed serially by points rather than by train loads.

Lieutenant General Lewis H. Brereton had quarters on McDill Field and was busy writing a book justifying his part in the events at Clark Field in the Philippines when the Japanese attacked. He had taken the remnants of that force to Egypt as the nucleus of the Ninth Air Force. He told me to carry on with the routine details and came in about once a week, or when called for important matters.

General Douglas MacArthur

While I was a cadet at West Point, Brigadier General Douglas MacArthur, replaced Colonel Samuel E. Tillman as Superintendent. Until I became a first classman, I only saw him at a distance, but his impact came early when he introduced the Intermural Program wherein every cadet tried his hand at a variety of sports. In 1927, General MacArthur was President of the United States Olympic Committee. I maintained an interest in his career over the years.

Mrs. MacArthur attended the weekly hops at Cullen Hall and I danced my duty dances with her as a first classman, for we had been trained in the social graces. General MacArthur would appear with her, dance a few dances and then disappear. When we graduated, General and Mrs. MacArthur held a reception for us in the garden of their quarters.

When General MacArthur was Army Chief of Staff during the Thirties, his reports to the Congress came to us in the Technical Library at Randolph Field, to be read with interest because of their lucid writing. One in particular gave his view on organization:

> . . . Manifestly, there is nothing sacrosanct in particular details of organization. So long as well defined, logical and easily understood methods are employed, there can be many variations as to organization with no adverse effects upon desired results. It seems, though, that some people, especially those of an academic turn of mind, often become obsessed with the idea that some particular organizational plan guarantees perfect results, and that any organizational variation is certain to lead to inefficiency and extravagance. Such a conception is, of course, absurd. The human element always dominates details of organization . . .

I watched with interest MacArthur's progress during the New Guinea Campaign when we were bypassing Japanese Islands to let them wither on the vine with their supplies cut off. I was certain that this was like General MacArthur's way of thinking. During 1945, Colonel Brown, his Headquarters Commandant, returned to Tampa from Brisbane, to retire for a second time. Brown called on me about some American Legion business in connection with their fights at the auditorium, for he was Commander of the local post. I took the opportunity to get his first hand view, and he assured me that General MacArthur's method was to tell his staff what he intended to do and ask them to prepare a plan. He would review that plan and it would be modified if necessary until he was satisfied, then it would be put into action. Colonel Brown also gave me an update on MacArthur's Chief Nurse, Jane Clement, our good friend from Langley Field days. He said that Jane was always on the go visiting her nurses throughout the command, dressed in trousers and flight gear.

General MacArthur's father had been a general in the Civil War with an outstanding record, earning the Medal of Honor. Raised in a military family, MacArthur had the habit of excellence, distasteful to egalitarians. As a cadet, he graduated first in his class and Captain of the Corps of Cadets. In World War One, he was the youngest divisional commander, leading the Rainbow Division. He had the habit of stating what he intended to do beforehand and then making good to the chagrin of his enemies. As a consequence, people were partisan, those who thought highly of him, as I did, or those who kept hoping that he would stub his toe. He was an avid student of history, trained and conditioned in the belief that there is no middle ground in war, only victors and vanquished. MacArthur intended to be a victor.

The Alaskan Department

I was pleased with my assignment to the Alaskan Department to command the Eleventh Air Force, for I knew very little about that area and what I knew had been gleaned from reading Jack

London's stories in my youth. The Third Air Force provided an airplane to fly me to the staging base at Great Falls, Montana, where I changed to a Military Air Transport C-47. The air route to Alaska was along the Alcan Highway via Edmonton, White Horse and Fairbanks, known as the inside route. On a later flight from Anchorage to Washington I flew the outside route which was down the coast to Yakutat for fuel, then turning Eastward by way of Prince Rupert to Edmonton. It was ninety degrees when I left Tampa and twenty-five degrees at Anchorage four days later.

I was welcomed at Elmendorf Field, Fort Richardson, by Generals Robert Bathurst, Chief of Staff and Harry Johnson who was commanding Fort Richardson, with Colonel Leslie Mulzer of the 90th Air Depot. Before going out to Adak to take over from General Brooks, I had a conference with Lieutenant General Delos C. Emmons, the Department Commander. General Emmons asked me to look around before I settled down and give him my views on the future military role for Alaska, particularly for the Aleutian Chain. General Bathurst briefed me on the general situation and Colonel Mulzer fitted me with a fur parka and hat Alaskan style.

General Brooks had sent his command airplane to take me to Adak. It was a conventional B-24 bomber fitted with some extra seats and fuel tanks. I spent the first night on the way at Fort Randall (Thornborough Field) at the end of the Alaskan Peninsula and I toured their facilities. At Adak I was met by General Brooks, Air Vice Marshall Heakes who had been visiting General Brooks, Colonel Detwiler of the Station and Lieutenant Commander DeWolfe who was in command of the Navy facilities. After a few days of meetings, a visit to Amchitka, and a reception at the Eleventh Air Force Officers Club, General Brooks departed for the States in his B-24 and I took over on October 27, 1945.

Alaska was in a holding pattern at that time with people moving out faster than in for the entire area was loaded with people who had a high point score based on months of duty. Their score was the basis for loading on the transports as they arrived to take them to the States. I inherited a Philippino chef from General Brooks who had a private mess, my high style lasted until the next transport when my chef went home and I moved to the Officer's Mess close by my quarters.

My Chief of Staff was Colonel Edgar T. Selzer, naturally known as "Bromo," an old time fighter pilot. He had selected a pilot aide for me who was checked out for flying the Chain, Captain Averill F. Holman, who had flown a P-47 in Europe. That type had the sobriquet of "The Jug" and the pilots liked that huge engine out front to absorb hostile bullets. I was set to tour the stations on the Chain, heading west for the first group and then east after a few days at Adak. Bromo told me that he had seen a postwar plan for permanent buildings on Adak to cost in the neighborhood of one hundred million. I took a look and that made me shudder, for should the Army ever invest that much money in permanent facilities, they would never get out of using them. I could see General Emmon's point in taking a look-see.

It was about that time that someone had studied a globe to discover that the shortest route from the Russian Heartland to our Mid-Western cities was over the polar regions. Ultimately, that led to the Distant Early Warning Network across that route. I took a look at my globe to see that the Aleutian Chain was well off to the west. But the important thing was that the Aleutian Chain was on the great circle route from Seattle to the Orient for military flights to Japan. I considered it likely that Northwest Air Lines would extend their flights West from Anchorage when conditions settled down.

My recommendation to General Emmons was that all the flying fields on the Chain be maintained operational with enough people at each field to look after the landing lights, refueling and weather service. We needed them for the troop carrier C-47s. Military flights to the Orient used C-54s which could use Adak and Shemya, overflying the intermediate stations unless forced to land by weather. Further, that no permanent construction be done on the Chain until the situation clarified, any money for permanent construction should go to the Mainland stations at Anchorage and Fairbanks, Elmendorf and Ladd Fields.

I learned later on that my recommendation to General Emmons was not at all popular with his staff in the Alaskan Department, but that was the way matters worked out. Adak finally became a Navy station for search and rescue work and they built permanent housing for their people. Besides, Adak had an excellent harbor.

The Eskimo who lived along the Yukon and Kuskokwim Rivers were unique in that they never used the wheel in their progress out of the stone age. Their kayaks and dog sleds were replaced by the airplane flown by *bush pilots* who landed on gravel bars and open meadows at first and then had aircraft which could use wheels, skis or pontoons. The Norseman was a popular type just before World War Two. Bob Reeve, one of the early bush pilots had been in the Army Air Service and then resigned to go to Alaska. After the war he had organized Reeve Airways, had made some charter flights to the Pribolof Islands, and was interested in the possibilities of flying out the chain for civilian flights. I told him that I did not see much civilian traffic along the Chain, but that he was welcome to use our facilities should he obtain the approval of the Alaskan Department. His twin, Dick, had also been an Army pilot who stayed in the Air Corps. He had flown a B-18 into a thunderstorm over Illinois to become a casualty of the weather.

I learned that Colonel Lawrence V. Castner who had been General Buckner's Intelligence Officer during the Aleutian Campaign had retired and was then living in Anchorage, so I paid him a visit on my next trip to Anchorage. I knew Castner as a cadet in "B" Company. His major call to fame was that he had organized the Eskimo into a lookout organization along the coast, and it worked. The interesting part of his story was that it took a special approach in eliciting information from the Eskimo, a round-a-bout approach to avoid a hint of the specific point of your interest. Otherwise, they would tell you a tale designed to keep you happy. They were excellent observers of the specific details of their environment, concrete items and that was the approach.

On the Kiska Operation he had been with General Buckner for that landing. I was curious about the factors leading to the decision to land when it was clear from the radio silence of the Japanese that they had probably gone. At that time, the two divisions, combat loaded had been cruising around offshore and psyched up for a landing. Since there was still some doubt, the decision was made to go ashore, rather than to sail back to Adak and Amchitka to unload with greater morale problems than with a landing.

General Simon B. Buckner directed the Army's program to bolster the defenses against a possible attack by the Japanese using the Aleutians as stepping stones to the Mainland, and air units were able to come to the defense of Dutch Harbor to surprise the Japanese. The story of the buildup and the Aleutian Campaign was told by Brian Garfield in his book the *Thousand Mile War,* published in 1975 by Ballentine Books.

Flying Aleutian Weather

One thing I learned in Alaska was that one did not trifle with Mother Nature's weather, high winds and extreme cold, with impunity. The idea was to know the weather and accommodate one's plans to suit the circumstances. Flying during the early days of the Aleutian Campaign was perilous because of the scanty information. After the Kiska operation the Navy established weather ships well out to the west for the attacks on the Kuril Islands. Aleutian weather was treated with respect by the pilots.

Newly arrived pilots were given a refresher course on instrument flying and the Ground Control Approach Landing System we were then using at Elemendorf Field. This course was conducted by the 54th Troop Carrier Squadron under Lieutenant Colonel Lewis G. Grossmith, Jr., the Commander. This squadron was our Aleutian Air Line transporting mail, spare parts, people and light cargo for stations along the Chain. The Ground Control Approach (GCA) was a short range radar with an operator to talk down the pilot to a landing under foggy conditions, the newest thing out.

After their checkout, the new pilot flew as copilot on the troop carrier run to learn the landing patterns at each station under an experienced pilot, and a feel for the weather. The next step was to the B-24 squadron on Shemya, the Fighter Group flying P-38s under Colonel Davenport who had been on Doolittle's Tokyo Raid or for administrative flying at various bases. My command airplane was a C-47, the general utility aircraft on the Chain. It had been modified to provide a sleeping compartment and airline seats.

Weather problems boiled down to fog in the summer and high winds during the winter months. The warm Japan Current passed about one hundred miles south of Adak. The cold seawater from the Bering Sea to the north, came down between the islands to meet the Japan Current. The cold air off the Bering seawater mingled with the warm moist air and the result was fog. It could be patchy or extensive depending upon the wind. While there had been experimentation with fog dispersion, such as a line of oil burners along the runway at Amchitka, there had been no reliable method to cope with the fog before the GCA equipment.

Winter winds over 75 knots were common, often with sleet. In

February of 1946 there were four storms in two weeks with winds to to 130 knots when the gauge broke, strong enough to roll up the steel planking on an abandoned landing strip on Adak. In such conditions everyone laid low until the storm was over and the local radio broadcast suitable warnings. All the weather fronts were of the warm air type, layers of clouds but no turbulence other than caused by the ground forms, the mountains, and nothing like thunderstorms.

In some respects the winter weather was harder on surface shipping. During February 1946, there were fifty foot waves south of Adak and two tankers broke in half, the *Donboss* a Russian ship and the *Sackett Harbor,* one of ours. The Russians towed the part remaining back to Vladivostok, while the stern half of the Sackett Harbor ended up at Anchorage to provide additional electric power for the growing population.

We practiced accommodation by selecting a suitable landing time from the weather map and working back to the takeoff time. I recall one time we were at Cold Bay near the end of the Alaskan Peninsula and faced with three fronts running close together with about six hours from the center of one to the next. We selected the halfway time to make a landing on Adka shortly after daylight. That called for a takeoff at three in the morning, and it worked out nicely for it was practically calm at Adak when we landed between the fronts.

Not all flights were in the clouds or flying between two cloud layers, for I had several trips in the summer where we had a cloudless sky and could see all the islands, mostly volcanic in origin. Only two smoked or steamed, Sitkin about thirty miles from Adak had a hot granite dome and emitted steam from the snow. Mt. Shishaldon, about half way to the Mainland, emitted black smoke. We flew over to take a look at the cone one clear day and could see the red-hot lava bubbling in the crater. The Aleutian Chain was part of the great volcanic arc which ringed the North Pacific from Seattle to Japan.

Ladd Field at Fairbanks was established as a winter test station for Air Corps equipment, and provided my first experience with Ice Fog which occurs during intense cold spells when water vapor from any source converts to crystals directly. When the temperature dropped to thirty degrees below zero, activities were delayed and took about twice as long to perform outside. When the temperature dropped to fifty degrees below zero, outside activity practically ceased. Construction continued during the winter because the contractor first erected a temporary shelter so that the permanent construction took place in a temperature above freezing. As one would expect, construction costs were about double those on the mainland.

The Navy had a program for training landing craft crews at Cold Bay in preparation for the assault on the Kiriles. That program had been discontinued before I arrived in Alaska. The ingenious airmen were using the maple flooring from the Navy quonsets to smoke Dolly Vardon trout in a homemade smokehouse. I sampled their smoked trout on one of my visits and it was delicious.

Adak

August 30, 1942, a combat assault team landed on Adak at Kulak Bay to find the island uninhabited. The engineers drained a shallow lagoon and laid pierced steel planking on the sandy bottom to make an air strip for fighters and bombers. Ellis Craig came ashore directly behind the assault group with an air base detachment to prepare accommodations for the arrival of the aircraft when the strip was ready. The Eleventh Air Force staged their bomb attack on Kiska, with fighter support, on September 14, 1942, all in two weeks. Craig joined my staff for a second tour in Alaska during 1946, then a second lieutenant. The assault was staged at Fort Glenn on Umnak Island, some two hundred fifty miles to the east, near Dutch Harbor.

With an excellent harbor, Adak became the main base for the campaign to expel the Japanese from Attu and Kiska. It was also the base from which the Army planned to launch an invasion of the Kiril Islands to assist the progress of General MacArthur by drawing Japanese ground and air forces far to the North. With VJ-Day, the invasion plan was terminated but the facilities had been largely completed. There were twenty huge warehouses to show for that effort. Adak was about one thousand miles west of Anchorage and about five hundred miles east of Attu.

The name Adak did not appear in any army document and the official title was U.S. Troops APO 980. The post commander was Colonel Augustus M. Gurney and his domain included the port facilities and various service units. The Eleventh Air Force and its Air Base Squadron were tenants of the station.

The Air Force had its separate area on the slope to the north of the airfield, complete in itself for housing the officers and enlisted men, with a headquarters office building. My quarters were similar to a stateside home, four bedrooms and two baths. Prior to my arrival it had been occupied by General Brooks, his Chief of Staff, Brigadier General Isaiah Davies, and their two aides. They had their private dining facilities with a Philippino chef. The airfield which had replaced the strip laid in the lagoon was the equal of any in the States to handle the B-29 bomber and used jointly by the Army and Navy. The major Navy facilities were docks and repair facilities in Finger Bay on the opposite side of the airfield from the army side. The Navy commander was Captain DeWolfe, a Naval aviator who had several PBY's for reconnaisance purposes.

The operations building of the joint airfield had separate areas for the Army and Navy passengers, incoming and outgoing. The weather and flight control activities were consolidated and manned by half Army and half Navy personnel. With the influx of new personnel, DeWolfe had some rumbles about scheduling duty assignments and hours. We resolved that issue by a joint policy which set up the minimum positions by type to be manned during duty hours and left the scheduling to those doing the work. When there was no air traffic in the Aleutian area during the night, the operations activity was shut down, other than for the weather office.

Gurney, DeWolfe and I worked together on any mutual problems. There were no memoranda or letters written during my tour. We got together, decided on a course of action and that was the basis for any communication. Gurney reported to the Alaskan Department, as I did, with DeWolfe reporting to the Commandant of the Naval District on Kodiak. Gurney and DeWolfe were ardent cribbage players and I could play that game as an average player. We would get together in the evenings from time to time for dinner and cribbage. On one occasion they were so intent on out-doing each other that I won the pot, all eighty-three cents.

What did I do to while away the evenings other that my visits with Gurney and DeWolfe? I revived my old hobby of processing my own film and making prints of snapshots taken on various trips. The chemicals were available at the Post Exchange and the water temperature was ideal, about sixty-five degrees. I had a small library in my quarters related to Alaska which included *The Friendly Arctic* and other books of Vilhjalmer Steffansson. I could borrow classical albums from the local radio station for my record player. When amateur radio operation was reauthorized in 1946 I had my station on the air; that story being told elsewhere.

When Edith arrived on station, we had the normal stateside social activity which was largely confined to the Air Corps group living on our hill which was remote from the main post. Edith enjoyed bridge, so she would have a bridge game going while I operated my ham radio station.

Early in 1946 we had instructions to convert buildings for dependent housing, light housekeeping style. A double quonset could be made into an apartment size home by adding a kitchen and bath, time consuming rather than difficult. The original hospital area was converted to enlisted and civilian dependent housing. We had few problems in our area for the senior officers had prefab buildings about sixteen feet square, ordinarily occupied by two bachelors. The policy was that all dependents would arrive on one transport load from Seattle. There was rivalry between the Army and Navy as to who could be ready first. DeWolfe was behind his schedule because he had fewer buildings to begin with and not all amenable for conversion. He got a query from the Navy Department and in his dispatch explaining the delay, he concluded with these words:

> . . . this station is fighting a losing battle for existence, not that the situation is catastrophic, but merely approaching same.

This was new to me, but I learned that it was customary in Navy usage. It would have been frowned upon in any Army message.

Edith joined me on the first contingent with several others for the Eleventh Air Force area. Life on Adak then became similar to Army life on the frontier during the Indian wars. One had to make do with whatever was available on the station. We had a congenial group as the Bodles and Beatties had been with us at Key Field, and Oma Fay had joined her husband Tex Holman, my aide.

When Edith and I would have a dinner party for high ranking visitors, all the ladies would pitch in.

Our small officer's club was built of four quonset huts joined to the sides of a prefab center building sixteen feet square. The front quonset was the entry and cloak room with its opposite mate the utility and store room. One of the two side huts was a social room and its opposite was a ballroom. The bar was in the central building. The ladies took over some improvements by making slip covers for the furniture. Social activity was mainly among the families on our hill, and with acquaintances made on the transport trip.

One of the early projects for all the ladies on Adak was to prepare for the Christmas party for the children, a post affair. Planning had to be done by the end of September in order to have the items on the dock at Seattle before the last transport left in early December. They worked through the Post Chaplains. Since I made frequent trips to Anchorage, I could bring back small items, but the bulk had to come by transport.

The winter before the dependents arrived was not barren of social activity. There were the Army nurses and Red Cross girls numbering about a dozen. The party that I went to was staged by the doctors of the base hospital, a dance with a spaghetti supper which the doctors cooked in the hospital kitchen. They had a combo of piano, banjo and violin, but they did not hesitate to stop playing to dance, so it would be the piano and one of the other instruments. It was a "Lil Abner" party with costumes based on the characters in that strip. The prize costume was that of the Base Surgeon, Lil Abner himself. He had a nurse's union suit with a volley ball as his paunch, hard to keep in place when dancing, and a wig made of silk stocking and surgical cotton. Every thirty minutes or so there would be a loud ringing of a bell and a shout of "Let's get fried," calling for a trip to the punch bowl.

The Air Force group returned that obligation with a dance in our club, but phonograph records this time for music. That was in February when we had a series of winter storms. While the dance was on it was snowing heavily and we were marooned on our hill, so the nurses and Red Cross girls could not get home to their quarters in the hospital area. I moved out of my quarters and turned them over to the ladies, bunking with one of my officers. One benefit of my kitchen, seldom used was that the ladies cooked breakfast and served it buffet style, visiting until the roads were cleared. Our mess hall was close by so we had no problems with eggs and bacon. They made themselves at home and played records on my record player. That was the highlight of the winter.

The most interesting visitor whom Edith and I had, early in 1947, was Simeon Oliver from the island of Atka about one hundred miles to the east. He and his wife were the teachers at the Eskimo school. Early in the war all the Aleuts on the Chain had been removed to the mainland, and recently moved back to Atka into a brand new village. He was on Adak for some business and we had him as a guest. Oliver was half Norweigian and half Eskimo, his native name being "Nutchuck." He had been orphaned early and raised at the Methodist Orphanage in Dutch Harbor. He had been sent to the University of Illinois for his higher education in music, but the capital left him by his father was wiped out by the depression, so he became the sustaining artist at Radio Station KWKH, Shreveport, Louisiana, one of my favorite stations while at Randolph Field, as we discovered. We had a classical music concert that Sunday afternoon and he enjoyed Schumann's A minor Piano Concerto, and he played a few excerpts for us on our piano. Since Edith wanted to buy some blue fox furs for a neck piece, Oliver persuaded the Chief of the Atka Group to sell us six pelts. The Eskimo were the only source and each pelt had to have their seal attached. We sent them to Seattle to be processed.

Our principal visitor that summer was General Eisenhower, then Chief of Staff of the Army. He was escorted by Lieutenant General Howard A. Craig who had replaced General Emmons as Department Commander, his party staying in the VIP quarters on the main post. He was interested in seeing everything for it was his first visit on the Chain. We had no facilities for a parade, but we had arranged a muster at Castle Theater in the Port area where he could address the troops. He then toured a number of barracks and mess halls in that area. No tour had been arranged, we just asked him what he would like to see and he would head out to get every day fare. I conducted the tour of the island for him.

As part of the entertainment program, Edith and I had a small dinner party in the Air Force area to be followed by a reception. The ladies had pitched in to help and everything went off nicely for General Eisenhower was an affable and interesting dinner guest. When we moved to the officers club, there was no receiving line for he just moved around greeting everyone with no formality.

We also had General Carl "Tooey" Spaatz who was to be the first Chief of Staff of the Air Force when it became a separate branch. General Spaatz and his party were on their way to the Orient and were not particularly interested in looking over the real estate, or installations. He took a perfunctory tour of the high spots, and then moved on. We did not entertain him at our Air Force Club.

That summer we had a group of volcanologists on the Chain, but they were out visiting particular volcanos. Mount Moffitt on Adak was classified as dormant, so it was not of as much interest as Sitkin thirty miles to the east. As one of the experts explained it, Sitkin had a granite dome which sealed off the hot molten rock below and that caused the melting snow to steam almost constantly. That was the type that very well could blow out the dome in an eruption.

We had an unexpected visitor in 1947 when operations were shut down during the night. The radar operator picked up an approaching aircraft from the west at about ten thousand feet in altitude. This target passed over the field and spiraled down to two thousand feet over Kulak Bay, still in the overcast. It then departed heading north through the pass between the islands. While we had a flight of P-38s on Adak, there was no purpose in a scramble as the cloud deck was solid above one thousand feet and went to above ten thousand. It was my view that the Soviet pilot was using "pressure pattern" flying to take advantage of the tail winds around a high pressure area, for their reconnaissance aircraft did not have the range to visit Adak and return from the Kuriles without refueling. Next morning I took a look at the weather maps and that was the case. The situation was quite rare, but the Soviet pilot knew how to take advantage of the weather.

I well remember my first earthquake on Adak shortly after arrival. I was sitting in my office when I heard a distant rumbling sound like a truck with hard rubber tires speeding down the highway. The rumble increased rapidly in intensity, then the building began to vibrate and shake, followed by a diminuendo, all in about ten seconds. They were frequent in the Aleutians so we came to ignore them.

Edith returned to the States on the October transport of 1947 and returned to San Antonio to stay until I was relieved. The Air Force had problems in finding a replacement for me; one prospect could not leave the States, another elected to retire. When Brigadier General Frederick von H. Kimble arrived in December, I was able to leave for San Antonio and I was the bearer of Christmas gifts in the form of a dozen frozen salmon for delivery to recipients at Tinker Field and Kelly Field, all former friends in Alaska. I was able to spend the Christmas holidays with my family in San Antonio for Clayton was a student at Trinity University.

The Alaskan Air Command

The ability to plan depends upon the ability to predict the future. With all the turmoil incident to the demobilization in Alaska, my command function was to keep operations going on a day-to-day basis, for no one knew what the future would bring. My recommendations to General Emmons were the basis for my actions, mainly establishing priorities for the use of our various stations. The 54th Troop Carrier Squadron was our lifeline, so all the stations were needed for the immediate future.

On my first tour of the bases I saw acres of trucks and motor vehicles left by the combat units which had returned to the States and none of the engines had been treated for open storage, so they were junk in my view. On Attu there were gullies full of the engineer equipment used in building the many airfields, obviously worn out from hard usage, only to be valued as scrap steel. The commander at Amchitka kept one mess hall as a special exhibit to show visitors the haste when the men were moving out to board the transport for home. Dirty dishes, breakfast food boxes and other signs of their breakfast were still on the tables undisturbed for several months when I saw them. There were acres of empty buildings on the Chain. About the only thing we salvaged were the diesel hot air stoves used to keep the quonsets warm. These were overhauled in a shop and available for exchange whenever a stove began acting up to avoid a fire. It was my view that we were not in the salvage business except when it was for our benefit.

Shemya, our Westernmost base just east of Attu was interest-

To General and Mrs. Lynch:

We shall always remember
the 'musicale' of a Sunday
afternoon in your Adak home.

Warmly,

Nutchuk and Ethel

[Atka - April '47]

ing. It was an ancient volcano with its top probably fifty feet above sea level at the most, two by four miles and relatively even on top. The airfield ran along the entire south side of the island, suitable for B-29s or larger craft. The housing was along the north side with the quonsets down in the gullies to escape the winds. There was only an open cove at the northwest corner, useable during the summer months for freight and supply boats. This was the point of departure for the bombing raids on the Kiril Islands, so they had Ground Control Approach equipment because they had more fog than Adak.

Two months after my arrival, the Eleventh Air Force became the Alaskan Air Command under the Joint Chiefs of Staff. The only change was that I was now responsible for the operation of Navy air units when in the Alaskan area, however, there were none at that time.

I had a new command airplane, a C-47 fitted out with a sleeping compartment and airline seats, to carry about twelve in comfort. On my first trip to Elmendorf Field I returned through Kodiak to pay my respects to Admiral Daubin who was the commander of the 17th Naval District. Daubin and his Chief of Staff, Captain Fitzgerald were submarine commanders, both Dutch Harbor and Kodiak being submarine bases. We got along well together and on one trip we stayed over to fish for silver salmon. They were the only species of salmon to strike on a lure. Should Admiral Daubin be busy when I arrived unannounced, Fitzgerald would hand me the commander's file of messages for he knew that I was entertained by the appended comments. On one occasion we knew that there was a strong front over Attu with very high winds and wondered how the station was making out. It is not polite to suggest that a commander may be having trouble so Admiral Daubin sent a command dispatch asking how the weather was on Attu. The answer came back in about five minutes, "Nothing flying today Attu but quonsets." I was on Attu about two weeks later and asked the Navy commander about that message. He told me that just as the query came in he looked out the window to see a quonset sitting at the end of the runway in takeoff position. No one was ever able to determine where it came from, or saw it in flight, but it must have been airborne for more that a quarter mile.

It took about one hundred thirty-five people to operate a flying field as a separate station making all the various reports and that was the strength at most of them, so there were no extras to work on salvage or surplus material. I wrote mission letters to each station to state priorities: first, the health, safety and welfare of the personnel. That included food and living conditions. Second came the maintenance and operation of the flying field. Third priority was to provide the necessary base facilities to support those priorities, and last was any work on surplus material or empty buildings. I felt certain that their hands would be full on the flying field work. My intention was to block any moves to use their personnel for other purposes.

Several weeks later I made a tour of the stations and asked the commander what he thought of the priorities, and they were satisfied that they had clear instructions. Then, I asked where his copy of the letter was, and as I had suspected, it was filed away. I told them that the letter was intended to be kept in the center drawer of his desk for it was his shield. Should some staff officer arrive on station and tell him to do something not appropriate under those priorities, he should hand the letter to that officer and tell him that "You must see General Lynch and get his approval first."

Another move to help the outlying stations was to change Umnak and Amchitka to satellites of Adak, that is all station type records would be handled at Adak. They would requisition on Adak for airplane parts rather than on the depot at Elmendorf, for instance. I had been through the supply at Adak and could readily see that it needed a house cleaning for there were obsolete parts which I could recognize. Colonel Leslie Mulzer who commanded the depot on the mainland cooperated by sending three civilian specialists to identify the parts in the warehouse, for that was the key to the whole program. They had cards of three colors, one represented "Keep in stock at Adak," another color said "Ship to depot," and the third color meant "Dump it!" They only spent a minute or so at each bin to identify the part and attach its proper card. Two teams followed the civilians, one team took the parts to a special area for packing to be shipped to the depot by our freight and supply boats. The second team took the parts to the loading dock and put them in a truck to be hauled to the dump when the truck became full. Nothing was done to the keep at Adak parts until later on, after the parts had been packed and shipped to the depot.

I saw the lights on in the Air Corps Supply one evening and stopped to take a look. Lieutenant George Conley, the Supply Officer and several of his helpers were re-binning the parts. When I arrived they knocked off and cut the cake that Conley had obtained at the mess hall and we had coffee and cake to wind up the evening. I learned that this had been going on for some time, purely on a voluntary basis and had begun when one of the men had dropped by to help when he saw what was going on, and it mushroomed. It intrigued me because it was a social affair rather than a workfare, an enjoyable evening. They were unaware that they were teaching each other the supply business because no one had had extensive supply training.

The standard Army cake was baked in a large square pan at least twenty-four inches per side and the finished cake was about two inches thick; a true sponge cake as I recall. It was served plain or with a glaze icing, cut into squares of two or more inches.

In the spring of 1946, General Emmons sent me to Washington to deliver the Troop Basis for the Alaskan Department, the Air Corps section being the larger part, and I was familiar with all the stations. I was his deputy to explain any details or justify the figures. We flew the outside route to Edmonton turning east at Prince Rupert to pass through a gap in the mountains. That was at night so I had an opportunity to test the sleeping compartment. We went on to an Air Corps base at Madison, Wisconsin, before stopping overnight. Holman had picked up a spare crew who were headed for the States. The conferences lasted several days including a weekend in Washington. My foster brother Sam Langley was then on duty in the Chief's Office, so I spent the weekend with him, including a visit to meet his fiancee who lived in Silver Spring, Jean Snyder.

We returned by way of Kelly Field so that I could spend a day with my family and brief Edith on living conditions so that she could decide what to bring with her. Tex Holman wanted to get some work done on the airplane and pick up some hard to get parts in Alaska. I also picked up a small amateur radio transmitter which Edith had in our goods in San Antonio for that was all I needed to get back on the amateur bands from Adak. There was a suitable receiver in my quarters, an all-wave type which covered the amateur bands. Edith and Clayton were living in San Antonio as he was a student at Trinity University. When Edith moved to Adak, Clayton moved in with the family of one of his friends, also a student at Trinity.

There were several changes in 1947, Lieutenant General Howard A. (Pinky) Craig took over the Alaskan Department from General Emmons, Major General Joseph H. (Hamp) Atkinson took over the Alaskan Air Command and decided to set up the headquarters at Elmendorf Field, or at least General Craig and Atkinson decided. There was to be an Aleutian Sector in the reorganized command and a Yukon Sector for the mainland stations. I remained on Adak and about half my staff moved to Elmendorf to help get the new organization going, including Lieutenant Ellis Craig. I now wore two hats for I was the Post Commander as well as the Aleutian Sector commander. Colonel Frank G. Jamison had been transferred from Shemya to Adak as my deputy, so he ran the station. I stayed away from station problems unless Jamison should raise a problem. He was experienced and I practiced General Larson's method of delegation. General Atkinson had much the same ideas as I had regarding the functions of the stations on the Chain.

I made another trip to Washington to deliver the personnel needs of the Alaskan Department, this time at the request of General Craig, since he was yet a newcomer. We did not tarry on that trip but went to Washington and back with no detours.

The summer of 1947 brought a group of scientists who were making a study of potential problems with radar and radio in the Arctic region. The design of the Distant Early Warning Network was under way and they were looking for problems due to snow and ice fog as well as the normal propagation. Since I had the best airplane in Alaska for such a tour, as well as having been all over the area, I was elected to be the tour guide and provide the transportation. It was an interesting and pleasant experience. Brigadier General Tom Rives of the Signal Corps was in charge and he had been a fellow student at the Air Corps Tactical School. The head scientist was Doctor Edwin Bowles who was scientific advisor to the Secretary of War. Doctor Stratton of the Radiation Laboratory, Massachusetts Institute of Technology was knowledgeable about radar. Doctor Tradup of the Bell Telephone Laboratories was naturally involved in communications on a wide scale. Doctor Beveridge was an expert on antennas and propagation; all were tops in their fields. They had done their homework before coming to Alaska and knew precisely what they sought. It was interesting to stand in the background and listen to them talk to the people in the field, say radar operators. One would never know that Stratton had designed their gear. They did know Doctor Beveridge because we had his antennas on the Chain. When the locals would point out his antenna, Doctor Beveridge would ask, "Does it work?"

We arrived at Nome when the St. Lawrence Eskimos were living on the beach with their Umiaks close by, with every family having their battery radio. The scientists were intrigued by the way the natives had adapted their skin boats to accommodate an outboard motor, as well as watching the natives carve trinkets from ivory with a semi-production line basis. The neophytes did the rough work and the elders finished the piece. The Eskimo used tooth powder to polish the ivory.

I had only one problem that might be classed as serious. I heard that a chaplain on Shemya had been fraternizing with enlisted men and selling them whiskey, so I turned it over to my inspector Major Frank Nims to find out what the true story was. Enlisted men had a regular ration of beer, but there was no source on the Chain for an officer or an enlisted man to buy whiskey. Whiskey had to be purchased on the mainland, and some officers had it through various ways. Nims turned up enough evidence to support a court martial for the chaplain. I knew from my own experience that the War Department was reluctant to court martial a chaplain unless the offense was blatant or too aggravated to ignore. Some chaplains got into trouble and the procedure was that the record would be sent to the Military Delegate, Bishop Spellman at that time. He would check with the denomination concerned and write us that the *Ecclesiastical Sanction* of the offender had been withdrawn. That meant that he was no longer authorized to perform the duties of a chaplain.

I decided to pass the problem on to Major General Charles Carpenter, the Air Force Chief of Chaplains, so wrote an appropriate letter of transmittal for the inspector's report. I was already due for a trip to the mainland, so I hand carried the report and General Atkinson agreed on my course, writing an appropriate endorsement. We sent it on to Chaplain Carpenter by air mail special delivery.

I had decided to send the chaplain back to the states for separation under a paragraph in Army Regulations dealing with surplus officers, and arranged through my channels to delay his arrival at Seattle for at least a week to provide time for Chaplain Carpenter to act. I heard later that this officer had been met when he stepped off the plane at Seattle, he was handed his orders for separation and his final pay to become a civilian within an hour of his arrival.

Sometime later I received a letter from the Adjutant General detailing the circumstances and questioning the use of the surplus regulation. I presume that someone had complained. I pondered the answer for some time and finally settled on this endorsement, "I did what I considered necessary under the circumstances." I was on Adak to make decisions and saw no reason to explain my decisions. When I next saw General Atkinson he said, "I wondered how you were going to get off that hook!" I never heard anything more about it.

I do not mean to pick on chaplains for we had one on Adak who was outstanding. Chaplain Cassius Ellis (Captain) had been on duty at Shemya when his unit moved out but had too few points to go home so was transferred to Adak to cover a shortage. He was junior to Chaplain Landerdahl (Major) and by agreement, he took over the Air Base Chapel in the Port area where the troops lived. It was not long before his Protestant services ran to a full house, including officers and their families who drove past the Post Chapel to get to the Air Base Chapel. Maybe they liked Mrs. Ellis's music for she was an accomplished musician, or he gave better sermons, I do not know. Chaplain Ellis and his wife were an asset to the command, well educated and a pleasant couple to talk to at various gatherings. As far as I was concerned, and Edith as well, their color made no difference. As you may have surmised, the chaplain who was railroaded to the states was a Negro trouble maker, but color had no bearing on the offense.

Ham Radio in Alaska

My usual routine while on Adak was to spend my mornings in my office and the afternoons visiting around the base. When the weather was good, which was not often, I would visit the remote areas where the combat units had been living before their return to the States in the spring of 1945. It was apparent that those buildings were worthless for many roofs were collapsed due to the snow load. Other days I would wander unannounced into some activity, introduce myself and ask to be shown around and to tell me what they were doing. I gained the impression that those visited were happy to see someone interested in what they were doing.

I met a number of amateur radio operators on such visits. One was in charge of the local broadcast station, WXLB. Others were in communication type activities such as the Alaskan Communications System operated by the Signal Corps. I confined my visits to the base proper which was known as U.S. Troops, APO 980. The Alaskan General Depot had units to operate the port and a heavy construction unit to repair the radio antenna systems should they be damaged by the storms.

General Emmons sent me to Washington to justify our personnel requirements in 1946. That was when I learned that the amateur radio bands had just been reopened. On my return trip I stopped at Kelly Field to visit my family and pick up a Meissner Signal Shifter which had not been packed away with my other Ham radio gear. This unit was a low powered transmitter with a variable control of the output frequency. Since I had a commercial type all wave receiver, all I needed to get back on the air when I arrived at Adak was a suitable antenna.

By the time I got back to Adak and began listening on the amateur bands, I could hear stations in Japan and Java obviously U.S. Troops using modified government equipment. That was no problem for the ingenious Ham. They could use their pre-war call with a suitable modifier. I heard Generals Curtis Lemay and Francis Griswold operating airborn mobile, but did not work them. I did hear Colonel Roland (Rosy) Akers, W4ZZZ, while he was on his way to Tokyo and was able to exchange greetings with him as he passed by south of Adak.

I applied to the FCC for an Alaskan call and received KL7DM. This was an asset for other stations would be looking for me when I sent the general invitation for a chat which was *CQ* in the Morse code. One evening in March 1947 I called CQ with my KL7DM and heard about a dozen stations calling me. I replied to the loudest signal, then the next loudest and so on until I had completed exchanges with everyone. I checked my *QST* and learned that I was in the middle of the DX contest sponsored by the American Radio Relay League. I moved my signal a bit and called CQ again with much the same result. Before the evening was over I had logged 60 stations and sent in my log so that the calls could be verified.

Adak is located almost on the International Dateline and the time difference to the west coast was four hours and six hours to Texas. I made a schedule with Fred Westervelt, W5MY, who was commanding a medical regiment at Fort Sam Houston. We used the 7 MHZ band with an all dark path, so it was four in the morning at Fort Sam Houston and ten in the evening on Adak. We made the exchanges as planned but did not make it a regular schedule. Stations to the south and west were easier to work because of the time difference. Hawaii and New Zealand were due south with good signals since it was an over water path. One evening I heard an amateur station in Dutch Harbor working a South African station at Cape Town. Since this was on the 14 MHZ band, I spent some time listening. The signals from South Africa were strong and steady while those from Dutch Harbor were considerably weaker and with a quavery sound. This told me that I was hearing the South African on direct path or halfway around the world while the signal of the Dutch Harbor station was travelling all around the world to reach me. Dutch Harbor was 500 miles to the east of Adak.

I was spending the night at Ladd Field, Fairbanks, in January 1946 when there was a beautiful display of the Northern Lights (Aurora Borealis). The entire northern sky from horizon to zenith was covered with flickering lights of changing colors of violet and rose in great streamers. The aurora is due to sunspot activity with magnetic storms which wipe out or disturb high frequency transmissions over long distances. We could not see the aurora from Adak but did have the blackouts during that winter.

We had a large number of civilian employees on Adak working for the Army and Navy. They had been under military control until 1947 when the Congress placed them under civilian jurisdiction. This presented some potential problems as the nearest magistrate was at Dutch Harbor and the uncertain Aleutian weather raised the possibility that he could not be present when needed to conform to the time tables.

On my next trip to the mainland we landed at Dutch Harbor to visit the U.S. Commissioner, Mr. Fletcher. His office was in his

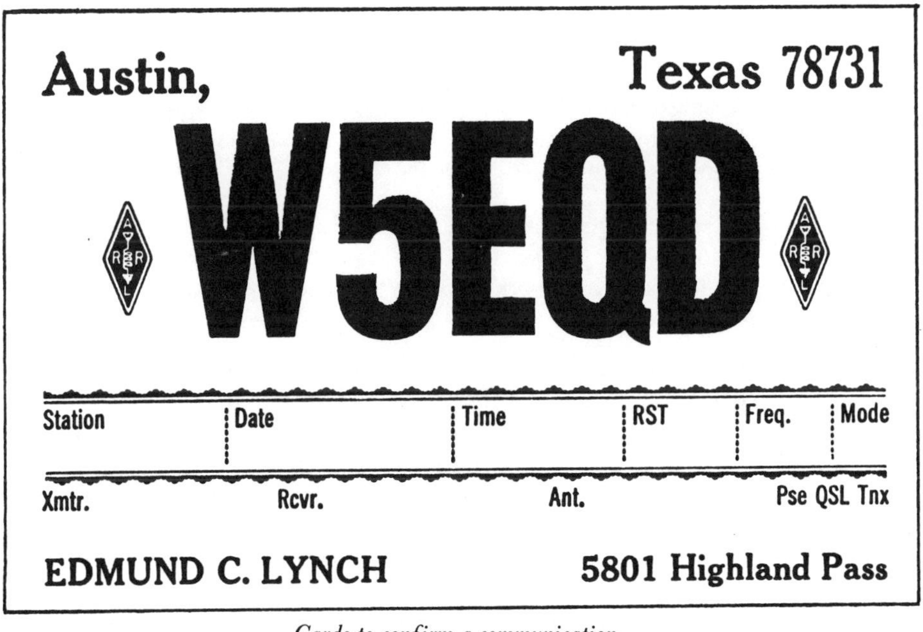

Cards to confirm a communication.

home and when I arrived I could see a ham radio antenna, so knew that he was an amateur radio operator. We spent thirty minutes viewing his equipment and in getting acquainted. It took about three minutes to solve our legal concerns for he told me just what to do. His call was EL7ET which had been issued before World War Two and that prefix had been changed to KL7 when I got my license.

Lettuce

Like Don Quixote I had a penchant for tilting at windmills and engaged in two duels both unsuccessful and relating to the transportation of perishable vegetables to Alaska by air. My first bout came shortly after my arrival in Alaska when I became aware of a fifty percent spoilage at Ladd and Elmendorf Fields. In simple terms, the transit time from the growing field to the dining table was too long when water transportation from Seattle was used. The only possible means for shortening that time was to use air transportation. As a matter of fact, the fresh vegetables in the Anchorage shops were brought in by commercial air, because I checked that point.

My error the first attempt was in not being tactful and in telling the Quartermaster how to run his business. In my paper I stated my view as follows:

> The service [Quartermaster] should be operated for the convenience of the troops it serves and not permitted to indulge in practices to make their work easier by placing an added burden on the using troops.

The point here being that the commissary would unload deteriorated perishables through a "forced issue," rather than screen out the edible vegetables for issue and disposing of the inedible at the commissary. That procedure made the commissary look good at the expense of the troops who were in effect, supposed to have consumed that issue, and I did not like it.

About one year later I was paying my courtesy call on the skipper of the transport which had just arrived from Seattle. I had looked over the side to see hundreds of lettuce heads floating in the water jettisoned from the refrigerated storeroom. The skipper told me that he estimated that about two thirds of the lettuce arrived in Alaska in too poor a shape to place on the table, for the storage and transport limit for lettuce was about six weeks.

I revived my proposal to ship only lettuce by air to sharpen the focus, that it would be shipped by air to Anchorage and then we would move it out the Chain by troop carrier. My theme was that buying only one third of the lettuce would provide savings that would offset the higher cost of air transportation. Since it would arrive in Anchorage only a few days after it had been harvested, it would be in top condition and any extra expense could be offset by feeding more appetizing lettuce, with more value for the troops. I sought to keep the argument on less, but better lettuce for the total cost.

I hoped that General Atkinson's indorsement would save this venture, but alas, that proposal was turned down. Again, there was no interest in looking after their customers.

Three years later, while on duty in the Defense Department, General Atkinson came by my office and said, "Eddie, do you remember that paper you wrote on supplying lettuce by air? We did get approval to use air shipment just before I left Alaska."

I had not been unduly irked when the proposal was turned down, for I understood the vast inertia of the procurement system and the many people involved. To me, it was sheer wastefulness and I could not get direct attention on the part of the Quartermaster General, for command action would have settled the matter in minutes.

As a paraphrase of what we were taught to say as cadets: Whenever possible the troops should be supplied with fresh lettuce.

The Advanced Management Program

Edith and I had a pleasant sojourn in San Antonio over the Christmas holidays. She had rented Sketch Henley's home across Greenlawn Drive from Gussie and Daddy Baker's home, for Sketch had gone to Kentucky for a month to visit her folks. Clayton moved in with us for the holidays and we had numerous parties to attend and one to return. Clayton was a drama student at Trinity University and I helped him build a wire recorder to use at rehearsals to permit the students to hear how they sounded and to make improvements.

Our leave was soon over and we headed for Kerrville to visit with my brother before starting the long trip to Washington. It rained off and on every day changing to snow at Richmond, Virginia. The bright spot of that trip was our visit with Mr. Sargeant at Narrow Lane Inn who was happy to see us again. We visited a few days with Catherine and Roland Birnn who were still living on Westover Drive, and Edith went house hunting in Arlington which was closer to the Pentagon.

My new assignment was assistant to Lieutenant General Edwin W. Rawlings, the Deputy Chief of Staff Comptroller, a new concept in the Air Force organization. Before I had time to settle down Brigadier General John Gerhart, Director of Statistical Services, and I were sent to the Thirteenth Advanced Management Program at the Harvard Business School, a fifteen week course designed to round out the specialized background of mature businessmen destined for promotion. Mr. Eugene Zuckert, the Assistant Secretary of the Air Force had been involved in that program from its beginning as he was then Assistant Dean. The Air Force had fourteen students in that class, the other twelve were colonels from various commands and activities. The class of one hundred thirty-eight also included nine from the Navy and three from the Army. Business students came from New Zealand, England, Denmark and Switzerland. We were housed together in Hamilton Hall. My roommate was Harry Chippendale, Superintendent of the refinery on Aruba of the Dutch West Indies. A neighbor was Carl Reistle, Jr., who was to become president of the Humble Company. Our subjects were in the areas of marketing, personnel, production and industrial relations.

The Harvard Business School had been using the case method since the Twenties and I was interested in that method for teaching. A typical case presents in story form a condensed history of a real company in an impartial, factual manner with selected financial data. The student's task was to analyze the situation presented in order to deduce his conclusions about the problem or problems involved. The function of the instructor was to guide or steer the class discussion toward bringing out the salient points. He would volunteer no information, and would answer questions with a simple yes or no in most instances. The instructors were sharp young men who knew how to be provocative when the going was dull.

While I enjoyed the problem solving in all of the cases, the one which interested me the most dealt with a former student of the business school who told his story in a series of letters to a former professor. His ideas for various improvements were met with indifference and eventually he had been fired. The entire discussion of that case centered on the point, just what responsibility the school had to acquaint the student with the realities of the business world. The first statement by one of the students was, "It seems to me that the business school failed to prepare this man for the real world." During the discussion my mind flashed back to the lectures which I had as a first classman before graduating, designed to orient us to the outer world and to keep us out of social or financial troubles.

Shortly after that case I spent a weekend with Marion and Duke (E. Y.) Blewett at their home in Durham. He was then Dean of the College of Liberal Arts, the University of New Hampshire. Edith and I had met them during the war in Washington and we had visited back and forth, and we still keep in touch through Christmas greetings. I told Duke about the case and the lectures which I had had as a cadet and we discussed the issue at great length. A year or so later, Duke wrote to say that he had instituted a comparable program. Senior professors held voluntary coffee seminars to discuss the future and where they stood at the moment.

Benefits from the course were intangible or subjective. I heard many perceptive comments on the cases, some points that I had not considered, and how differently some others viewed the material. It broadened one's outlook. One of our students was Wilfred Kirk, a branch manager for National City Bank. He was a sharp dresser and looked the part of a successful banker. He was elected our class treasurer to collect the entertainment assessment for the cocktail hour when we had guest speakers. His announcement was curt and to the point which irritated several, but I got along well with him and we had dinner in town several times in a small group. The night before the class was over there was a group of us sitting in the Hamilton lounge trying to pin down what had happened to us in the fifteen weeks, what we had gotten out of the course. When it came to Kirk's turn he said, "This course has taught me to have more consideration for the opinions of other people." That attitude alone, if taken to heart, would make him a better branch manager.

The Air Force had a reserve training facility at Bedford, Hanscom A.F.B., which provided all Air Force pilots in the Boston area with aircraft for proficiency flying, by appointment. The winter weather in Boston was little better than that at Adak, less the high winds, so I kept to the local area, maybe flying to Stewart Field at West Point for lunch on a weekend. As the weather improved in the spring, I could schedule an overnight flight to Bolling field and expect to return to Bedford Sunday afternoon. A staff car would take me to and from the airport by prearrangement. Needless to say we toured all the historic points around Boston and I saw my first Rope Walk at the Charleston Navy Yard, a relict of sailing ship days.

Manage or Command?

Stuart Symington, Secretary of the Air Force, had used the expression "Management Control Through Cost Control" in his testimony before a Committee in Congress and it went over big. That statement meant management through estimated costs at the working level. Cost control in this context was derived by using actual historic cost data which had been adjusted for future changes, inflation would be an example. The resulting cost information was used as a yardstick or standard for measuring a manufacturing activity such as making a widget. Its accuracy depended upon the ability to estimate the modifying factors.

When I arrived as General Rawling's assistant, he had a group working to make Mr. Symington's statement into a practical procedure. We had no difficulty in accumulating all the historic costs associated with a bombardment group and its base support for it was a well defined package. The problem was that the diversity of Air Force activities was such that no meaningful force-wide modifiers could be developed for future costs at the Air Force level, such as the civilian airlines use for fluctuating fuel costs today. That project died a natural death when Mr. Finletter became Secretary of the Air Force.

The Air Force was unique in having a Deputy Chief of Staff Comptroller similar to those found in large business firms, General Rawlings having graduated from the Harvard Business School. The primary responsibility of the comptroller was to supervise the preparation of the annual budget and then operating under the appropriation.

With this new concept there was considerable education going on. Gerhart and I had been sent to the Advanced Management Program with twelve colonels from various Air Force activities. Senior officers in Headquarters were given a short course at George Washington University. The Technical School at Lowry Air Force Base began training officers and enlisted men for the work at the base level. I gave the graduation talk to the first class at Lowry Field in 1948. As a result of this emphasis, the term management became quite popular, for it seemed businesslike and denoted efficiency. I had no difficulty in using the term for fiscal matters, but did not consider it equivalent to our military terms of command and leadership. I thought it was a euphemism.

The best distinction between command and leadership that I have read was that of Robert Dubin in his book *The World of Work*. He said that there are two functions in command; the first was the giving of orders or issuing instructions for work to be done; and then the followup to see that the work was done properly. Since the work to be done dictated the instructions, the personality of the commander was not a significant factor. Dubin identified two functions in leadership; first that of building and maintaining morale, and secondly, accommodating the organization to change. Leadership did depend upon the personality and social skills of the leader. I had been using the *Principles of Leadership* by Ordway Tead which came out in the Twenties and applied psychology to leadership personality factors. Tead was using the same concept of leadership as Dubin.

It was my view that fiscal control and activity (operational) control were two different things, primarily because the ends were different calling for different means. The first effort toward management control in the Air Corps was in 1939 when Byron E. (Hungry) Gates was Executive Officer and searching for a method to keep General Arnold informed about various projects under way, such as the expansion of the tactical units. Gates called in Professor Ed Learned of the Harvard Business School as a consultant. He, in turn, brought in several bright young MBA graduates of the school, including Robert McNamara who would become Secretary of Defense after World War Two. The efforts of that group created the Office of Management and Statistical Control. This was superposed on the Army's system for gathering information and had no input from the field, and the MBAs had no military experience. As a consequence, that office was generally known as, "Hungry Gates and his shoe clerks." As a sidelight showing the persistence of ideas, Mr. McNamara came up with a cousin of Mr. Symington's idea some thirty years later, but the title was now "Cost Benefit Analysis," and not well received. In 1948 the title was "Statistical Services." While there had been sentiment to do away with it after the war, it did serve a useful purpose in personnel accounting which was taken over from the Adjutant General when the Air Force separated.

An interesting and different approach along these lines was described to me by my neighbor on Westover Drive in 1941. Harland (Spike) Hennessy had been a systems analyst with IBM on the west coast before he came on duty in the Navy Department. On one assignment, the owner of a small brewery in San Francisco wanted to know, "How well am I doing?" Spike studied the operation and concluded that the significant indicator was the number of empty longnecks returned for refill, so set up a tally using punch cards. The trend line moving upwards would be reassuring to the owner and indicate that things were going well. Should the trend line have a downward slope, that would indicate that trouble was brewing (no pun intended) and that it was up to the owner to begin asking questions to determine the *Why?* Someone has to take action after reading the figures.

In the Third Air Force we had monthly strength reports that showed some categories of enlisted men were surplus and other categories in which there were shortages. Month after month the surpluses would increase and the shortages would increase. General Larson had noticed this trend and asked for authority to retrain the surplus to alleviate the shortages, but his request was denied. In theory the Office of Management and Statistical Control was supposed to correct such situations. They had created a data base but no one was reading the numbers.

Washington Once More

Housing was in short supply in postwar Washington, but Edith was able to lease a house in Arlington off Lee Highway in the Cherrydale section. During that year's lease, she kept looking around for a permanent home. The new developments to the west in Fairfax County were too far out for her taste. By the end of the year she had found a new house: 6298 15th Road North in Arlington near Seven Corners which was in Falls Church. It was a dead end area with about eight homes with woods and a small stream at the end of the street. It was under Veteran's Priority so we used Clayton's entitlement to make the purchase.

Edith had selected the place because she could count about a dozen couples who lived within a mile or so, and all old friends. Kitts and Jack Davies from our Panama days, my classmate Nathalie and Conny Conway, the Beatties from Key Field and Adak, Elizabeth and Fred Westervelt from Fort Leavenworth. The Davies were old friends of Swede Larson and he always stopped by when he was in town. Our social activity centered around the Falls Church area rather than downtown Washington, although we were members of the Army and Navy Town Club.

The house was a two story brick house with three bedrooms and one bath. The full basement was divided so that one side could be made into a separate apartment except that there was no bath. Our next door neighbor on the west side had a toilet installed and I knew the cost, but when I asked the plumber for a bid, he quoted a much higher price. When I talked to Reuben Johnson of Westover Drive about doing the work, he said that he did not have a license to work in Arlington County, and that my high bid was due to the fact that the plumber did not want to do the job. Reuben then said, "Why don't you do it yourself? I can furnish the material." So, I installed the bathroom, the most difficult part was cutting through the basement floor.

The following Christmas we had a party and Gin and Reuben were among the guests, so I told him to inspect my plumbing job because I could say that it had been "inspected," by someone unidentified. After Reuben took a look he said, "If an inspector sees that he will want to know who did your work, because they do not run pipes straight up and down anymore!" The house was inspected after we had moved in and I trailed the party to the basement. The vertical stack was dead ahead as we walked down the stairs. The inspector turned to the plumber behind him and said, "You almost got that straight!" I knew that Reuben was up to date on the state of plumbing, a realist.

The small apartment was completed and provided many happy hours of evening and weekend work. I had my amateur radio gear in that apartment, so it took about two years to complete the entire plan. We had a sofa bed for Clayton to use when he came home for a visit.

Clayton was then working at Abingdon, Virginia, with Robert Porterhouse and the Barter Theater of Virginia. That was a repertory company which spent the summer playing in their theater in Abingdon and then toured various cities in Virginia during the winter. Clayton was doing the electrical and sound work with the company, sometimes filling in on bit parts. When the company played in the high school auditorium in Arlington, we had the troupe in for a party with our local friends who all knew Clayton.

One of the troupe was from Winchester, Virginia, and brought a bushel of peaches from his family orchard. They were dead ripe and had to be processed promptly for freezing. I did the special syrup to prevent the color from turning, and the blanching to remove the skins, while the leading lady sliced them into the freezing containers, turning out very well despite the hustle and bustle.

Edith and I had left Rusty with the Scattergoods when we moved to Tampa and he had lived with them until they had orders to move from Washington to Germany for duty. We had stayed away from the Scattergoods after we came to Washington to avoid upsetting Rusty. When we heard of the change in station, Edith got in touch and they were happy to return Rusty to us. When we arrived to take him back, he recognized us promptly though it had been four years since he had seen us. He settled down in our large back yard with a chain link fence, but we let him roam at times in the nearby woods. His favorite spot was in the center of the living room floor. Lucy and Jack Price from Langley Field days lived in the neighborhood and when they came by he recognized them as well. Rusty lived out thirteen years, but the last year he developed a weak heart and took digitalis. On a cold winter night with ice and snow on the ground, he finally was unable to get up on his feet to walk and the veterinarian at Fort Myers told us that he had reached the end of the road.

Lieutenant Colonel Joseph Kusner was our neighbor on the east side, a most interesting person. Before the war he had been professor of mathematics and astronomy at the University of Florida, Gainesville, having the doctor of philosophy degree. During the war he taught air navigation for the Air Force. The war over he had accepted the presidency of Farragut College, a new college being established in a surplus navy training facility in Idaho. He had assembled a faculty and proposed to operate the college in a businesslike way with a budget or spending plan to live within their resources. It was clear to him that he was on a collision course with the faculty on this issue, they did not like it. In the nick of time he received an offer from the Munitions Board to work on the design of a mathematical model, he accepted and was off the hook.

A model, in this context, is a set of mathematical equations designed to replicate the way certain variables behave in the activity to be modeled. The equations may represent a curved relationship in that variation, or a linear variation. This involves the use of the calculus, a study of continuously changing quantities. The model is an approximation of the real thing, and the idea is to use limited numbers of significant variables to simplify the computer's calculations. For instance, there are several models of the National Economy to aide in economic forecasting each providing its approximation to be applied with informed judgement to the forecast. Kusner wanted to set up several models and evaluate them through trial and error, an approach referred to as successive approximations by mathematicians, but the higherups sought perfection the first time around. Joe spent most of his time on organization studies while we were neighbors.

Joe and I rode to work together almost every morning so that Edith could have the car, and this was an opportunity for many interesting conversations. When the *new math* became the rage I commented one morning that I would have to go back to school, and Joe said, "What do you mean, there is nothing new. They have just changed the names we know!" We did not always return home together because of our schedules. When I was late I rode the bus out

Wilson Boulevard to a stop about three blocks from the house.

Shortly after I returned from Alaska I was invited to a talk show on the Dumont Television Network station, the subject being the future of air transportation. The moderator was Frank Blair just getting started in the TV business, the other participant was from a civilian airline. My contribution was the way the airplane was used by the Eskimo in getting around and the story of the bush pilots who had opened up Alaska for air transportation. I also did a session of the Georgetown University Forum, much the same but for radio broadcast. The tapes were circulated among a number of stations in that area. Frank Blair moved to WNBW-TV in 1951, and then moved on to The Today Show. Clayton got a job with WNBW-TV, so Frank Blair visited with him several times before we moved on to Austin.

Clayton stayed with us in his basement apartment until he became settled and looked around for an apartment, finding a suitable one in Georgetown. I helped him redecorate and we furnished some things to get him started. While he was working with the Barter Theater he was home over the Christmas season for it was a period between the fall and spring tours. For several years he had a temporary job with the Falls Church post office for Christmas mail, so was well acquainted with our neighborhood.

I attended the state funeral for General of the Armies John J. Pershing in the ampitheater at Arlington Cemetery in July 1948, a hot and humid day. Pershing's most significant decision had been to keep intact the American Expeditionary Force that went to France in World War One. Our Allies wanted to use our troops as fillers in their existing forces, but *Black Jack* was adamant. General Pershing got his start fighting the Sioux Indians on the frontier after he graduated from West Point in 1886. He was in on the dawn of the Air Force because the First Aero Squadron conducted reconaissance for the Punitive Expedition he led into Mexico in 1916.

Upon retirement the Air Force would send our household goods to suit our choice which was to San Antonio, where it remained in storage for three years. When we left Washington, the real estate market was depressed, so it took months before we were able to sell our house in Arlington.

Potomac Valley Radio Club

After my return from the Harvard Business School in the late spring of 1948, Elizabeth and Fred Westervelt took Edith and me to a Saturday luncheon meeting of the Potomac Valley Radio Club held in a Falls Church restaurant. We met a number of congenial souls and I joined the club.

This club had been organized a year before for the specific purpose of competing in amateur radio contests such as the one I had stumbled upon in March 1947 while operating from my quarters on Adak. In such contests the basic points are earned when there is a two-way exchange of specified information with another amateur radio station either in a foreign country or within the United States. Contests with foreign stations are known as distant or DX contests. The base score of points may be increased by a multiplier, somewhat like a handicap when applied to the power utilized.

The members were all experienced CW (Morse code) operators and worked in government agencies in the Washington area such as the National Bureau of Standards, the Federal Communications Commission and the military services. Victor Clark, W4KFC, was head of the Coast Guard Radio and Radar Laboratory. He had accumulated over 200,000 points in the Sweepstakes Contest the previous fall, the top score for a single operator. I had been recruited because Fred Westervelt knew that I was a long-time CW operator. It did not take me long to realize that I was a neophyte in that group and had much to learn.

The Frankford Radio Club in Philadelphia was also a contest minded club and had an accumulated score for the club of over one million points in the sweepstakes. The goal of the P.V.R.C. was to beat Frankford by a comfortable margin. Being engineer types, the effort was well organized and planned for a year ahead. Committees were set up to help members get their gear in top shape. Vic Clark passed on his shortcuts for keeping records, to speed up that part of the contest. Each meeting ended with members pledging a contribution and that was summed to determine where we stood and the need to recruit additional help. My pledge was 50,000 points and I barely made it, and the club did win with over two million points.

The sequel to that contest was most interesting. There are some who argue that competition has destructive elements, but not so here. The Frankford Club was invited to a dinner in Washington to discuss the contest and to share impressions on contesting. While equipment does have a bearing, the basics for winning are skill, perseverance and hard work. The two clubs worked together to improve the rules and details for the various contests for several years that I know of.

At the luncheon meeting we met Amanda and John Boland. He was a retired captain in the U.S. Navy having graduated from Annapolis in 1936. They had a 75-year-old home in Falls Church not far from our home in Arlington. Elizabeth and Fred Westervelt lived in Arlington and were also within a mile or so from our home. We were close friends during my tour of duty in Washington and could be found together in any amateur radio activity. Both Fred and Jack had obtained their first Ham license when they were fourteen years of age and the three of us were in agreement that the fraternity needed more young blood to stay vigorous.

The Federal Communications Commission had proposed a Novice Class of amateur radio license, good for one year and with a code requirement of five words per minute. The concept was that a learner could get on the air and build up his code speed by communicating with other novice operators. That would enable the novice to upgrade to general class which called for a code speed of thirteen words per minute. I knew from my own experience in teaching the Morse code at Randolph Field that this idea made sense, and we all agreed on that point. The American Radio Relay League opposed the FCC proposal, so we got busy. The three of us knew many amateurs around the country who were influential, so we wrote them to spread the word in support by writing the FCC. The League finally changed their stance and the novice license became reality. It justified our faith because a few novices achieved a code speed of twenty words per minute during their first year.

During the Thirties, the Army Signal Corps had an affiliate of Ham radio operators called the Army Amateur Radio Service which drilled on the proper method of handling military messages. This idea was revived after the war as the Military Affiliate Radio Service (MARS). When I moved to Mrs. Rosenberg's office in

1950, I became a member of the Department of Defense Committee on National Guard and Reserve Affairs. Mrs. Rosenberg authorized me to attend the American Radio Relay League National Convention and make a speech in support of the MARS program. That convention was at Seattle (1951).

The 1952 National Convention was held in Houston, Texas, and again I put in a good word for MARS, stressing its value in National Defense as well as its benefit as a hobby. I said:

> It is my view that the active support of an interesting hobby contributes a great deal to an individual's well-being because it provides a means of relaxation and stimulates an interest to improve one's proficiency in a line outside of the work at which you earn a living. Also, I value the friendships which I have made outside the military through Ham radio. I have been an active supporter of all measures to keep amateur radio strong and vigorous.

Once a member of the P.V.R.C., always a member for the club kept track of members who had moved away from the Washington, D.C., area. The first weekend in June of each year had been dedicated to an *On the Air Reunion* where members compete to see how many other members they can communicate with. For the 1987 reunion there were 510 names on the list. Two of the charter members became president of the American Radio Relay League, Victor C. Clark and Robert Dennison.

Manpower and Organization

I became Director for Manpower and Organization under the Deputy Chief of Staff for Operations early in 1949, the basis for my promotion to Major General. This was a new office created by merging the former Manpower Group and the Organization Branch. The Deputy Chief of Staff for Operations was Lieutenant General Idwal Edwards.

My first problem before I had an opportunity to settle down

was one of organization. We had a liaison officer from my staff who regularly attended the hearings of the Military Affairs Committee, Mr. Carl Vinson of Georgia being the Chairman. He returned to my office to tell me that Mr. Vinson was vexed and impatient because the Air Force had not sent him the language for their organizational bill which he had requested more than a year before. That was news to me and I pulled the file to learn the background. The files showed that two boards of officers had studied the matter and made recommendations, but there was no evidence of any action having been taken by General Vandenberg. I suggested to General Edwards that General Vandenberg telephone Mr. Vinson to placate him on the delay.

What I saw in the file puzzled me for there was no evidence that the normal procedure had been followed, the report of the first board had been filed away and a second Board of Officers convened to write a second report little different than the first one. I then learned that both boards had recommended the Army title, Chief of Staff, United States Air Force, while General Vandenberg preferred the title the Navy used, Chief of Air Operations. Mr. Vinson preferred the Army style of title because he considered that Chief of Air Operations clouded the issue of civilian control at the top through the Secretary of the Air Force, and Mr. Vinson was adamant on that point. The proper procedure would have been for Vandenberg to have used his preference in the language and sent it to Mr. Vinson for the hearing and to testify in support of that language so that he would be on record. In the final writeup of the bill, Mr. Vinson would have the language he wanted in any case for he had the final say. For some reason unknown to me, General Vandenberg had done nothing for more than a year.

At any rate, General Vandenberg did not placate Mr. Vinson and about two weeks later I had a copy of Mr. Vinson's bill on my desk when I arrived one morning. The first page had Chief of Air Staff as I expected, but as I read on I was amused for he had incorporated any number of changes which he knew would be very distasteful to the Air Force, clearly his device to punish General Vandenberg in a polite way for dragging his feet.

I sat through the hearings in a backup role. General Vandenberg did make his speech in support of Chief of Air Operations. On that point, Mr. Vinson asked, "General, you are the top dog in the Air Force, are you not?" To which Vandenberg replied, "Yes." Mr.

Vinson then returned with, "Now general, do you mean to tell me that when you tell someone to jump, they don't jump? I don't see what the fuss is all about!" That settled the matter as far as Mr. Vinson was concerned, from then on he blandly substituted the language from the reports after detailed testimony had been provided on each point that he had introduced as a red herring. The Air Force had their bill after a tedious hearing which had lasted a week or more. Had General Vandenberg written in his preference to the Board's report, there would have been the same interchange with Mr. Vinson, but then Mr. Vinson would have asked whether he was satisfied with the rest of the bill and that would have ended the hearing in about an hour, for Mr. Vinson knew what was in that report.

Other hearings were in the offing on the B-36 Bomber. It was anticipated that the Navy might testify to the effect that more aircraft carriers could do a better job for the money. I was placed in charge of a small research group to develop a briefing book on the capabilities and limitations of a typical carrier task force, a search through various publications and organizing that material for easy access. It was clear that the aircraft carrier was a splendid and impressive sight steaming along escorted by cruisers and destroyers. However, a large portion of the fighters aboard were dedicated to the protection of the carrier, which was a veritable floating fire bomb with all its fuel and ammunition. Midway was a battle of aircraft carriers and the heyday of such operations. We looked at the total tonnage of ships sunk, commercial and military during World War Two, by various means and the airplane was the least effective weapon, whether land based or carrier based, despite the fact that Japanese Zeros with torpedoes had sunk two British battleships off the China coast. The submarine mine was the most lethal of all weapons, with the submarine next (some submarines laid mines).

In the course of our study we sent a young officer to interview a mine specialist in the Navy Department for sources about the effectiveness of submarine mines. He was in a small out of the way office and was happy to see someone interested in his specialty, and incidentally, I became aware of the social hierarchy in the Navy, that it was inversely related to the lethal effectiveness of their weapon. Those who worked with submarine mines were at the very bottom and the submariners were next, both because they used sneaky weapons quite good for sinking ships, often with little or no warning before the explosion. Battle carriers and battleships were at the top of the social structure, the most desireable assignments. Destroyers and cruisers were intermediate, the larger the ship the greater the prestige. The aggregate figures in our study obscured the reality of particular combat situations during World War Two. One of my Austin friends was in The Royal Navy and had eight destroyers sunk under him in the Mediterranean when the British were fighting Rommel in North Africa, all destroyers were sunk by German land based aircraft flying out of fields in Italy.

That briefing book was never used. General Curtis Lemay was the first witness to testify at the hearing on the B-36. General Lemay had an inscrutable face, chewed a cigar rather than smoking it, the stub sticking out the corner of his mouth. The first question was long and rambling, but it boiled down to, "General, what do you think of the B-36?" General Lemay leisurely removed the cigar stub from his mouth and said, "I'll be flying in the lead airplane," and waited patiently for the next question. For all practical purposes the hearings were over for his seven words could not be challenged.

During the demobilization process the Manpower Group had been concerned with adjusting personnel among peacetime activities, to balance over and under staffing. Manpower Boards had visited various bases to make surveys while I was in Alaska. Colonel Ralph Stearley, the base commander at Elmendorf Field had told me about such boards, and I had gathered that they were only a partial success. With the change in organization the emphasis had shifted to Manpower Requirements in connection with the annual budget reviews, the Deputy Chief of Staff for Operations being responsible for personnel in units, while the Deputy for Personnel was concerned with personnel as individuals. In essence, a budget review is comparative since one knew the past year's actual experience and any changes should be related to some change in condition, or to provide for an added function.

We had an interesting small scale experience after I took over the Directorate. The former Manpower Group had two industrial engineers on its staff for utilization work, but we had no mandate to do a survey on the civilian personnel in Air Force Headquarters. At every budget period there would be pressure to hold down civilian employment in Air Force Headquarters and, at the same time requests for more people. When we received such a request, I would call on the Section Chief with one of our industrial engineers and say that I was loaning the engineer to him to help him make-do with the number of people he then had, or to justify his request for more people, if need be. The engineer was to remain on our payroll and there would be no reports to me because he would be working for the Section Chief to help him out. In a number of cases there was no need for additional people. When there was, we would have data to back it up.

This procedure generated an interesting aspect. Industrial engineers were trained to first make an inventory of what was going on at the time they arrived on the scene, analyze the situation, design improvements, put the improvements to work, and then report on the way the improvements worked. One of the analysts complained to me that he could not write any details in an orderly manner because, when he made a suggestion for improvement, the employees would put it to use right away, the improvements were piecemeal. I pointed out that he was really training the workers to examine their work critically. Ordinarily the easy way is the better way. The engineers were teaching work simplification and improved flow. In one case, each worker would make a trip to the file to obtain information needed to process a paper. The analyst made up a worksheet so that the first one of the group to consult the file would extract information for the others in that section. The word soon spread that our engineers were helpful and they spent their time teaching supervisors and employees how to use work simplification and analyze flow.

Colonel J. B. Stowe, a Branch Chief, had been a flying cadet with me at Brooks Field in 1923. I remembered him because I had been riding in the rear cockpit when he made a bad landing at Smithville, Texas, on our cross country flight. He had flown under the railroad bridge over the Colorado River, too. Weldon Ellis, my deputy had lunch with him one day and said that Stowe had been taking pills for his stomach. That sounded like stress to me so I had lunch with Stowe to catch up on what he had been doing over the years. It was apparent to me that he preferred doing things out in the field rather than to work on papers in the Pentagon. Jack McCormick was Deputy Chief of Staff for Personnel, so I told him about Stowe and said that I would release him should a good base commander's job turn up. When Albrook Field in Panama became vacant, I asked Stowe if he would like it and off he went. Six months later he was back for a base commanders conference and he had his old sparkle back and was no longer taking pills.

The Department of Defense

My three years with the Department of Defense were devoted to managing the budget for military and civilian personnel. The tour began with devising an organization for the Office of the Assistant Secretary of Defense for Manpower and Personnel occupied by Mrs. Anna M. Rosenberg, the first secretary. Then I was assigned to that organization as Director of Manpower Requirements.

As Director of Manpower and Organization for the Air Force, I had gone through the budget process which began in the fall of 1949 when President Truman told the Secretary of Defense his limiting figure. Mr. Lovett then apportioned that total among the Army, Navy and Air Force. Little policy guidance was provided, so there was much cut and try with numerous meetings before a program was developed to fit the money cost. The end result was a political solution, certainly not rational. The last minute adjustments in the Department of Defense Budget were made in the dollars, sometimes arbitrary, without going back to check on the effect on the operating plan involved.

I knew that Mrs. Rosenberg had been appointed Assistant Secretary of Defense for Manpower and Personnel in March 1950, so was not surprised when two young men came calling to find out what we were doing in the Air Force. They were scouts from her Industrial Relations firm in New York City and asked numerous questions about our operations. I was free in my answers on technical points. A few days later, Mr. Eugene Zuckert, the Assistant Secretary of the Air Force called me to his office and said that Mrs. Rosenberg had selected me to help in the organization of her office on a temporary basis and could I help out. I told Mr. Zuckert that I could see no obstacle for I had a good deputy, Brigadier General Aubrey Moor, and he could keep things going. There were no orders issued, I would stop by my office from time to time and visit with Moore to keep in touch while he ran the show.

Mr. Zuckert took me to Mrs. Rosenberg's office to introduce me and I was off on a new assignment as it turned out. Admiral Sherman had provided her with Colonel McGlashan of the Marine Corps who had been working in the Navy Bureau of Personnel. He was a very capable officer and well versed in what went on at the grassroots level. We worked very well together, for we had not been in her office more than an hour or so when she handed us a request for an increase in personnel from the Army. I handed a copy to McGlashan and took one myself and suggested that we go our separate ways to study the matter and then get back together to determine what we should advise Mrs. Rosenberg. It was interesting that we had each come to the conclusion that the Army already had the people on board and this was to validate an overstrength, not to procure more. It was a guess on our part because of what was *not* said in the paper, reading between the lines, and we so informed Mrs. Rosenberg who clearly understood the point. We then suggested a question to smoke out that supposition and told her how we thought that the conversation would go, and how to behave in that environment, new to her. Mrs. Rosenberg dominated that conference and from then on would ask our opinion on any unusual matter that came up. I think that McGlashan and I developed a protective instinct at that first meeting to keep her out of trouble. But Mrs. Rosenberg had the knack to grasp the central issue very quickly.

McGlashan and I had been through the last budget cycle and knew that there was room for improvement from the service point of view. We spent hours kicking the ball around. It was clear that the major asset with Mrs. Rosenberg on the scene was that she would balance the dollar emphasis of the Comptroller by representing the operating plans of the services at the department level in the final adjustments. That was a decided plus. But that meant that we had to resolve the internal relationships between Mrs. Rosenberg and the Comptroller as the first step.

Mr. Cooper was the analyst who dealt with personnel programs in the Department of Defense Comptroller's Office and our purpose was to convince him that his work would be easier and it would be helpful to the services if better policy guidance was issued by the Department of Defense and that Mrs. Rosenberg's office could assist in developing such guidance. Furthermore, joint reviews would not increase the number of meetings and feedback on the policy guidance would be helpful to everyone involved. As an analyst, Cooper worked with ratios based on dollars, while the services worked with jobs and people which, of course, cost money. We went back over the past budget to show him examples of better policy guidance which would have reduced many arguments based on differences in viewpoint. With a general agreement that we could develop better guidance, we moved on to the internal procedure or relationships between the Assistant Secretary for Manpower and Personnel and the Assistant Secretary of Defense (Comptroller) in the formulation of the budget, specifically the development and evaluation of the requirements for military personnel and direct-hire civilian employees. This procedure was written up and the Secretary of Defense, Mr. Lovett approved it. This was the bottoms up approach worked up by the people who would have to do it.

After that, the Secretary of Defense announced this relationship to the Secretaries of the Army, Navy and Air Force, and that Mrs. Rosenberg would be concerned with the operating programs of the services. This was a statement of principle with no procedural details. As all the Secretaries agreed, we were then ready to move ahead on details. Our premise was that other operating details would follow the trend set for the budget, the critical line.

The final organization had two major sections, Manpower Requirements and Manpower Utilization. I was then transferred to the Department of Defense to become Director of Manpower Requirements. I became involved in manpower procurement through Selective Service and voluntary enlistment, and most anything else relating to the military operating plans. Utilization was mainly concerned with the civilian personnel programs of the services. By this time McGlashan had served his time in Washington and had been replaced with Colonel Dan Godbold, another Marine and equal to McGlashan in every way. He became my deputy and we continued to advise Mrs. Rosenberg as needed. For the procurement side, I got in touch with Colonel Charles Collier who was then an administrator at a Veteran's facility in Arizona and he was happy to come back on active duty to work with General Hershey and me. I also acquired Mr. Bonus from the Army's Adjutant General's Department. He had a doctoral degree in statistics and I had known him since 1940. My secretary moved over from the Air Force to join me.

I construed my role in the Defense Department to be helpful to the services. Mr. Truman would present the Department's Budget to Congress in his annual message in January and then we would have hearings before the Apropriations Committee chaired by Mr. George Mahon of Lubbock, Texas. I had made my first presentation for the Air Force in 1950. The next year, as a Department of Defense representative, I would lead off with a summary stating the Department's view; then introducing each service representative to justify their segment of the budget. I held rehearsals beforehand to insure that we put our best foot forward and checked the effectiveness of their charts. Then, I sat through all the hearings ready to move in should any difficulty develop. Since I had reviewed their programs, I was familiar with detail, even the Navy and Marine Corps part. My unit had all three services represented, the Navy providing a captain in rank while the Army and Air Force officers were colonels. My position was to be rotated among the services.

Another assignment at the Department of Defense level was to the Committee for National Guard and Reserve Affairs. At one meeting the Air Force representative said that they were increasing their ROTC program to produce more second lieutenants. I did some mental calculations and told them that they would be in trouble with Mr. Vinson's policy for they would be unlikely to have officer positions for the increase when they graduated. Mr. Vinson was adamant that any young man who had been draft deferred on the basis of a National Guard or reserve program would be called to active duty for one year as long as the draft law was in effect. My warning was pooh-poohed. When that increase came out of the ROTC program in 1956 the Air Force had to call the graduates to active duty as enlisted men because there were no officer vacancies available for them, and Mr. Vinson had the last word.

Chaplain Hewlett, my staff chaplain at Key Field was an excellent chaplain by all standards in my judgement for he spent most of his time out on the flight line or mingling with the troops much like my friend Chaplain Carpenter at Langley Field who organized a baseball team and wrestling matches for the enlisted men. The war over he had taken an assignment as pastor for a Southern Baptist congregation in rural Missouri. He had written me in Alaska to report on his status and I could read between the lines that he was frustrated by the narrow concerns exemplified by card playing and similar social activity. I just sent his letter on to Major General Charles I. Carpenter who was Chief of Air Force Chaplains. In my note I said that, should he need a chaplain I could recommend Hewlett highly, and further that I thought his military experience had so enlarged his vision that he would be more comfortable back in the service if needed.

As I entered my office one day I was greeted by laughter for the girls were being entertained by Chaplain Hewlett reenacting his reception by the base commander when he reported on active duty as Chaplain for Warren Air Force Base at Cheyenne, Wyoming. The base commander's theme for about twenty minutes was to the effect that his prior chaplains had been a pain in the neck for him. Needless to say, Hewlett changed his attitude. He had been reassigned to Germany for duty and had stopped by on his way to visit Chaplain Carpenter and me.

The Administration changed when General Eisenhower became president and John Hannah, president of Michigan State University took over from Mrs. Rosenberg. I was scheduled for retirement on February 28, 1953 and that ceremony at Bolling Field went off as scheduled. However, I was called back to active duty for the budget sessions before the Appropriations Committee were coming up and I was needed. That task ended by July and I was able to leave for Austin, Texas.

Anna M. Rosenberg

Anna M. Rosenberg, the first Assistant Secretary of Defense for Manpower and Personnel was an Industrial Relations Specialist who had come up through the school of hard knocks and had her own firm, Anna M. Rosenberg Associates. She had cut her teeth working with the employees of her husband's clothing factory in New York City and the benefits of her activities had spread, so her personal business grew. During World War Two she was head of the New York State War Manpower Commission, also having risen through the ranks from New York City. Politically, she was a dedicated Democrat and had risen to National Democratic Committee Woman, well acquainted with the Democratic leaders around Washington in the House and Senate.

Early on she told me that the only reason that she had accepted the appointment was that Mr. Truman had personally urged that she do so. She also said that she had come to Washington in fear and trembling. It did not take her long to get her feet on the ground because she would take files home with her to study for background. She soon remarked, "I now find myself knowing more about some problems than the experts!" She had an acute intellect and was able to penetrate to the central issue and avoid distractions from side issues.

Since I had been directly involved in personnel problems in the Washington area for ten years at that time, I was quite familiar with the background and knew where to find any information that I needed. McGlashan, and later Dan Godbold, and I would brief her on the history of certain personnel problems that had a tendency for recurring, and we would sometimes debate solutions, but Mrs. Rosenberg made her own decisions. It was a pleasure to work with her because she was pragmatic and a realist, typical of one with political skills.

On one occasion we were working with a Committee of the House on language for a reserve forces bill and she had promised the committee some material at ten the next morning when they convened. Riding back to the Pentagon in the limousine I remarked, "You realize that it should take two days to do a first class job, but Dan and I will have something for you in the morning." We did work until about eight that night and were on hand at seven-thirty the next morning when Mrs. Rosenberg arrived. She then reworked that material to her satisfaction and we were ready to leave for the hearings at nine-thirty to deliver the goods.

On that same bill we were asked to propose some language. John Adams, Counsel for the Department of Defense was with us and on the way back to the Pentagon, Mrs. Rosenberg suggested that we meet at four that afternoon to firm up our proposal. Since Adams was a guest at that meeting, Mrs. Rosenberg asked him to lead off, so he read his version, rather legalistic. Mrs. Rosenberg then said, "Now John, you know very well that will not do because

Congress is allergic to any increase in the power of the President!" Dan and I had carefully skirted that issue in the language we had worked up.

When Mrs. Rosenberg arrived she instituted afternoon tea in her office at five when the office normally closed. Should she have had callers during the day, they were invited to return, one I recall was Bernard Baruch for an interesting discussion at a social level. business was not ordinarily a subject. Mr. Lovett, the Secretary, would pop in and out for tea and a cookie. General Omar Bradley was often present when he became Chairman of the Joint Chiefs of Staff. General Hershey usually made his visits late in the afternoon to stay to tea. McGlashan and I were always present for when there were no visitors we had a review of the day's work and discussed what to do the next day. Later on when her office was fully staffed there would be in and out traffic on their way home in the evening.

Mrs. Rosenberg endeared herself with the military services by pushing a pay raise through Congress almost single-handed, after she was assured of President Truman's support. Charles Tyroller, her administrative assistant, had prepared a worksheet showing just how each member of the Congress would be likely to vote. Just before the vote, Tyroller's count showed that the margin for the pay raise was slim. I sat in the background in her office one evening when she had Admiral Sherman, Generals Lawton Collins of the Army and Hoyt Vandenberg of the Air Force in a working session to tip the balance in favor of the bill. She ran down the list of those uncertain and, in each case, asked whether those present knew that member or knew of anyone who could influence his vote. The end result was telephone calling list for each, including Mrs. Rosenberg. She also telephoned the Administration leaders of the House and Senate to urge them to get behind Mr. Truman and pass his bill. The bill did pass with a small but comfortable margin, and it was clear to me that her last minute push was conclusive.

Mrs. Rosenberg was demanding at times and also considerate. She set an example of dedicated work. I was in her office one morning when General Omar Bradley came for visit. In the course of conversation he asked whether I was attending the convocation at West Point celebrating its one hundred fiftieth anniversary. I said that I had considered going but had cancelled my plane at Bolling. General Bradley said, "Come with me for I have an airplane with plenty of space." Mrs. Rosenberg urged me to accept and I did. It was a pleasant experience to tag along with a five-star general.

Before Mrs. Rosenberg left the Defense Department at the change in administration, her final accolade was to recommend me for the legion of Merit for my work in her office.

The Manpower Pool

The Korean War brought emphasis on manpower procurement because we had to worry about the turnover rate. Young men inducted by Selective Service only had to serve for two years. On the other hand, men who enlisted did so for a four year period in the Army and Air Force. The Department of Defense was using both induction and voluntary enlistment with the result that the turnover was closer to three years. The bait was that the man who enlisted could obtain the service of his choice and also a choice of his first station. Men who were inducted had no choice of service or of first station. The Department was happy about this arrangement, but there were numerous complaints about the dual system, but none from General Hershey.

General Hershey was a frequent visitor in Mrs. Rosenberg's office and he would tease her, saying that he was the best recruiter that the Defense Department had, which was quite true. He understood the problem of turnover, and also knew that we were approaching the bottom of the barrel. It was well that we had no truth squads listening in for what General Hershey said in our office did not match what he said in public because that was designed to pacify his local boards. Shortly after Charlie Collier had joined our office the three of us were sitting in Mrs. Rosenberg's office and he was enjoying reminiscing with Charlie, it dawned on me that the three of us had been working together for ten years and knew more about manpower procurement for the Army at least, than anyone else in Washington.

President Truman had been urged by several of his visitors to stop this dual recruitment and he was able to fend them off because Mrs. Rosenberg had been careful to explain the problem of average turnover to his satisfaction. But he would call her on the telephone after such a visit to keep her informed. Dan Godbold and I were in her office at the time of one phone call and when Mr. Truman hung up Mrs. Rosenberg asked us if we could do something to help the president.

I thought of my letters to the station commanders in Alaska to be kept in the center drawer to fend off visiting staff officers and explained the idea to Dan. We went back to Mrs. Rosenberg to find out whether she could hand carry a paper from her to him, and to explain how he was to keep it in the drawer of his desk to refer to for answers on the dual recruitment operation. She said that would be no problem so we wrote up a memorandum from her to the president, person to person, which listed about ten questions and their answers, placing the toughest question first, for we had numerous questions which we had answered for her. Each question had its own answer and the text was double spaced for easy reading. We made only three copies, one for Mrs. Rosenberg in case the president quizzed her and one for his desk. She delivered that paper and he understood its purpose, helpful, for he had great confidence in Mrs. Rosenberg. That paper worked.

Except for the policy issue, everything was wrong with that paper. It was person to person and outside channels, it was in memorandum form not used for papers to the president, it was repetitious and double spaced for easy reading. However, it was a special solution for a special case and worked.

The controversy stemmed in part from the fact that there was no firm figure as to the size of the manpower pool. The Selective Service figure was based on registrations, but there was no assurance that all young men had registered at age eighteen. The Army had their figure worked up from population data which were not specific as to year of birth. One day Mrs. Rosenberg asked me if I could clarify the confusion.

Since we were concerned with a ten-year period between 1932 and 1942 when the birth rate was low, I decided to go back to the census data and made up a spread sheet for the ten years, posting births for each year. I obtained infant mortality rates from the Army Surgeon General, these were in five year groupings, and reduced each birth class for deaths, carrying forward the remainder cumulatively. At age eighteen I used the Selective Service data to estimate the number physically qualified. My figure was different and lower than the other two and caused some comment. I had my statisticians review the work before I gave it to Mrs. Rosenberg.

I became an expert overnight and made the presentation a number of times, once for a Committee of Congress. I always took along my worksheets for anyone to see, and explained the process. My method was laborious for the entire population, but I had a firm fix for the 1952 estimate, so we knew where we stood.

The Manpower Pool was the centerpiece of a speech that I made to the Reserve Officers of California at their State Convention during April of 1953. Representative Leroy Johnson of Fresno, a member of the House Armed Services Committee, discussed the Reserve Program that we had worked on a few years earlier in the Defense Department. Colonel Morris J. Brummer, Air Force Reserve and president of the California Department, had worked with me in the G-1 Section of the General headquarters Air Force at Bolling Field in 1941.

Retirement One

My flying career began with propeller driven aircraft. Thirty years later when I retired, the Air Force was moving into the jet engine age. I had been overtaken by technical progress and it was time to move on to other things.

I was fortunate for my thirty years were filled with varied assignments, many of an original or independent type and I enjoyed the doing of every one of them, particularly when I could use my own ideas and judgement. I had attained general officer grade, far beyond my expectations in June of 1922.

Mrs. Rosenberg personally arranged an interview for me with the Central Intelligence Agency to consider a civilian administrative position that was available. But, I had reservations about any civilian employment in a defense related activity. I had been planning other activities after retirement.

That plan was to teach at the university level after obtaining the degree of Master of Business Administration to provide a transition. When I left Washington in July 1953 I had my letter of admission to the Graduate School of the University of Texas at Austin and was ready to go to work that fall.

Just before I left Washington I sent Mrs. Rosenberg a birthday greeting signed by all the members of the Manpower Requirements Division. In her acknowledgement she said:

> . . . I was surprised to hear that you are going back to school to get your Master's Degree in Business Administration. I honestly believe you know more about management and administration than the people who are going to teach it . . . My very best to you . . .

General Nathan Twining, Chief of Staff of the Air Force, sent me on my way with a complimentary letter which speaks for itself.

DEPARTMENT OF THE AIR FORCE
OFFICE OF THE CHIEF OF STAFF
UNITED STATES AIR FORCE
WASHINGTON, D. C.

Major General Edmund C. Lynch
6298 15th Road, North
Arlington, Virginia

Dear Eddy:

Upon the occasion of your impending relief from active service and reversion to retired status, I offer my most sincere congratulations to you for the many years devoted to the service of your country and for the permanent record of outstanding accomplishments that you have contributed to our growth and development.

Your sterling leadership during the development of the Air Force from its formative stages is a matter of record and merits the highest praise. You are one of the Air Force pioneers whose efforts were of major importance in making air power a reality.

Your skill and hard work during World War II greatly contributed to the victory that was achieved. I have noted with great pride your successful accomplishment of the many difficult missions which have been assigned to you these past several years. Your judgment and courage as an Air Force leader have been of inestimable value to the Air Force and to the nation.

We are counting on you as an alumnus to maintain the same active interest and support of the Air Force that you have provided during your years on the active list.

My staff joins me in extending best wishes for many years of happiness and success.

Sincerely,

Nate Twining

N. F. TWINING
Chief of Staff, United States Air Force

Career Two

The University of Texas

Academic Life

William R. Spriegel

William R. Spriegel, Dean of the College of Business Administration and Distinguished Professor of Management at the University of Texas, was my graduate advisor. Spriegel had been a World War One pilot earning his wings at Kelly field in 1918 and remaining active in the reserves through flying at Selfridge Field until physically disqualified in 1939. I had met him in 1949 when he visited Air Force Headquarters to inquire whether we had any organizational studies that could be done by his college. Spriegel had worked in industry before embarking on his doctoral program under Walter Dill Scott at Northwestern University. Scott was this country's first industrial psychologist and his text *Personnel Management* had been published in 1923. Spriegel had taken over that book from Scott so that we were using his latest edition. Spriegel was also acquainted with Hugo Diemer who had published his text on *Factory Administration* in 1910. Lillian M. Gilbreth was a house guest of the Spriegel's on two occasions when she passed through Austin on one of her trips across the country, and I twice had the pleasure of chatting with her on her visits.

My academic program at West Point had been the basic civil engineering program, so my letter of admission listed a number of courses needed to make up the undergraduate requirement, as well as those for the Master's requirement. At our first meeting I asked Dean Spriegel to make up a list of courses for me that would satisfy the total requirement and that I would get to work for the issue was to graduate. Toward the end of the list he pondered for a moment or two and then said, "I think that you should take a course under this man," and jotted down a number. That man was Professor Eric W. Zimmermann and the course Foundations of National Power which I thoroughly enjoyed.

I had two distinct identities those two years as a graduate student. Being a retired Air Force officer, Edith and I were invited to many social functions of the Spriegel's at their home, some including all the Faculty of the College of Business Administration. As one of Dean Spriegel's graduate students, we attended the social affairs he held for his students. Maree and Jack Spriegel took us under their wing and introduced us to the town group through the

Knife and Fork Club, where we met Mayor Harry Akins and his wife.

When Edith and I returned to the campus for the fall term in 1954, I had a message waiting for me to see the Dean. He wanted to know whether I would teach the freshman course *Introduction to the Study of Business* and I was happy to agree. That was a survey course, purely descriptive with not quite ninety students. Since I had visited several plants of the industries described, I was able to color my lectures with details. My title was Lecturer and I now had an office space in Waggener Hall with two doctoral candidates who were teaching assistants.

Dean Spriegel had known from the beginning that my goal in seeking the degree of Master of Business Administration was to prepare me for teaching at the college level. Before I had graduated in June 1955, Dean Spriegel had invited me to join the Management Department Faculty, a real compliment and my first and only job offer. I asked to start in the fall of 1956 because Edith and I had planned an extensive vacation trip to last about nine months.

When Spriegel stepped down as Dean having attained the age of sixty-five, he moved into an office adjacent to mine, so we were able to visit easily. When I began my research on the early history of personnel management in the Sixties, his close association with Dr. Scott during his doctoral program was most helpful to me, not to overlook reminiscing about other old timers in the field whom he had known.

Student Life

Edith and I had our household goods shipped to San Antonio for storage while I was a student as we planned to rent a furnished apartment while in Austin. While working on the move to Texas, I was fortunate to meet Major General Otis Benson in the Bolling Field Operations Office just as he had arrived in his C-47 airplane from San Antonio. He was moving some of his chattels to Washington for he was being transferred to the Pentagon. Otis had been our next door neighbor at Randolph Field and we had flown together on a number of cross country flights. He had his crew take several footlockers to San Antonio for us and leave them with Gussie and Daddy Baker.

The Bakers had a guest house at the rear of their home, so we put up with them until we had located an apartment on Thirty-third Street in Austin, close to the University. They loaned us a 1949 model television for Edith's entertainment while I was studying. We were settled and I had reported to the College of Business well before the fall semester began.

At that time the graduate student took the senior level course and wrote a paper of about twenty pages on a related topic for his graduate credit. I was competitive and intended to make "A's" so expended more effort than was necessary, mainly on the papers, for the course material was easy. My reason for taking the degree (under the G.I. Bill) was that I could study how the professors handled their classes from the student's seat, to learn how to do things the civilian way, and to get some feel for the way the students thought about their life, what was important to them, or their point of view. Several of my instructors were working on their doctoral programs as teaching assistants, one in elementary accounting.

Weekends were for social activity. We visited Gussie and Daddy Baker about once a month, or whenever there was a party of old timers to attend in San Antonio. We were frequent guests at the Spriegel's parties, and we toured the countryside, so there was plenty to do and some visiting in the apartment building.

We spent Christmas with Edith's brother and his family at Corpus Christi. During that holiday we drove over to Rockport, Texas, to see Major Andy Byron who had been my Adjutant General in the Eleventh Air Force. He had retired and was living at Hunt's Courts on the bay side. He told us about the fishing and the summer activity, so we decided to spend the next summer at Rockport and put our deposit on the cottage close to the fishing pier, at the heart of things.

During the winter I built two fiberglass fishing rods from kits, so we were set for a relaxing summer from June through August. We would sit on our front porch and observe activity on the pier to determine whether the fish were biting, for it was pleasant in the early morning breeze. We would fish for our food, usually early in the morning, filet the trout or redfish and broil them over charcoal that afternoon. Knowing that I would have time on my hands, I had registered for two courses that summer. One was a problems course under Professor Mumma for which I worked up a supervisor's training program on getting along with his workers, or leadership for small groups. The other course was a correspondence course to complete my accounting requirement.

Since Hunt's Courts were crowded over the weekends, we usually went to Corpus Christi to visit Edith's brother and family for he was off work. Gussie and Daddy Baker had moved their trailer to North Beach at Corpus, so we would visit with them at times. There was a fishing pier at their trailer park and the fishing was good.

My innovation as a student was to carry my sponge rubber chair cushion from class to class as the oak chairs in Waggener Hall were hard and I wanted to be comfortable. Soon there were several others who had their cushions, too. In talking to students I learned that their work schedule was the central issue when they were working to pay their way, and courses were fitted around that schedule. The subject matter of a course was secondary as long as it counted for their program. I spent my time listening and never volunteered information about my past. I sat next to one student for an entire semester and just before the finals he said that he understood that I had been in the Air Force. When I said, "Yes," he then asked, "What type did you fly?" He was apparently not interested in other details.

I enjoyed all the courses that I took and found the material interesting. However, Spriegel's two seminars were special for he was strong on going back to the original sources, the writings of the pioneers. In the Personnel Seminar we were introduced to Vilfredo Pareto's work, *The Mind and Society,* in which he presents the notion of non-logical thought and decision because most human behavior is based on emotion rather than logic. Pareto was influential in shaping the experiments conducted by the Western Electric Company at their Hawthorne Plant near Chicago, in which the Harvard Fatigue Laboratory participated.

During one seminar Lillian M. Gilbreth was a guest at Spriegel's home and she came to the seminar to talk to the students about the early days in the management movement. She said that Frederick Taylor's ideas were met with resistance because many of the early practitioners were entranced by his technique and made no effort to understand Taylor's philosophy in the use of his techniques. They were concerned with means rather than ends. She deplored that approach and her comments reminded me of the *Sorcerer's Apprentice.*

In the Production Seminar Spriegel had assigned about eight books and various students had reported on them in class, handing out their customary outlines which had been duplicated for the other members of the class. During the class discussion Spriegel had made no comment or explanation. When it came time to study for the final examination, I had a stack of papers but could discern no clue as to what all that stuff meant. Knowning that Spriegel had some purpose in assigning the books, I decided that the authors were the important thing, but the students had not done much on the front part of the books. I went back to the library and paid close attention to the title page, preface and chapter headings. The final examination was on the relationship of the various authors in the evolution of management thought and I was loaded.

My competitive spirit paid off for I was elected to Beta Gamma Sigma the honorary scholastic fraternity for Business Administration students, similar to Phi Beta Kappa for the Arts and Science students. Some five years later, I was elected Secretary of the local chapter and served in that capacity until I retired in 1971.

As a student, I was also elected to Sigma Iota Epsilon, the honorary scholastic fraternity for students in the field of management. I became National Secretary of that fraternity in 1961 for a five-year term.

Constructive Conflict

Dean Spriegel had earned his Doctor of Philosophy Degree under Walter Dill Scott this country's first industrial psychologist. In his graduate seminars he introduced his students to the true pioneers many of whom he knew personally. One interesting personality who was at least a generation before her time was Mary Parker Follett. She had graduated from Radcliff College in 1898 with concentrations in economics, government and philosophy. At that time, psychology was a branch of philosophy. She began her public life working with the Roxbury Neighborhood House of Boston preparing boys and girls of poor families for entry jobs in shops and factories. That led to an interest in vocational guidance and her work with the Boston Placement Bureau and the Vocation Bureau of Boston. Through this work she made many friends in the business community and was invited to speak to various groups on the application of psychological principles to personnel problems in the period before World War One.

Miss Follett's basic theme was that an industrial organization must be grounded upon a recognition of the motivating *desires* of the individual and of the group. It was her view that day to day living, whether for an individual, a business or a society was an evolving process in which the happenings of one day became the basis for starting the next day; a dynamic process. Her concepts were based on the individual, his instincts and habits and desires.

Her lecture on Constructive Conflict was new to me for she considered conflict to be the essence of life when dealing with people for it was the consequence of the interaction of desires. Her idea was to make it serve a useful purpose. Miss Follett began by stating the three methods for coping with conflict; domination, compromise and integration of interests. Domination could be effective in the short run by suppressing the conflict, but it did not deal with the source of the conflict. Compromise was based upon each party giving up something for the sake of peace. But, people do not like the giving up part. It dealt with the situation as it existed and was not creative. Her proposal that interests be integrated centered on the desires of each party to the conflict, what they really wanted; or the ends rather than the means. The desires having been identified and agreed upon, both parties join to invent a solution which satisfied both parties. That conflict had then been settled and the next conflict would occur at a higher level.

As the process begins, each party to the conflict stated in specific terms what they sought to achieve, customarily work oriented rather than theoretical. This brought the differences out in the open where they could be compared or evaluated by both parties. That was not easily done because of the language used. Or, many minor claims would obscure the underlying problem. In this evaluation and re-evaluation there was a circular process at work in that the behavior of one party could create a new situation calling for a response, an evolving situation. Each party was learning something from the other party.

Once the desire of each party had been established to the satisfaction of the other party, then they join to invent or create a solution. The desires having been satisfied, the next conflict would occur at a higher level with prior experience to fall back on.

For those readers whose curiosity may have been aroused, the source was *Dynamic Administration; The Collected Papers of Mary Parker Follett,* Henry C. Metcalf and L. Urwick, Editors, Harper and Brothers 1942.

Eric W. Zimmermann

Dean Spriegel, while advising me on my graduate program, had said, "I think that you should take a course under this man." It was clear that the professor rather than the subject was the issue. Professor Eric W. Zimmermann was that man and the course was Foundations of National Power. Zimmerman was internationally recognized as an authority in his field, Resources.

He had come to the University of Texas from the University of North Carolina in the Forties. He looked typically German with craggy features and a strong accent, perhaps sixty-five years old or more. I had no problem with his accent for I sat in the front row on an aisle seat. He had no pretensions of renown, truly humble. In his lectures he laid out the material in simple terms for the students to make their own judgements. His method was Socratic, and in one instance, when a graduate student asked a complicated question, he thought for a moment and then asked a series of questions which led the student to answer his own question.

Professor Zimmermann did not wear his hearing aide while lecturing because it bothered him. When a student would raise his hand to ask a question, he would say, "Wait until I get wired for sound." He was the first person who I had observed who could write in Greek script faster than I could write in English. He lectured as a broad based social scientist roving over many fields with emphasis on culture. A rare sample of what a true social scientist could be.

Zimmermann had developed his unique concept of resources because he had become dissatisfied with the inventory approach as used in economics, that resources were fixed. In the field of international trade, he thought that social guidance theories had greater bearing on international trade than market specialization according to Adam Smith. His view was that resources evolve through the interaction of nature, man and his culture. Nature provided the substance; man had a need for that substance; and, man had the technology to put it to his use. While nature set the outer limits, man and his culture would determine that portion of the substance that would be available for human use. Knowledge was the key, and command over energy, especially inanimate energy, with electricity holding the central position, determined the availability of resources. Man was both the agent and the beneficiary of his particular culture, running back in time to when man first had fire. This process of wresting resources from nature would not come easily because there were *resistances* to be overcome; the innumerable and often insurmountable difficulties faced by man. Resistances were also those of nature, of man, and of his culture, but culture was often the major obstacle.

Resources were means to ends. For the individual, the end would be to live a good live. For a nation, the ends would be to maintain and improve both the internal and external position in terms of order, progress, prosperity and security. Each nation developed its unique culture suited to its needs. He warned against the glib notion that cultures could be easily transferred.

In the Western world, Zimmermann traced the cultural shift resulting from the progressive change in an agrarian society to an industrial society along these lines. In an agrarian society numerous children were an asset, but in an industrial society numerous children create problems or resistances. His favorite expression for such change was, "From Grand Babies to Grand Pianos." He stressed that such cultural changes come slowly, much slower than changes in technology.

I also took his course on the Conservation of Earth Materials. Our text was the May 1952 issue of *The Annals* of the American

Academy of Political and Social Science. The entire issue was devoted to "The Future of Our National Resources." I learned that, while conservation was an essential function and important, nobody knew just what it was all about. The reason was that it meant different things for different people, and there were different ideas as to what should be done. Zimmermann noted that Coolidge was the first president to do something about conservation when he created the Federal Oil Conservation Board. His directive to that board pointed out that the oil industry had to be prosperous to assure that this country had an adequate supply of oil. For the first time, Coolidge associated prosperity with conservation. Zimmermann considered the market approach was condemned to failure because it was a short-run approach. It was his view that conservation, to be effective, should be controlled by and through end uses, but the average customer in 1954 was not yet ready to go that far. In a democratic society, individuals cannot be compelled to act against their own interest for the sake of creating values which would accrue too late for them to enjoy. Zimmermann knew that the supply of oil was exhaustible, but he was an optimist and believed that technology would come to our rescue and that nuclear energy would substitute for it in time.

Professor Zimmermann did not accept the traditional view that international trade was *egalitarian,* that is among equals. Resource development determines whether a society grows strong or remains weak. An agrarian economy is weak, while an industrial economy is strong. Alexander Hamilton sought to promote manufactures that would render the United States independent of foreign nations for military and essential supplies, and that was at a time when our universities were teaching British economics, the exchange theories of Adam Smith.

In sum, national power rested upon a healthy and literate population. Public health was a basic asset; for it was the foundation of literacy as well as of the ability to understand and to use technology. Our most precious resource was knowledge, and knowledge grows through being shared. Productive power was the true source of wealth, and such productive power was ever changing.

Dean Spriegel was correct. The exposure to Professor Zimmermann in three courses was an illuminating experience for me. He reshaped material that I already knew into a different context, and

Resources 364: A

Reading your answers gave me a great and rare thrill. I congratulate you on your ability to benefit from my teaching.

Best wishes

Cordially E.W.Z.

with new meaning. It was truly an intellectual experience and the highlight of my two years as a graduate student at the University of Texas.

Airstream Vagabonds

For our second year in Austin we had a furnished apartment at 32nd Street and Red River, in the Northwood Terrace Apartments. That building has been demolished for an addition to St. David's Hospital. Edith and I had already decided that when I graduated we would take an extended trip to visit our retired friends to see how they were getting along. Since we did not wish to stay with our friends, the thing to do was to take our own housing, an Airstream trailer towed by our Ford Ranch Wagon.

That purchase was made in San Antonio, so we towed it to

Austin to load up before our May rent ran out in 1955 and we moved to Kerrville for a visit with my brother and his family. I had the idea for writing a book on retirement through gleaning "does and dont's" from the experience of those we would visit in our travels.

From Kerrville we headed for Denver, Colorado, for a month's visit. Our son Clayton had moved to Denver when KOA-TV went on the air since the staff was drawn from WNBW-TV in Washington, D.C. He was due to graduate from the University of Denver. Our close friends from Randolph Field days, Peg and Dave Davasher were living in Denver and my cousin Mary Lynch, plus many others, several in Boulder. We parked the trailer at Aurora on the east side of Denver near Lowry Field.

The Davashers had a Volkswagon with a rag top which they brought back from Germany, so we had an open view as we rode to Central City or Estes Park. On the way to Estes Park we stopped at Boulder to visit General Rush B. Lincoln and his daughter. That was a very busy month and most enjoyable for Edith had not been in Colorado before.

From Denver we headed for Keystone, South Dakota, for another visit which ran over a month with Harriet and Robin Day. Their summer cabin was close to Mount Rushmore. Robin had been base commander at Ellsworth Air Force Base when he retired and had acquired a cabin at Keystone for their summer home. They spent their winters in Florida near Stuart where the fishing was good. We were at the height of the tourist season and parked our trailer beside the Days' cabin for sleeping quarters. The State Fair was on while we were visiting so we went to Rapid City for the rodeo and the Indian dancing, but much time was spent watching the tourists and a small group of Indians on the main street of Keystone. I picked up some good ideas on retirement from Robin.

The tourists disappeared after Labor Day and we stayed until a light snow told us it was time to move along for our next stop which was Salt Lake City. Our route went through Rock Springs, Wyoming, where we parked the trailer to take a side trip to Yellowstone National Park to watch Old Faithful perform. While late in the season we were able to get a cabin and the cafeteria was still open. On the way to the bath house that night I saw a black bear rummaging in the trash.

The trailer park at Salt Lake City was close to the downtown section, so we stayed a week; most parks having weekly rates. We toured the area and took a close look at Great Salt Lake, and attended a concert at the Mormon Tabernacle. The Pioneer Museum was most interesting for it brought home how little the first immigrants had carried on their backs or in their two-wheeled push carts. We also visited Fort Douglas where I had stayed in 1940.

Our next extended visit was at San Jose, California, to see the Fitzmaurices. Our route was via Las Vegas, Nevada, Barstow, California, and north up the San Joaquin Valley to San Jose.We did not tarry at Las Vegas but spent an extra day to enable us to cross the desert at night. That was an interesting leg because all the filling stations and eating places along the way were open and the traffic was heavy.

We broke the trip with a short stay at Fresno to see Kay and Jack Brummer who had duty with me in the GHQ Air Force at Bolling Field. After his tour in England he had returned to Fresno Air Force Base. At the end of the war he had reverted to reserve status and entered business in Fresno. They took us for a full day's trip to see the redwoods and Yosemite National Park.

We spent several weeks at a trailer park in San Jose. It was a new one having been bulldozed out of an apricot orchard and one could pick fruit by leaning over the fence. We violated our rule by staying with Marge and Jim at their home for we were together morning, noon and night. The four of us visited Marie and E. D. Jones who were living in an apartment in San Jose. We had lost touch with them as E. D. had retired in 1939. He was then managing a furniture store at the edge of San Jose. The Fitzmaurices took us to see San Francisco and dine at Fisherman's Wharf, including the Officers Club at Fort Mason where we had landed from Panama. We also had lunch with Gertrude and Lee Tucker at Hamilton Field where he was the commander.

Evelyn and Oakley Kelly were next on our list so we headed for Los Angeles. They, too, had been neighbors at Randolph Field. Oakley still had the propeller from the T-2 transport airplane over their mantel, made into a souvenir with a clock in the hole for the engine hub. That was from the airplane in which Oakley and John Macready had set a World Endurance Record in 1922. During the war, Oakley had been the Air Force Representative at the North American Plant in Los Angeles.

San Diego was the last major stop on the west coast to visit the zoo and General McNarney, not in that order. General Joseph T. McNarney had been my boss while I was on the War Department

General staff and then president of the Consolidated Aircraft Company at San Diego. I visited his office to pay my respects and to tell him what I had been doing during the past years. On our way to San Diego we stopped over at Riverside to see Gay and Lonnie Koontz also old timers from Randolph Field. Gay raised cats and we left with two Siamese kittens because Edith thought that one would be lonely. The Siamese are like dogs in that they will walk with you on a lead, so we got collars and began to train them.

As it was nearing the first of December we headed for San Antonio, stopping at Tucson to see Marge and Clyde Rich, also of Randolph Field days. Clyde had been commander of Davis Monthan Air Base and retired in Tucson. The highlight of that stop was that the temperature dropped to twenty-five degrees and our water hose froze solid.

The first part of December 1955 was spent in a trailer park in San Antonio so that we could visit various friends. We visited my brother and his family at Kerrville putting up at the Bluebonnet Hotel and leaving the trailer in San Antonio. We then moved on to Corpus Christi to spend Christmas with Edith's brother and his family.

Our enthusiasm still high, we left shortly after the New Year to make our grand tour of Florida with the first major stop at the Clearwater-Sarasota area. Catherine and Roland Birnn who had lived across the street from us on Westover Drive were living in Clearwater. Roland had a motor boat and was head of the local Coast Guard Auxiliary, so we cruised the area with him one day. Ruth and Kewp Sharon of Randolph Field days lived nearby. Our main visitees were Frances and Stowe (Sut) Sutton who lived at Sarasota. They had been with us in Panama, and Frances was Marge Fitzmaurice's sister. There we were in the clutches of seven Infantry colonels and their wives, so we had a party every night and needed a breather before we arrived at the Miami area.

How did we locate a trailer park in a metropolitan area? We had a directory of parks with the telephone numbers. The difficulty in the Miami area was that many parks rent spaces on an annual basis and do not take overnighters or short termers. We wanted to stay in the North Miami area near Hollywood. The day before I had made a list of all the trailer parks and telephone numbers. When we got to the edge of that area we parked on a side street near a pay phone. Most of my calls were negative. Just before I ran out of numbers or nickels I had a cheery response, "We are happy to have overnighters. Where are you now?" As luck would have it, we were only a block away from that park which was in Ojus. From that park we visited Marie and Walter Myer who had been with us at Pope Field and also at Kelly Field.

We then headed north on U.S. Route One to Stuart, Florida, at the mouth of the St. John's River. Harriet and Robin Day had a place for us at their trailer park called The Fishing Hole, for it was full of fishermen. Robin had a motor boat so we went out with them to the edge of the Gulfstream where the fish would feed, catching quite a few mackerel. Robin had a commercial fishing license and sold his catch keeping a few for our dinner that evening. He told me that such sales just about paid for his fuel and bait.

After we left Stuart, we headed directly for Austin. Since our route went through Orlando, we stopped for short visit with Ray and Harlan Holden of Pope Field days. They gave us a quick tour of that area to see the orange groves. We parked our trailer on Airport Boulevard in Austin and lived in it while hunting for a house and then waiting for our household goods to arrive from San Antonio to our new address on Briarcliff in northeast Austin convenient to drive to the University.

How did our nine month trip turn out in retrospect? Nicely. It had not been tiring for we limited ourselves to about 300 miles per day. While visiting we had kept our mornings free, generally visiting in the afternoons and evenings. We had done what we had set out to do, but were happy to settle down in Austin. We had seen nothing or heard nothing on our trip to change our minds.

While I had accumulated considerable interesting material, my book "How to Retire Gracefully" never got written. I was too busy putting in a new lawn and preparing my material for teaching that coming fall semester.

Pinch Hitter

When I checked into the Management Department ready to go to work in the fall of 1956, I learned that I was not the only ex-military member on their staff. John R. Beishline who had retired from the Army in 1955 as a Brigadier General, had earned his Ph.D. at Ohio State University in Management while on active duty. Beishline was a West Point graduate of 1931. Betty, his wife preferred the east coast to Austin, so they moved on in 1957 when he became chairman of the Management Department at New York University.

Ed Mumma was still chairman of the department and had considerable amusement through comparing our different styles. Over the three years that he had known me, he knew that I never made any mention of my past experience unless it was in answer to a direct question, for I had made a complete break with the past. In contrast, Beishline frequently made reference to his Army experience in class. He had been G-1 Personnel of the Ninth Army in Europe.

As a newcomer, I thought it desirable to make my role clear and told Mumma my thinking knowing that it would get around in the department. Through my graduate work and prior experience, I felt qualified to teach any of the courses the department offered. I told Mumma that I considered myself a *Pinch Hitter* and would be happy to fill in wherever needed, that I did not intend to establish any particular field to compete with others on the faculty. In the course of fifteen years I did teach all courses other than Collective Bargaining and Wage and Salary Administration.

As was customary for a newcomer I began at the bottom teaching several sections of our basic management course, the core course titled *Industrial Organization and Management.* That eased me in for I only had one preparation to make. One of the subjects in that course was a discussion of Statistical Quality Control related to process control in the volume manufacture of identical parts. That system was based on the application of sampling theory devised by Walter A. Shewhart of Massachusetts Institute of Technology following World War One. Briefly stated, the principle was that a properly selected sample would represent the entire lot of the items produced. The goal was to keep that process within limits so that no bad parts were made. For example, in the case of a shaft of specified diameter with a dimensional tolerance plus or minus, all parts within the range of the tolerances would fit and be good parts. Those measuring in excess, either under or over, would be bad parts.

Since no bad parts were to be made, the deviation of the sample from the central desired value was plotted to show the trend. When the trend line moved close to the upper or lower limits, the process would be shut down for correction. One reason that Shewhart's system did not find wide use in this country was that managers were reluctant to permit quality control personnel to shut down production for a correction. One of Shewhart's students, Leslie E. Simon, West Point 1924, did apply quality control as taught him at M.I.T. to the manufacture of ammunition at Picatinny Arsenal, Dover, New Jersey, in 1933. Simon later wrote a book on the subject, *An Engineer's Manual of Statistical Methods*.

The following semester I worked with Ed Mumma teaching one section of Supervision, how to attain the cooperation of your workers. Knowing that Mumma was an excellent teacher, I sat in the back row of his class which preceded mine to become acquainted with his style. Our textbook had been designed for training supervisors during World War Two and was augmented by training material developed for the Armstrong Cork Company, film strips and accompanying records presenting the timeless problems confronted by an industrial supervisor. It was interesting to note that the ladies classed the material out of date because of the clothing worn by the women in the film strips, while the men took the same track based on the vintage of the cars that appeared.

The magic words in supervision are:

We and Us.

The pride course of the Management Department was our capstone course Business Policy, designed to integrate the functions of Marketing, Production and Finance.

Business Policy was taught by the case method and the case book was supplemented by a business game developed jointly with the Statistics Professors in the college. The computer program for this game would accommodate seven companies to compete in a fixed market against each other for market share or sales. Competition was measured by the number of salesmen hired and the money allocated to advertising, the two variables. The student team made decisions as to the production needed to support their estimated sales and the financing to support the effort. A detailed manual had been published for this game with instructions for the students and the instructor. The student teams were ordinarily four: president, production manager, marketing manager and financial officer.

Professor Bernard H. Sord was the leader in teaching Business Policy, but I knew what was going on because I was office mate with Burnie in Waggener Hall. When Burnie left for a year in Italy to teach under a State Department Program, he recommended me to take over while he was away. I considered that a compliment. My task was to explain the game, answer questions and monitor the decision sheet that each team submitted to insure that it was complete; when the results were returned, to explain what happened. The computer program would print out an operating statement and a balance sheet for each company. The students enjoyed playing that game. I could bail them out when they got in a hole or suggest means to keep the game going. The eye opener for me was that senior level students did not remember the basic core material that they had had as juniors. I would have to review some basic principles in marketing and accounting as well as in management. In sum, I think that I learned more from teaching that course than the students did.

When Burnie returned from Italy he was elected chairman of the Management Department. However, Dean John Arch White asked him to serve as Associate Dean for graduate studies. Since no one in the Management Department would step forward to take over the chairmanship, Burnie asked me to do so. I demurred on the basis that I was not qualified to recruit faculty for the department and we were on the lookout to fill several vacancies. Further, I was too low in academic rank to participate in the Budget Committee. We worked out a deal where I became Acting Chairman as far as the papers were concerned in the president's office. In reality I ran the department for the next three years, except for recruiting and the preparation of the budget.

I enjoyed the confidence of Dean John Arch White and represented the college on a number of committees, the major one was the Educational Policy Committee. Also, I was Campus Chairman for the Texas Personnel and Management Conference held on campus each October. It was governed by a committee representing government agencies, business and academe, with the Management Department the action agency. From my beginning title of Instructor in 1956, I was advanced to Assistant Professor in 1959 and then attained tenure in 1965.

Momentous Years

Edith and I spent the spring vacation of 1957 in Corpus Christi taking the trailer to have a quiet and uneventful visit. When we arrived home Sunday afternoon, Edith complained of feeling unwell so we slept in separate rooms as I would leave early for my eight o'clock class. Later that morning, classes being over, I returned home to discover that she had died peacefully in her sleep. Edith had been under treatment for high blood pressure since 1949. She was buried in the Mission Burial Park near Stinson Field in San Antonio and close to her parents. Edith always considered San Antonio home.

Not being needed to teach that summer, I had decided to take a long trip, but where? My sister-in-law Virginia and I persuaded my brother Raymond that he should take his leave and go with me to Philadelphia for he had not been back since moving to Texas thirty years before. We took the direct route and drove up the Shenandoah Valley to Harrisburg, Pennsylvania, to turn east on the turnpike for New Jersey and avoid local traffic. We parked the trailer in Camden several days while visiting relatives and then moved to the Philadelphia side of the river to visit around Sharon Hill where we used to live. On our way to the trailer park in South Philadelphia we were pulled over by the police. When the patrolman came up he said, "I see that you are from Texas. Do you know Tex Ritter? He is a cousin of mine." That eased our tension and we chatted about Texas and Tex Ritter. Then, we had a police escort to our park which was a block or so ahead. I had met Tex Ritter when he was just beginning his singing career.

Our visit ended, Ray caught the bus for Texas while I moved on to Washington to park at Potomac Park for a week of visiting. Mr. Cooper was the only one I looked in on at the Pentagon. He was happy to see me and learn what I had been doing. He told me that I could walk into my old office the next morning and be quite at home, for the problems that we had been working on in 1953 were then on top of the stack again.

From Washington I followed U.S. Route 301 as it was off the tourist route and avoided large towns. At Statesboro, Georgia, I angled across that state to Chattahoochee to pick up the highway along the Gulf coast. I dawdled along the way for hurricane Carla was heading for the Gulf coast and I intended to cross Louisiana after the storm had moved inland. Even then I cut it rather fine for when I arrived at Kinder, Louisiana, the electricity had been restored but six hours before. My meal at the cafe that evening was ham and eggs with toast.

The Air Force had a large number of officers enrolled in both undergraduate and graduate programs in 1958, such students being on active duty. We had several pursuing the Master of Business Administration degree. Captain B. J. Smith who was also an amateur radio operator, had invited me to a party at his home, so I met most of the graduate students including Robert Jones who was rated as a navigator. Jones asked me to escort his favorite aunt who was to attend his graduation that spring. His aunt was Beatrice Dortch, a Navy widow, and I escorted her to the large graduation party for the group at Bergstrom Air Force Base and other student parties. We were mutually attracted to each other. On my part it was her accent which was just like that of my Philadelphia relatives, not surprising for her mother had been raised in that city. She had enjoyed the same social life as I had in the Air Force and also enjoyed the university life. She had visited Austin the year before and was acquainted with several town people. Beatrice and I were married at the Base Chapel at Bergstrom with a small reception at the Officers Club. Her first husband had entered the Naval Academy from a small town near Corsicana to graduate in 1927, so she was familiar with Texas.

During the spring I had planned a fishing trip for that summer, for I had spotted a place near Estes Park in Colorado on our trip in 1955. My fishing trip became our honeymoon trip. Trailer travel was quite new for Bea, but she was a good sport and willing to learn. As before, we headed out for Denver and the Black Hills knowing that it would be cooler. Our main purpose was to get acquainted with each others friends and relatives in the Western area. After we left the Black Hills we went to Phoenix, Arizona as Bea had relatives there, and then on to San Diego a purely Navy town. Since Bea did not care for my Siamese cats, we visited Gay and Lonny Koontz to return them on the way to Los Angeles.

After our visit with Marge and Jim Fitzmaurice at Menlo Park, we went on to Sacramento to visit Liz and Bob Jones for they had married shortly after we did and were now on duty with the navigation school. We crossed Nevada to Provo, Utah, and then on through the mountains to Denver, before heading for Texas. I had a Chevrolet pickup to tow the trailer for that trip and it could handle any road grade that a passenger car could make.

Bea adapted readily to university life having the social skills service wives learn in moving about and working with different people, her former husband having been a captain in the Navy. She was an accomplished bridge player.

Through General Hershey, Edith and I had become acquainted with Maggie and Morris Schwartz for Colonel Schwartz was the State Director of Selective Service. When General Hershey came to Austin on his official visits, he asked Colonel Schwartz to include us in any social activities incident to his visit. Maggie was an ardent bird watcher so Bea and I joined the Audubon Society. Magnolia Green, president of the Violet Crown Garden Club, was an aunt of Liz Jones, Bob Jones' wife, so Bea became interested in growing African Violets. She was also active in the faculty wives group of the college and was in charge of the afternoon tea to welcome the newcomers the fall of 1959.

The summer of 1959 we headed for Annapolis, Maryland, so that I could meet her family. Our route was through Pensacola, Florida, a Navy town where she had been residing before our marriage. We went on to Moorestown, New Jersey, to visit my Aunt Nancy and Bea was surprised to learn that my aunt knew her mother's family, the Tylers. Bea also discovered two cousins on her mother's side who lived close by. That was a quick trip and two months remained of the summer, so we hitched up the trailer and headed for Denver and the Black Hills where it was cooler. The highlight of that visit was the Passion Play at Spearfish, South Dakota, with a full moon rising over the open air theater.

That was our last long trailer trip. During the school year we kept the trailer parked in Kerrville and used it as a weekend cottage while visiting my brother and his family. We continued to take our summer trips, one year to the east coast and the next to the west coast or to Colorado to visit friends at the University of Colorado at Boulder. Our Eastern trips were usually to Syracuse, New York, to visit Helen and Mo Cross. Professor Maurice Cross had been a visiting professor at the University of Texas after retiring from the University of Syracuse. Mo and I were office mates while Helen and Bea were in a bridge group.

Sigma Iota Epsilon

The Personnel and Management Conference in October was a total effort for the Management Department, including seniors and graduate students. Members of Gamma Chapter of Sigma Iota Epsilon acted as guides and aides for the conferees, identified by their arm bands, while other aspiring initiates helped in diverse ways. I did my stint in 1953 by waiting on tables at the Luncheon Meeting held in the Student Union.

Maurice C. Cross organized one of the founding chapters at Syracuse University in 1924 among his industrial management students. That chapter dealt with local interests to become Beta Chapter when the National Organization became effective in 1928.

"Mo" Cross was my officemate for the two years (1957–1959) he taught as a visiting professor at the University of Texas, so I learned much about the early days of the management movement through casual conversations. He told me that when he attained the age of sixteen, he went to work for the railroad. From what he saw being done he thought that there must be a better way to run a railroad, so he went to Ohio State University to find out, ending up with a Doctor of Philosophy Degree in Industrial Management. Cross organized the Management Department at Syracuse in 1922.

The mainspring for the National Organization came from a chapter at the University of Illinois sponsored by Professor Arthur G. Anderson, also formed by his industrial management students. They became Alpha Chapter and had decided upon Sigma Iota Epsilon for a name based upon "Spoude" for earnestness, "Idrea" for knowledge and "exoche" for excellence.

At about the same time (1927), Professor Chester Lay at the University of Texas had organized a chapter of the Taylor Society. The interest of this group was in general management. Chester had heard of the activity at Illinois and wrote Professor Anderson to join in the National Organization, and Anderson brought in Syracuse. The Texas Chapter became Gamma Chapter, and Alpha Chapter was at Illinois. Chester Lay was a frequent visitor at the University of Texas and I knew him from various meetings around the Management Department, often luncheons when he was on campus.

Professor Joseph Bailey of the Management Department was elected National President in 1961 and asked me to serve as National Secretary. My major task was editor-publisher of the *Manager's Key* which was published twice each year. That journal had been started by Professor Cross in 1929. The copy for an issue was developed by one of our fifteen chapters. I whipped it into shape and had it published.

Joe Bailey was a member of the Academy of Management and his goal as National President was to have Sigma Iota Epsilon affiliated with the Academy as its student branch and that goal was achieved in 1964. I had suggested a short history of Sigma Iota Epsilon to be published in the journal to be helpful when the matter came before the body for adoption, that was easier said than done. There was no history in the files which I received, but many bits and pieces spread over thirty years. Fortunately, all three founders were active and I knew two of the three, so organization of my bits and pieces was done by questionnaires sent to Anderson, Cross and Lay. They all approved my final version which was published in the *Manager's Key* for December 1964. My comment in that issue was to the effect that the founders of S.I.E. had been more concerned with problems of the moment than with keeping detailed records of their actions. That issue was dedicated to the three founders, and included their biographies.

One of my unfulfilled desires was to write a paper on the involvement of the Army Ordnance with *Taylorism* as the term was used before World War One. The Army had several arsenals to manufacture heavy ordnance, such as guns for the Coast Artillery, beyond the capability of the civilian steel industry. The managers of such establishments were enthusiastic about applying Taylor's ideas to the extent that their employees lobbied Congress to prohibit the use of the stopwatch in work measurement through an amendment to the Army's Appropriation Bill for 1912. That prohibition remained in effect for thirty years.

During World War One there was enough concern about the low productivity in the Munitions Industry, including the manufacturing arsenals, to cause the War Department to establish the Morale Branch within the War Department General Staff (told elsewhere). I thought that it would be interesting to examine the relationship between these two events. But, time ran out on me.

Walter Dill Scott

Ever since working on updating the Army's Classification and Assignment System in 1939, I had been fascinated by the fact that a group of university psychologists and businessmen had devised that system and had it working within six weeks. Furthermore, that system was sound in that no basic changes were required for its use in World War Two. That group was under the leadership of Walter Dill Scott, Professor of Psychology, Northwestern University. Walter Van Dyke Bingham had been his deputy in 1917 and was the resident psychologist in the War Department and we were acquainted. Edith and I had been guests at two garden parties the Bingham's held at their home in Washington.

Early in 1967 I decided to look into this matter since fifty years had elapsed. My first goal was to identify the expertise that Professor Scott had brought to the committee, and secondly, to identify changes that might have occurred over that fifty years. It required more than two years of research although I had thought it to be easy since my colleague, Dean Spriegel had studied under Professor Scott for his Ph.D. at Northwestern. Before World War One the term "employment management" had been used where we now say personnel management. Many of the items I dug up were in psychological journals or in the literature of vocational guidance. The result was a paper, *Walter Dill Scott: Pioneer in Personnel Management* published by the Bureau of Business Research at the University of Texas in 1968.

Trained under Wilhelm Wundt in Germany, Professor Scott established a psychological laboratory at Northwestern in 1900. He was one of the few who believed that psychology should be used for the benefit of society and his interest was directed to business problems. His method was pragmatic and direct. His graduate students would survey what businessmen were doing through interviews or questionnaires and study them in terms of psychological principles. This would be developed into knowledge or procedure which could be passed along. In the field of testing, Scott sought to design a test which would discriminate between successful and unsuccessful salesmen, for example. There was no problem in identifying those successful. His unsuccessful individuals were from those who had been fired or who were about to be fired. Several of Scott's students worked with him during 1917 on the system for the Army.

Scott's basic field in psychology was the Power of Suggestion or Suggestability, so he began with advertising to increase sales. However, he soon realized that the selection and training of salesmen was the issue.

During the years 1910 and 1911, Scott wrote a series of articles under the general title, *The Psychology of Business,* published in *System* magazine (Now *Business Week*) and later published as a book, *Increasing Human Efficiency in Business.* This was the first treatise on motivation and productivity that I could find in the literature. It was a how-to-do book designed for the business manager; how to develop and maintain cooperation. The focus was on the worker and his needs. The only other significant publication before 1917 was that of Hugo Muensterberg's *Psychology and Business Efficiency,* published in 1913. His focus was that of the business manager, how to adjust the worker to his work through selection and training, and with consideration for monotony, attention and fatigue.

As a consequence of his work through the psychological laboratory in dealing with business problems, Scott was well known in the business world, and he, in turn, knew good managers among that group.

The committee also developed a Personnel Manual to be used in the operation of the system and for training personnel. Scott became president of Northwestern University in 1920 while a number of the committee members formed the Scott Company as consultants to spread the word to the business community. Scott was the senior author on the text *Personnel Management* published in 1923, the state of the art up to that date.

Employment Management came of age in 1916 with the first National Conference of Employment Managers which was held at Minneapolis, Minnesota, June 1916. The first local association of employment managers was organized at Boston in 1911. This association was a forum where experience and information could be shared, paralleled by research and development. The idea spread rapidly throughout the Northeastern and Midwestern industrial areas of the country. After World War One the term Personnel Management was used.

Edward L. Munson

I came late upon *The Management of Men* by Edward Lyman Munson while seeking information on the early history of Employment Management during 1967. Published in 1921, it had received little attention in the field of personnel psychology, largely because it was considered tailored to the military view.

Munson was one of the early thinkers who believed that the benefits of psychology could be extended to society as a whole as well as used beneficially by the Army. Munson, a medical doctor, had developed a deep interest in psychology well before World War One. I could find no reference to him in the literature prior to the publication of his book. There being only two major texts dealing with psychology and business prior to 1918, it was likely that he was familiar with at least one of them. Munson's view in his book is more like that of *Increasing Human Efficiency in Business* by Scott than Hugo Muensterberg's book. At the very end Munson says, ". . . to disregard the factor of human relations is to disregard the mainspring of human behavior." Munson stressed leadership based upon psychological principles.

A Morale Branch was created by War Department General Orders Number 94 on October 19, 1918 with Munson in charge. Its mission was to improve the efficiency of the soldier through the betterment of morale, but Munson said in his book that the pressing need was to improve productivity in the Munitions Industry. The Morale Branch was later consolidated with the Educational and Recreation Branch under the War Plans Division of the War Department General Staff. Munson was at that time a brigadier general in the General Staff Corps. Early in March 1918, he had proposed the need for a systematic psychological stimulation of the troops to promote their fighting efficiency, suggesting some general measures to that end. He was then commanding a Cantonment and had applied them himself.

Munson described his work as a handbook for the young officer and all future leaders of men, applying psychological principles to leadership and all that term implied. There was much detail on a Morale System, an Army staff function to identify an unwholesome mental state and devise a corrective plan of action. As a consequence, the general reader would get the impression that it was a justification for continuing the Morale Branch. It was viewed as designed for the military and received little interest.

I found Munson's discussion of crowd psychology most interesting for he covered both organized (the Army) and unorganized, the mob or riot. His analysis begins with the statement: "All men are either leaders or followers." Since followership is instinctive and leadership is defined, the task of the military leader was to understand human nature and to make it work for him. Principles of psychology show that *suggestion* works when based on an understanding of the follower. The unorganized crowd responded to the same principles. The crowd surrendered its responsibility to some stronger will and that leader swayed the crowd through mental images created and repeated. The St. Bartholomew Day Massacre was his example of an unorganized crowd. Munson's treatment of crowds is the only one I have come across in extensive reading of psychology.

His section on the Psychology of Pubescence dealt with the mental states of the typical male period of growth from age fourteen to twenty-four, most first enlistments. Munson said that that adolescence was characterized by instability of ideas and behavior, and he considered that their delinquencies were those of impulse and immaturity of mind. He advised troop commanders that the adolescent did well "when worked hard and played hard." I had learned the same thing without reading Munson, it was to keep them busy, keep them tired and keep them broke.

Munson discussed twenty instincts of which fourteen had relevance for the military. Instincts were primary inherited tendencies to act in such ways as to produce certain ends, and without foresight or prior education. Such instincts formed the basis of character. Efficient leadership would stimulate the desired instincts and divert those not desired into useful channels, rather to attempt to suppress them.

Munson's instincts were motivators now termed *needs* in the literature of today, usually considered in three groupings. The basic or survival needs were those relating to food, clothing and shelter. The intermediate grouping relates to social interaction, the need of belonging and sex for another. The ultimate need or motivator was that for self fulfillment. Munson's point was that the military leader should understand human nature and have it work for him rather than against him.

Two of his instincts interested me for I had seldom seen a reference to them, these were the *religious* and the *comic*. Munson said that the religious instinct was innate in mankind everywhere and found expression in admiration, wonder, awe and reverence toward omnipotency, including fear of the unknown. That instinct provided an expectation of reward for good conduct and punishment for faults, extended beyond all human limits. Religion supplemented public opinion in the control of conduct.

The comic instinct was peculiar to human beings and served as a safety valve for suppressed emotions. Human beings note the unexpected incongruities in the speech and behavior of others that could be regarded as ludicrous and evoke hearty laughter. Munson cited the humorous war cartoons by Bairnsfather as examples. Mirth at a common cause brings sympathetic understanding, he noted.

While Munson received little recognition at the time his book was written, his ideas lived on. His son, E. Lyman Munson, Jr., graduated from West Point in 1926. Munson Junior wrote a smaller book on leadership for junior and noncommissioned officers based on his father's work. I do not recall the title, but Colonel Wade Haslip who was then G-1 in the War Department General Staff gave me a copy in 1940 and a summary of its background. I passed that copy on to E. Y. Blewett who was working on a similar book for the Air Corps.

About Personnel Management

With Personnel Management so pervasive today, it is a general unknown that this organized folklore is a creation of the Twentieth Century, so a brief history may be of interest. The Industrial Revolution, with its factories steadily increasing in size, resulted in the owner-employer becoming divorced from his workers. That impaired his ability to know his employees as individuals.

The origins were in social welfare, applied psychology and vocational guidance. Social welfare came first and was concerned with the health and well-being of the worker, to help him live a good life. The Colorado Fuel and Iron Company of Pueblo, Colorado, established a Sociological Department in 1901 under Richard W. Corwin who was a medical doctor. He conducted classes in nutrition and housekeeping for the wives of their employees in order to promote good health.

Walter Dill Scott, this country's first Industrial Psychologist, sought to apply the findings of psychology to benefit society. In his book on motivation and productivity, *Increasing Human Efficiency in Business* (1911), he stressed the mutual interests of the employer and the worker in the success of the enterprise. This idea was later broadened to The Human Conception of Labor in his textbook *Personnel Management* (1923). Scott considered the power of suggestion to be influential on behavior in the work place because human behavior was based more on sentiment than logic.

Settlement houses were organized early in this century to help the newly arrived immigrants become citizens. They were mainly on the east coast and taught the children of the immigrants employable skills to help them move upward toward the American Dream. The Civic Service House in Boston was one of these. Its director, Meyer Bloomfield, was a social worker and became acquainted with Frank Parsons the father of vocational guidance. Bloomfield invited Parsons to set up their Vocational Guidance Bureau in 1908. Parsons died shortly thereafter and Bloomfield carried on his work.

While Civic Service House had classes to teach boys and girls employable skills for entry jobs, Bloomfield soon learned that there was no organized way to match their graduates with available local jobs. As a consequence, he formed the Bostom Employment Managers Association in 1911. This was a forum for the exchange of information and the discussion of mutual problems. The Vocational Guidance Bureau, as part of their work, gathered information on the various job fields in the Boston area. This was designed to help the students make an intelligent choice of their future career while still in school.

The Boston experience resulted in the Employment Management Movement as other local groups were formed in the Eastern and Midwestern industrial cities. By 1913 there were a significant number in existence and that was the generally accepted time when the three threads merged into Employment Management as personnel work was then known. By 1916 there was enough interest to have a national convention in Minneapolis.

With the new draft law about to take effect, the Army asked Professor Scott to head a committee to develop a Classification and Assignment System in order "to place the Right Man in the Right Place." Scott assembled a group of university psychologists and experienced businessmen who created a system and had it operating in six weeks, ready for the men to arrive. At the end of the war, seven thousand personnel specialists were returned to civilian life trained in the Army system. Again there was a labor surplus and there was little interest in Personnel Management, the generally accepted term for personnel work. It was not until the new war in Europe brought demands for increased production that the interest in Personnel Management perked up, the labor surplus had dried up about 1939, or a shortage could be foreseen.

After spending two years delving into the early history of personnel practices between 1900 and 1917, I became convinced that the elements had been well developed by 1923 when the first textbook on Personnel Management was published and that there had been no significant changes since that date. It was interesting to me that all the innovations had come through people who were outside the doing of everyday personnel work: social workers, psychologists and workers in vocational guidance.

Correspondence Learning

My first Army Correspondence Course taken in the early Thirties at Randolph Field had the title, "Control of Civil Disturbance," or what to do about a mob. I clearly recall the Army doctrine presented in that course to the effect that we should not confront the mob, but use military force from the rear. Troops were moved up with fixed bayonets to urge the laggards forward to push on the front ranks of the mob from the rear. The central idea was to get the crowd moving and keep it moving. When possible, to split the front using a barricade, but one kept the crowd moving until it dispersed. I suspect that the underlying purpose was to limit control by the leaders. In contrast to this notion, all crowd scenes on today's TV screens show confrontation between the crowds and the police. Maybe they have to defend an embassy, but a contingent of riot police with cattle prods might be an easier method of moving the crowd by using the timid rear-enders to push the leaders off balance.

I soon learned that Lieutenant Howard A. (Pinky) Craig was enrolled in the Command and General Staff School series designed for reserve officers, so I changed to that program. My investment of time and effort was very beneficial when I attended the Air Corps Tactical School at Maxwell Field, and again at Fort Leavenworth. I was familiar with the language, form and symbols used in map problems, so I could move directly into the problem details.

While in Alaska I had promoted the Army Correspondence Courses as a means of coping with long hours indoors because of the weather on the Aleutian Chain, and to qualify for promotion. I found that very few were interested, but I made the effort. I knew that correspondence courses were not for everyone because the successful student needs self-discipline to work through the course. The ability to write clearly was also needed.

When Professor Kenneth Olm of the Management Department left for the University of New Mexico for a year's stay as a visiting professor, he plumped a large envelope on my desk and asked that I locate a replacement for the basic management correspondence course which he had been teaching. It was our policy that only full time faculty members would teach such courses. However, all our faculty were then involved and I took it over. I taught that course for seven years, continuing after I retired in 1971.

I learned a great deal from teaching that course, mainly that it forced me to sharpen up my own thinking before writing suggestions to the student.

Retirement Two

I returned to full time teaching when I stepped down as Chairman, preferring to sit in the rear at faculty meetings to observe what was going on. Our newer members had not worked in business but had spent about nine years in college between high school and the end of their doctoral program, perhaps with teaching assignments along the way. It became apparent to me that the newcomers and I were not tuned to the same frequency as we would say in amateur radio.

The late Sixties were a period of ferment and turmoil and there were frequent discussions in the faculty meetings of teaching for change. It was my view that the ability to cope with change was a state of mind, and not a technique, so we could not teach it. The ability to cope with change involved visions of the future and what could be done about making such dreams come true. We could help the student by doing a good job in teaching problem solving and analysis, and that could be done through the usual courses.

For every biennial catalogue revision we had a review to determine whether we were up to date. Simply put, this was to answer the question, "Are we doing the best we can for our students?" I was the chairman for the committee to review our Personnel Management Program. Ordinarily we concentrated on looking for gaps or overlaps in our courses, but that year the discussion began on our objective or purpose and it was quite general. I suggested that everyone write their version of what they thought that it should be for discussion at our next meeting. As a teaser, I stated my idea of our purpose, "To train an individual for executive work in personnel recognizing that the program would not make him ready to assume full responsibility, but that it would prepare him for final training under an experienced manager." That language came from the description used at the Amos Tuck School, Dartmouth College, for a five year program which they began in 1915. Our then current version said much the same thing but was not quite so explicit. It then dawned on me that they had textbook knowledge, but that they were not familiar with the activity in a business environment.

While I could have continued teaching on a modified service basis, I decided that the time had come to close my book and retired at the end of the spring semester of 1971. I had had a wonderful time working with the students at the University of Texas, enjoying a cordial relationship with my colleagues on the faculty.

Epilogue

As a lad of fourteen, my father took me to the National Guard Summer Camp at Mount Gretna with Company "B" of the Sixth Pennsylvania Infantry, for he was the captain. We had an overnight train ride from Chester to Mount Gretna and I observed several footlockers treated with great care in the loading and unloading of the troop train. The next morning, "B" Company had their breakfast on schedule for our breakfast supplies had been in those footlockers. My father had anticipated and prepared for this contingency knowing that the commissary would not open until midmorning.

I also recall that he held a complaint session every afternoon sitting under the fly of his tent during the hour before supper. There was no formality, anyone could come forward and speak his piece about anything that bothered him. The First Sergeant at that camp, who served through World War One with that company, told me years later that he was considered "Hard but Fair."

Although my father had been tendered an appointment to West Point, his mother talked him out of it and he enlisted in the Pennsylvania National Guard to participate in the Homestead Riots, the guard having been called out. He was called to active duty for the Spanish-American War and trained at Camp Chicamaugua, Tennessee. He was again called to active duty in 1916 for duty on the Mexican border, training at Fort Bliss, El Paso.

I am dubious about the emphasis placed on high technology today. It is my view that technology should be subordinate to the human element. Wars are fought by human beings, conflicts involving courage, honor, fear and duty. A prudent analysis of Wellington's chances before the Battle of Waterloo would have shown that he should have lost that battle. Wellington had an edge in that the British foot soldier had confidence in him, was loyal and stood fast. Their loyalty was based on their knowledge that Wellington cared for them.

As my father's surrogate at West Point, my goal was to live up to his expectation, yet to be true to myself. Reflecting on the stories herein gleaned from a lifetime of learning, I wonder about their accidental nature in the many encounters and events that shaped my life to my benefit. I hope that my activities may have had a reciprocal benefit for those with whom I was associated.

My basic values were set at home during my formative years, honed and developed at West Point adhering to the ideals of Duty, Honor and Country.

You, Dear Reader, now have the ingredients from which to shape your own Omelet!